THE ECONOMIC SOCIOLOGY
OF IMMIGRATION

THE ECONOMIC SOCIOLOGY OF IMMIGRATION

Essays on Networks, Ethnicity, and Entrepreneurship

ALEJANDRO PORTES

EDITOR

RUSSELL SAGE FOUNDATION · NEW YORK

#30671445

The Russell Sage Foundation

The Russell Sage Foundation, one of the oldest of America's general purpose foundations, was established in 1907 by Mrs. Margaret Olivia Sage for "the improvement of social and living conditions in the United States." The Foundation seeks to fulfill this mandate by fostering the development and dissemination of knowledge about the country's political, social, and economic problems. While the Foundation endeavors to assure the accuracy and objectivity of each book it publishes, the conclusions and interpretations in Russell Sage Foundation publications are those of the authors and not of the Foundation, its Trustees, or its staff. Publication by Russell Sage, therefore, does not imply Foundation endorsement.

Library of Congress Cataloging-in-Publication Data
The economic sociology of immigration : essays on networks, ethnicity,
  and entrepreneurship / Alejandro Portes, editor.
      p.   cm.
  Includes bibliographical references and index.
  ISBN 0-87154-682-5 :
    1. United States—Emigration and immigration—Economic aspects.
  2. United States—Emigration and immigration—Government policy.
  I. Portes, Alejandro, 1944–
  JV6471.E27   1995
  330.973—dc20   94-20933
                                                                   CIP

The paper used in this publication meets the minimum requirements of American National Standard for Information Sciences—Permanence of Paper for Printed Library Materials, ANSI Z39.48-1992.

RUSSELL SAGE FOUNDATION
112 East 64th Street, New York, New York 10021

10 9 8 7 6 5 4 3 2 1

Contents

v

Foreword

$\mathbf{T}$HE TITLE AND SUBTITLE of this finely calibrated volume serve its
potential readers well. The title instantly directs attention to its principal scholarly aim—a linkage and partial fusion of ideas central to
both economic sociology and the sociology of immigration, fields
that are experiencing an energetic renewal and, I think it safe to say,
definite advancement. In turn, the subtitle signals us that the book
draws upon theoretically oriented empirical studies of immigration,
ethnicity, and entrepreneurship, thus providing readers with far
more than another set of wholly programmatic reflections on those
reemerging fields of sociological inquiry.

The title and general objective if not the subject of this volume
have inevitably put me in mind of the sociological essay, "Die sozial-
en Klassen im ethnisch homogenen Milieu," first published in 1926
by Joseph Schumpeter, that giant among twentieth century economists who lay much store on what he, like Max Weber, described as
"*Sozialökonomik.*" For, as I had forgotten but as the economic-sociolo-
gist Richard Swedberg remembered in his anthology of Schumpeter's writings,[1] when that essay, which Schumpeter numbered
among his six "most important works,"[2] finally found its way into
English a quarter-century later, I found myself gravely proclaiming
that it "builds a bridge carrying two-way intellectual traffic between
economics and sociology." Just as rather more recently I was privileged to observe the authors of this volume building a bridge between economic sociology and the sociology of immigration during
their year as Visiting Scholars at the Russell Sage Foundation.

During that year of participant-observation, it soon became plain
that the authors were an exemplary research team intent on examining the socio-economic phenomena of immigration as a strategic research site (SRS) for advancing certain frontiers of economic sociology in the course of making specific contributions to our sociological
knowledge of immigration. The considerable results of that collabo-

vii

rative work are admirably summarized and placed in broad theoretical context by Alejandro Portes in his introductory chapter, thus re-
lieving a mere foreword of that heavy responsibility. Still, there is
room for a few further expressions of specific interest and pleasure
in the volume when viewed from the standpoint of the history and
sociology of science.

The authors exhibit a keen sense of continuities and discontinuities in historically evolving socio-economic thought. Thus, their systematic research draws upon and significantly extends Karl Polanyi's
theoretical orientation that he liked to describe as his "substantive
[as distinct from formal] economics." Looking forward rather than
backward, it can be argued that the authors' own evolving theoretical orientation would profit from replacing the current, often adversarial, stance dividing the "New Economic Sociology" (so effectively
exemplified in this volume) from the "New Institutional Economics"
(so effectively exemplified by the work of Douglas North, Oliver
Williamson and, in his frequent use of immigration as a strategic
research site, particularly by the sociologist Victor Nee) with a less
competitive and more productive synergy. Such a move might resemble the Schumpeterian program for *Sozialökonomik* that comprises
"economic theory," "economic sociology," "economic history," and
"statistics." After all, we know that concrete socio-economic phenomena cannot be exhaustively accounted for by any one theoretical
orientation. Why, then, allow a misplaced contest among diverse
but complementary theoretical perspectives to reintroduce a latter-
day version of Whitehead's fallacy of misplaced concreteness? A dis-
ciplined pluralism, constrained by the norm of "socially organized
skepticism" that has long been institutionalized in science, seems indicated.

Several of the chapters in this volume that center on ethnic entrepreneurial patterns bring Schumpeter back to mind. Precisely because he had gone to some pains to exclude ethnic variation in his
analysis of class formation by confining himself to an "ethnisch homogenen Milieu" (as few contemporary economists would have
bothered to note they were doing), there is reason to suppose that
Schumpeter, as the prime mover of a theory of entrepreneurial innovation as the spur to economic development, would have resonated
to these studies of ethnic entrepreneurial patterns embedded in institutional structures. Along with their theoretical contributions to
economic sociology, the studies greatly advance a sociological understanding of our multicultural and multi-ethnic society. In doing
so, moreover, they counter the ethnic chauvinism that has each ethnic group insisting on its unique and preeminent contribution to

American society and culture. As we have cause to know, such excesses of defensive ethnic pride have a way of degenerating into an offensive ethnocentrism that in turn lays the foundation for balkanization and intense ethnic conflict.

In fine sociology-of-science style, Alejandro Portes notes that "the resurgence of the sociology of immigration has been event-driven. More precisely, it has paralleled the growing interest in the expanding immigrant populations in the United States and Western Europe and concern about the consequences of their presence. To the extent that immigration has been perceived as a 'social problem,' the growth of sociological research has followed the dynamics of other applied subfields of the discipline."[3] And as we know, it is particularly when great tides of new kinds of ethnic immigrants are sweeping onto American shores that immigration tends to be redefined as a social problem rather than experienced as a much-needed social asset. As familiar cases-in-point, we have only to recall the legislative rationing of immigration that followed upon the shift at the beginning of this century from a largely "old" immigration deriving from Northwestern Europe to a largely "new" immigration from Eastern and Southern Europe. Or in our own immediate time, we have only to observe the hostility expressed in certain quarters toward greatly increased Hispanic and Asian immigrations.

Such expressions of hostility toward new "immigrant hordes" recur despite periodic reaffirmations by one or another authoritative figure reminding us that "we are a nation of immigrants and descendants of immigrants." Perhaps the most memorable of such affirmations occurred in 1938 when, secure in his own patrician status, President Franklin Delano Roosevelt archly reminded his would-be fellow patricians of the ultra-conservative D.A.R. (Daughters of the American Revolution) that they too were descendants of immigrants:

> . . . it so happens, through no fault of my own, that I am descended from a number of people who came over in the *Mayflower*. More than that, every one of my ancestors on both sides—and when you go back four generations or five generations it means thirty-two or sixty-four of them—every single one of them, without exception, was in this land in 1776. And there was only one Tory among them.
>
> The text is this: Remember, remember always that all of us, and you and I especially, are descended from immigrants and revolutionists.[4]

Later that day, Roosevelt held a special press conference where he made it plain that he had been baiting those "revolutionists" of the D.A.R. for their regressive attitudes and behavior toward new immigrants and Negroes. It cannot be said, however, that Roosevelt's affirmation of universalist values soon altered the public behavior of the D.A.R. For only a year later that organization of ethnic chauvinists refused to allow the widely revered contralto Marian Anderson to perform at their Constitution Hall; this, although she was the first black to become a permanent member of the Metropolitan Opera Company.[5] A slowly changing composite of values, norms, expectations, and sanctions had evidently not yet fully worked its consequences on the D.A.R. and other like-minded groups. Powerful social networks composed of those who, like Roosevelt himself, were still taking ethnic pride in deriving from the first immigrants were, unlike Roosevelt, still translating that pride into exclusionary practices. Nor, of course, were these attitudes and practices confined to those social strata. Theoretically guided findings in this volume shed new light on such invidious patterns of attitude and behavior among groups variously located in the American social structure.

And now for a concluding admission: I freely confess that this enthusiastic but free-flowing foreword does not begin to do justice to the systematic and evocative contents of this collaborative venture into economic sociology via empirical studies of immigration, ethnicity, and entrepreneurial patterns. For a proper appreciation of that admirable achievement, one must turn first to the fine orienting Preface and then to the chapters variously vibrant with distinctive sociological findings and implications.

Robert K. Merton

Notes

1.   Joseph A. Schumpeter, *The Economics and Sociology of Capitalism*, edited by Richard Swedberg (Princeton: Princeton University Press, 1991), pp. 92–93. The same year also saw publication of two biographies: Robert Loring Allen, *Opening Doors: The Life and Work of Joseph Schumpeter* (New Brunswick and London: Transaction Publishers, 1991), 2 volumes; and Richard Swedberg, *Schumpeter: A Biography* (Princeton: Princeton University Press, 1991).

2.   Schumpeter's short list of his major works was recovered by his early associate at Harvard, Paul M. Sweezey, who also edited the English translation of that essay. For the list, see Paul M. Sweezey, "Schumpeter on 'Imperialism and Social Classes,' " in Seymour E. Harris, ed.,

Schumpeter: Social Scientist (Cambridge: Harvard University Press, 1951), p. 119; for the translation, see Schumpeter, *Imperialism and Social Classes,* translated by Heinz Norden and edited with an introduction by Paul M. Sweezey (New York: A. M. Kelley, 1951).

3. Alejandro Portes, this volume, at pp. 1–2. Portes's final sentence alludes to an observation in the early 1950s on the neglect of the sociology of science before it became widely defined as a social problem and the correlative observation on the renascence of interest in sociological research on immigration in the early part of the century that followed upon the great influx of new kinds of immigrants and their being widely defined as a social problem. See R. K. Merton, "Foreword" to Bernard Barber, *Science and the Social Order* (New York: The Free Press, 1952), esp. at pp. xvii–xx.

4. *The Public Papers and Addresses of Franklin D. Roosevelt, with a special introduction and explanatory notes by President Roosevelt. 1938 Volume: The Continuing Struggle for Liberalism.* (New York: The Macmillan Company, 1941), p. 259.

5. It may be remembered that Eleanor Roosevelt promptly resigned from the D.A.R. and then, as First Lady, saw to it that Marian Anderson would sing to a huge audience at the symbolically apt Lincoln Memorial.

Preface

THIS BOOK is the product of a year-long collective project organized under the auspices of the Russell Sage Foundation and conducted at the Foundation's offices in New York City. Recent developments in economic sociology have garnered a great deal of attention, renewing the promise of a fresh perspective on economic events and institutions. At the same time, work in this field has consisted primarily of exegeses of the sociological and economic classics, trenchant critiques of the current orthodoxy in economics, and conceptual discussions at a high level of abstraction. The renewed momentum of economic sociology runs the risk of stalling by failing to connect with bodies of empirical knowledge that infuse it with fresh ideas and novel research questions.

In parallel fashion, studies of immigration and ethnicity have experienced strong growth in the United States, fueled by a new wave of immigration, the seemingly intractable plight of domestic minority groups that were created by earlier migrant waves, and the contrast between the situation of these groups and the economic success of some of the most recent arrivals. The study of these phenomena has given rise to separate bodies of empirical literature. Although each body of research has developed its own theoretical perspectives and concepts, all have also developed propositions that are generally at a low level of abstraction. The basic goal of our project then, is to link innovations in economic sociology with the grounded propositions and factual knowledge accumulated by research on immigration, ethnic poverty, and ethnic entrepreneurship. We aimed at broadening the scope of each of these subfields by highlighting the interconnections among their concepts and thematic priorities as well as their fit with more general theoretical propositions. By the same token, the project sought to suffuse sociological thinking about economic processes with new insights stemming from fact-driven hypotheses.

To explore these linkages, the project brought together six social scientists who had worked extensively in one or more of the relevant subfields and whose scholarship combined attention to general theoretical issues with empirical research on relevant subject areas. Four members of the group spent the year in residence at the Russell Sage Foundation, while the other two attended several of the group's regular meetings and were kept abreast of its progress. Participants met frequently to discuss each other's research and every month they hosted an outside speaker, either a distinguished sociologist or economist, whose work had direct relevance to the year's collective project. The papers elaborated by each group member, the final versions of which constitute the chapters in this volume, benefited from these extensive discussions with our visitors and with each other.

In addition to regular participants and visitors, many of the project's sessions were attended by Robert K. Merton, the Foundation's scholar-in-residence, whose intellectual influence is evident in several of the following chapters. In addition to the contributions specifically acknowledged by different authors, we owe Bob a collective debt of gratitude for the enthusiasm with which he greeted the idea of this project, his unfailing support for it throughout the year, and the wisdom with which he steered us away from several serious pitfalls. Other members of the 1992–1993 "class" of Russell Sage fellows, in particular David Blau, Russell Hardin, and Robin Jarret, also deserve acknowledgment for their helpful comments on specific papers and their sympathy and support for the group's aims.

The introductory chapter provides an overview of recent conceptual developments in economic sociology and the sociology of immigration and some of their key interlinkages. Its aim is to familiarize the reader with central ideas and propositions, several of which are developed at greater length in subsequent chapters. In Chapter 2, Bryan Roberts explores how social definitions of time and normative expectations about the proper duration of migration episodes affect the economic prospects of immigrants and, in particular, their propensity toward entrepreneurship. Data from turn-of-the-century European immigrant groups and from contemporary Mexican immigration are used to support his main propositions. Saskia Sassen provides a review and critique of orthodox economic perspectives on labor markets and shows how the spatial delimitations that are usually assumed to circumscribe local markets are inappropriate in the case of immigrants whose networks render their perceptions and utilization of space much broader than those usually assumed in the economic literature. Sassen uses evidence from several recent immi-

grant groups to show how social networks connecting distant regions in countries of origin and destination give migrant workers
superior information and a more flexible use of economic opportunities distributed unequally in space.

These two chapters on the temporal and the spatial dimensions
of immigration are followed by two on the sociocultural underpinnings of entrepreneurship. In Chapter 4, Mark Granovetter draws
on studies of business development among ethnic minorities and
culturally defined groups around the world to advance a novel theory of the firm. His propositions on the role of normative expectations and socially conditioned trust are set in explicit contrast to indi-
vidual-centered theories that rely exclusively on personal skills and
market advantage. In the next chapter, Ivan Light and Carolyn Rosenstein put to test the "interaction" theory of entrepreneurship,
which argues that the rate of business creation among ethnic groups
depends on the fit between their "supply" of material and moral
resources and the "demand" for entrepreneurial services in the specific areas where they settle. Using census data, they examine empirically the bearing of aggregate sociodemographic characteristics and
key features of the economic environment of standard metropolitan
areas on rates of entrepreneurship for five major ethnic populations.

Chapter 6 by Patricia Fernández Kelly inverts the analytic focus
by examining the lack of entrepreneurship and the associated social
pathologies of the inner city, with special emphasis on adolescent
pregnancy. She argues that these problems do not arise out of anomie or the lack of social capital in the black ghetto but out of its
isolation from the rest of society, which renders the resources available through social capital inappropriate for economic success. Using
ethnographic data collected in two poor black areas of Baltimore,
Fernández Kelly shows how the rich but self-enclosed networks of
the ghetto create cultural definitions of situations, including teenage
pregnancy, which are at variance with those held by the mainstream. The same "cultural capital" that facilitates survival in the
harsh conditions of blighted urban areas thus becomes a major barrier to movement out of the inner city through mainstream employment.

Chapter 7 follows with an analysis of the adversarial culture
developed by inner-city youth and its impact on the children of
recently arrived immigrant groups. This chapter makes use of concepts advanced in the first chapter to fashion several theoretical
propositions about the adaptation outcomes of today's second generation. The clash between the history, outlook, and moral resources
of ethnic communities brought into close contact with each other

affects the outcomes of the "segmented assimilation" process confronted by children of immigrants. Data from a recently completed survey of second-generation youth in California and Florida are used to illustrate the chapter's main propositions.

Every analysis in this book combines empirical material, either primary or secondary, with extensive theoretical reflection. The theoretical discussions are not limited, as in standard research articles, to the implications of the analyses for a particular set of hypotheses, but extend to its bearing on broader sociological thinking about economic action and economic institutions. To be sure, not all the authors share precisely the same perspective or adhere to the same thematic preferences. Thus, while Granovetter and Fernández Kelly focus on group characteristics affecting the presence or absence of ethnic entrepreneurship, Light and Rosenstein analyze the interaction of such "supply" factors with a varying demand for entrepreneurs in different urban areas. Similarly, while these three chapters focus primarily on settled ethnic minorities, the emphasis in Roberts's and Sassen's chapters is on movement and contact across national borders and on the implications of these dynamics for immigrant labor market adaptation.

Nevertheless, the overall intent of each chapter fits with the original goals of the project. In the following pages, the reader will find novel theoretical notions, old concepts refashioned to meet new analytic demands, and the application to fresh research material of some of the most important ideas advanced by economic sociology. We hope that this effort will help integrate the relevant fields of study and provide them with a tighter focus.

ALEJANDRO PORTES

1

Economic Sociology and the Sociology of Immigration: A Conceptual Overview

ALEJANDRO PORTES

THE SOCIOLOGICAL perspective on the economy is currently experiencing a vigorous revival. Its resurgence has been due, in part, to mounting doubts within the discipline of economics itself that neoclassical theory provides a satisfactory framework for the explanation of numerous aspects of economic life. In part, economic sociology has gained renewed energy from the realization among sociologists that much of what is missing in the dominant economic approach is social in nature and, hence, within their purview. With some exceptions, sociology has left behind rigid versions of both functionalism and Marxism, and this has given the discipline new freedom to reconnect with its classical roots and explore what it has to say about different aspects of the contemporary world.[1]

This revival may be further stimulated by linking theoretical developments in economic sociology with related subfields where a body of relevant empirical research has accumulated. Of these subfields, few have experienced more vigorous growth in recent years than the sociology of immigration. Unlike economic sociology, which reemerged as an outcome of recent theoretical debates, the resurgence of the sociology of immigration has been event-driven. More precisely, it has paralleled growing interest in the expanding immigrant populations of the United States and Western Europe and concern about the consequences of their presence. To the extent that immigration has been perceived as a "social problem," the growth of sociological research has followed the dynamics of other applied subfields of the discipline. However, unlike most of those subfields, the study of immigrant adaptation possesses its own independent theoretical tradition dating back to the origins of the discipline.[2]

Sociological studies of immigration and ethnicity bear directly on theoretical developments in economic sociology because they provide a distinct set of empirical materials to draw on for the generation and refinement of general concepts and hypotheses. Seldom are the social underpinnings of economic action laid bare with such clarity as in the processes that give rise to immigration and determine its outcomes. The linkage was already apparent in early sociological studies of immigrant groups in North America, where the focus was on the social structures that organized the transoceanic journey and permitted the survival of newcomers in a hostile environment. Robert Park's "marginal man" was rooted in the immigrant experience, which gave the concept the heuristic power to become a central feature of sociology's theoretical arsenal. Classical studies of the socioeconomic adaptation of immigrants, most prominently *The Polish Peasant in Europe and America*, not only reflected the sociological ideas of the time but influenced theoretical developments for decades to come.[3] In the current climate of revived interest in what sociology has to say about economic life, the field of immigration represents, in Merton's term, a "strategic research site" (SRS)—an area where processes of more general import are manifested with unusual clarity.[4]

The task of integrating findings and hypotheses in the sociology of immigration with the more abstract concepts of economic sociology has not yet been systematically attempted. We believe that such an exercise can have a significant theoretical payoff. In order for the new economic sociology to live up to its promise, it must move beyond general sensitizing notions or critiques of the reigning economic paradigms and apply its propositions to concrete aspects of social reality. If it is possible to isolate specific areas of economic life that are best explained by a sociological perspective and identify the most useful applications of theoretical notions to this task, we will have contributed significantly to an emerging field. The remainder of this chapter attempts to lay the groundwork for this enterprise by reviewing central concepts in economic sociology and the sociology of immigration. I select a set of concepts from each subfield and investigate their interrelationships.

Five from Economic Sociology

Socially Oriented Economic Action

Economists and sociologists agree that economic action refers to the acquisition and use of scarce means. All activities required for the production, distribution, and consumption of scarce goods and services are conventionally characterized as economic.[5] There is less agreement, however, on the array of motives of economic actors and on the socially patterned influence of others upon their activities. The triumph of the neoclassical perspective in economics hinged on the adoption of a set of simplifying assumptions about human action that allowed the construction of complex mathematical models. Individuals are assumed to act in pursuit of their maximum personal utility, defined as the accumulation of scarce means. Competition between individual maximizers takes place on a level field—the market—where buyers and sellers meet. Market supply and demand are kept in equilibrium through the price mechanism. Any external interference with prices reduces the capacity of the market to allocate scarce means efficiently.[6]

Rationality in this system is defined as the unimpeded pursuit of gain by economic actors, be they individual or corporate. Many neoclassical economists are plainly aware that these are only heuristic assumptions which, they argue, lead to internally consistent and predictively powerful explanations of economic events. While agreeing that this is the case, other social scientists have observed that there are many situations where these assumptions neither hold true nor lead to accurate predictions. The field of behavioral economics has focused on the assumption of rationality and shown its untenability in various contexts. Most of this work has been conducted from the standpoint of individual psychology.[7]

Economic sociology has been less concerned with psychological constraints on individual rationality than with those created by the social environment. Research in this field has focused on the ways in which social influences modify the assumed maximizing behavior of individuals and lead to predictions differing from those of conventional economic models.[8] This perspective assumes that actors are rational, in the sense of pursuing goals through deliberately selected means, but that they are not socially atomized. On the contrary, social relationships enter every stage of the process, from the selection of economic goals to the organization of relevant means.

The most succinct classical formulation of this approach is found in the writings of Max Weber. In *Economy and Society*, as is well known, Weber distinguished three types of action: those guided by habit; those guided by emotion; and those guided by the deliberate pursuit of goals. The last of these, described as "rational" action, is in turn differentiated by whether its means-end structure is oriented toward the pursuit of individual ends (*zweckrational*) or the pursuit of some transcendental value (*wertrational*). This typology identifies the type of action assumed by neoclassical theory as simply one ideal construction among several, all of equal plausibility. Moreover, Weber also assumes that rational instrumental action is socially oriented in the sense that "it takes into account the behavior of others" and is thereby oriented in its course.[9]

"Taking account of others" is not meant by Weber solely in the sense of formal considerations attending market transactions but, more importantly, in the sense of substantive expectations linked to sociability. By virtue of membership in human groups—from families to churches and associations—individuals acquire a set of privileges and associated obligations that simultaneously further and constrain their selfish pursuits. Even more importantly, every interaction, including market interaction, creates sociability in the sense of generating over time a complex of stable expectations, status rankings, and emotions.[10]

The postulate of socially oriented economic action, therefore, is not simple but contains several related subarguments. For the sake of clarity it is convenient to list them as separate analytic types, although this does some violence to reality:

1. Economic action is socially oriented in the sense that it can be governed, in whole or part, by value introjection. Included in this category is not only the type of behavior dealt with in economics and sociology under the label "altruism" but also, and more generally, every action guided by moral considerations.[11] Morality or the acting out of collectively held values may influence both the character of personal goals and the selection of means to attain them.

2. Economic action is also socially oriented in the sense that the pursuit of material gain interacts with other self-centered goals such as the quest for approval, status, and power, all of which depend on the opinions of others. Wholly unrestricted maximizing behavior commonly meets with disapproval by others in the same social milieu, especially if it is pursued without regard to their own interests. The accumulation of the valued goal, wealth, may thus come into conflict with the realization of another valued goal, social status, and with the unhampered exercise of the power that

wealth itself confers. The accumulation of material means compels others to do one's bidding, but it does not by itself create the *auctoritas* that leads others to do so willingly. The Weberian distinction between power and authority thus bears directly on how economic action is conducted, insofar as authority is guided by concerns for legitimacy.[12]

3. Finally, economic action is socially oriented in the sense that even the unrestricted pursuit of gain is constrained by reciprocity expectations built up in the course of social interaction. The accumulation of social "chits" is central to the pursuit of economic advantage insofar as they facilitate access to information, capital, and other scarce resources. By the same token, such access is granted in the course of everyday transactions with full expectation that it will be reciprocated. Over time, each economic actor becomes surrounded by a dense web of expectations built in this manner. Nonobservance of reciprocity expectations carries the threat of immediate or delayed retribution either by the aggrieved party or by her associates. The existence of such social obligations does not guarantee that economic actors will not pursue their own self-interests, but it insures that they will conceal, as much as possible, those aspects of their actions that carry the threat of sanctions. Their behavior will be modified accordingly.[13]

The various types of social influence on economic action, of course, combine in a multiplicity of ways in concrete situations. Their analytic separation remains useful, however, both because of their implications for the prediction of actual behavior and because they help identify different stages of sociological theorizing about the economy. An "oversocialized" conception of action in which individual conduct is guided primarily by value introjection (type 1 above) became the focus of functionalist economic sociology. As elaborated by Parsons and Smelser, the economy was portrayed as existing to fulfill one of the key functional prerequisites of society, with economic actors oriented fundamentally by moral imperatives.[14]

This conceptualization did not prosper, in part because its theoretical categories were so abstract and its implications for individual action so stereotyped. Economists had no trouble pointing to systematic deviations from the expected behavioral pattern, and many lost no time in debunking what they saw as sociologists' "naive" view of human nature.[15] The reemerging field of economic sociology has not abandoned moral considerations as an aspect of social influence on economic behavior but has focused, to a greater extent than earlier schools of thought, on the remaining types described above (2 and 3), both of which assume self-interested actors. It has paid close attention to the structures from which values and norms, criteria for social approval, and reciprocity expectations stem. To these I now turn.

Embedded Transactions

The concept of embeddedness refers to the fact that economic transactions of the most diverse sorts are inserted in overarching social structures that affect their form and their outcomes. The concept originated with the Hungarian anthropologist Karl Polanyi, who used it to argue that the market, far from representing the universal form of economic organization, is just one historically situated form corresponding to modern capitalism.[16] The concept was then adopted by Mark Granovetter, who noted that while Polanyi had been right in pointing to the role of social forces in structuring precapitalist economies, he had been wrong in assuming that such influences ceased to operate in modern market transactions. Granovetter went on to summarize a number of research findings indicating how social expectations modified and even subverted the original intent of both market transactions and transactions conducted within firms.[17]

In later work, Granovetter distinguished between "relational" embeddedness, referring to economic actors' personal relations with one another, and "structural" embeddedness, referring to the broader network of social relations to which these actors belong.[18] The relational type of embeddedness includes the normative expectations, quest for mutual approval, and reciprocity transactions discussed above. The structural type calls attention to a factor of a different order of magnitude, namely the insertion of economic exchanges into larger social aggregates in which many others (aside from the actual participants in the exchange) take part. Such aggregates then become the source of normative expectations for particular transactions and the conferrers of valued rewards such as social standing and esteem. Compared with isolated individuals, they also provide a greater deterrent against violations of interpersonal reciprocity obligations.

From the myriad empirical examples that can be used to illustrate the significance of structural embeddedness, I select just two. The first is Ronald Dore's analysis of the decentralization of Japanese textile production and the emergence of "relational subcontracting" between spinning companies (the small merchant-converters who turn yarn into cloth) and an array of dyers, beamers, and weavers. Contracts between participants in this densely articulated production process are stable and not easily altered by the advent of cheaper alternatives that might be supposed to induce some to switch suppliers. Such "rational" market behavior is frowned upon by the community to which both merchants and suppliers belong. Instead of opportunistically shifting his business to cheaper suppliers, a buyer will point to them and encourage his long-term associate to imitate them:

> . . . the more common consequence is that other merchant-converters go to their finishers and say "Look how X has got his price down. We hope you can do the same because we really would have to reconsider our position if the price difference goes on for months. If you need bank finance to get the new type of vat we can probably help by guaranteeing the loan.[19]

Such behavior would appear irrational for isolated maximizers but is entirely explainable by the structural embeddedness of these transactions. To do otherwise would be to risk incurring serious social and economic penalties. Actors in this system can switch business associates, but only after making a demonstrable claim that their current associates have violated reciprocity expectations. Then the shift is socially legitimized as part of the collective sanctions against violators.[20]

The second example is closer to home and involves executives of a large American manufacturing conglomerate specializing in electronic games, toys, and computers. Morrill conducted a study of the corporate headquarters of this company that revealed the development of an adversarial culture among executives in response to outside takeover pressures and managerial innovations. Public confrontations between executives became commonplace and led to the creation of an elaborate ritual as well as a rich imagery to describe these encounters. Executives engaged in "shootouts," and entire departments "went to war," with initial skirmishes followed by the tossing of "hand grenades" toward the adversary camp.[21]

In this highly competitive environment, opportunistic behavior—known as "ambushing" or "flying low" to avoid open confrontation—was possible, but only at the cost of serious status loss. "Honor" became the executives' most prized commodity and was earned through straightforward behavior, making strong presentations in public debates, and above all, learning how to win and lose with grace. Those who adhered to this normative code became "white knights" or "white hats." Less honorable executives could win a skirmish or duel through guile, but were promptly dubbed "black hats" and often forced to move to a different department or resign from the company ("jump ship"). According to Morrill, the pursuit of honor in corporate joustings became so dominant that the substance of debates commonly took a back seat to the etiquette with which they were conducted:

> . . . challenges and counterchallenges indicated a "duel" would occur at the next team meeting. Besides carefully preparing their presentations, each of the principals prepared themselves through rituals common in such situations. All of the principals wore their lucky ties and "flack vests" to fend off "bullets" from the opposition. . . . The rest of the team knew of the "duel" via an agenda circulated three days prior to the meeting. As was customary, an uninvolved team member spun a gold ballpoint pen flat on the meeting table; the principal to whom the ink end pointed was allowed to choose the order of presentation . . .[22]

Such elaborate games may appear irrational when evaluated from the standpoint of the "real" goals of the corporation. To be sure, corporate profit seeking and individual income maximizing remain important aims, but plainly they must be pursued within the constraints of an elaborate social code that extracts severe penalties for deviance. Not interpersonal transactions but the larger social world of which all transactors are part becomes the prime source of expectations guiding individual action.

Social Networks

Social networks are among the most important types of structures in which economic transactions are embedded. These are sets of recurrent associations between groups of people linked by occupational, familial, cultural, or affective ties. Networks are important in economic life because they are sources for the acquisition of scarce means, such as capital and information, and because they simultaneously impose effective constraints on the unrestricted pursuit of personal gain. As an illustration of their first function, consider Dalton's analysis of the ways in which department heads in a large industrial corporation tipped each other off in advance about the "surprise" visits of central auditing staff and helped each other conceal what they did not want auditors to see or count:

Notice that a count of parts was to begin provoked a flurry of activity among the executives to hide certain parts and equipment. . . . As the practice developed, cooperation among the chiefs to use each other's storage areas and available pits became well organized and smoothly functioning. Joint action of a kind rarely, if ever, shown in carrying on official directives enabled the relatively easy passage of laborers and truckers from one work area to another . . .[23]

As an example of the second function (imposing constraints on maximizing behavior), recall the limits on extra work effort established by networks of industrial workers who develop norms as to what constitutes a "fair day's labor." Individual workers could gain extra pay and promotions by exerting themselves, but they are kept in line by effective pressure from their peers. First reported in the famous Hawthorne plant studies, the pattern has been noted since in a number of studies of industrial plants both in the United States and Europe.[24]

Social networks differ in several dimensions that have direct consequences for economic behavior. Size and density are the most important. Size refers to the number of participants in a network and density to the number of ties between them. Boissevain has noted that the larger the size of the network, the more difficult it is for all members to be interrelated and, hence, the lower the density. Relatively large and dense networks are, however, most effective in developing normative expectations and enforcing reciprocity obligations. This may be appreciated in the difference between the two types of networks portrayed in Figure 1.1: A's violation of reciprocal obligations to B is likely to incur a lesser cost (and hence be a more tempting option) when B is relatively isolated than when B is closely connected with a network of other members.[25]

Figure 1.1 also highlights another important dimension of networks, namely the relative centrality of members. Power tends to be correlated with this dimension. In the top diagram, A is subject to weak social controls and able to control flows of information among other network members. A is thus in a relatively stronger position to reap the advantages and avoid the costs of social interaction within this particular configuration. In the bottom diagram, centrality is much lower and hence the effectiveness of the network in creating common expectations and monitoring individual compliance is much greater.

Two other important aspects of networks are their clustering and multiplexity. These are illustrated in Figure 1.2. Clustering refers to the degree to which subsets of a network have greater density than

Figure 1.1   Density and Centrality in Social Networks

I. Low density, high centrality:

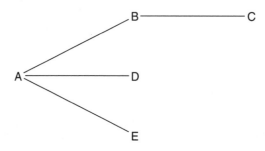

II. High density, low centrality:

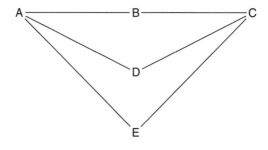

---

the network as a whole. These subsets are sometimes called cliques. Multiplexity is the degree to which relations between participants include overlapping institutional spheres. For instance, individuals who are work associates may also be linked by family ties, political affiliations, or club memberships. The top panel of Figure 1.2 presents a partially clustered, relatively dense uniplex network of the type commonly found in corporate offices and illustrated by the referenced studies of Morrill and Dalton.[26] Cliques are formed in these situations to defend common interests or aggressively pursue greater control over resources. They may be "horizontal" when they involve individuals of similar power and centrality, or "vertical" when a more powerful figure bestows special favors on subordinates in exchange for deference and collaboration. Cliques 1 and 2 in the figure approximate these situations.

The bottom panel of Figure 1.2 exemplifies a heavily clustered,

Figure 1.2   Clustering and Multiplexity in Social Networks

I. Partially clustered, uniplex:

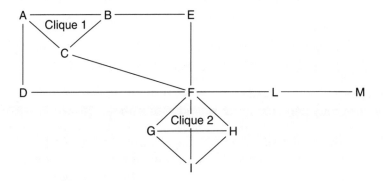

II. Fully clustered, multiplex:

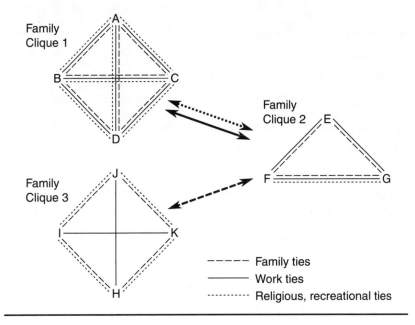

multiplex, dense network of the type found by Boissevain in the Maltese towns he studied. Clusters of kin are overlaid by multiple work, religious, and recreational ties. Family cliques are, in turn, heavily linked to one another by residential proximity, occupational pursuits, and church activities. In these situations, where "everyone knows everyone else," community norms proliferate and violations of reciprocity obligations carry heavy costs. Solidarity within family cliques is intensified as a way of differentiating them (and sometimes protecting their members) from an already dense web of "outside" relations.[27]

As these examples suggest, networks can link individuals within organizations and communities and across them. Networks are not the only social structures in which economic action is embedded and, in fact, they often emerge as features of larger aggregates. However, networks generally constitute the more immediate settings influencing the goals of individuals and the means and constraints in their paths. Depending on the characteristics of their networks and their personal positions within them, individuals may be able to mobilize a significant amount of resources, escape close scrutiny of their selfish behavior, or on the contrary, be tightly bound by group-enforced expectations.

Social Capital

Social capital refers to the capacity of individuals to command scarce resources by virtue of their membership in networks or broader social structures.[28] Such resources may include economic tangibles like price discounts and interest-free loans, or intangibles like information about business conditions, employment tips, and generalized "goodwill" in market transactions. The resources themselves are *not* social capital; the concept refers instead to the individual's *ability* to mobilize them on demand. The key conceptual characteristic of such resources is that, from a market standpoint, they are free to recipients. They have the character of "gifts" since they are not expected to be repaid by a certain amount of money or other valuables in a given period of time.

Resources acquired through social capital often carry the expectation of reciprocity at some point in the future. Unlike the expectations involved in market transactions, these expectations tend to have a diffuse time horizon, without fixed deadlines. In addition, the very character of the repayment is flexible since it may involve a "currency" of a different nature from that in which the original gift was made.[29] To illustrate the differences between market transactions and transactions underwritten by social capital, consider the example of money loaned to start a business. If the loan is from a bank, it is collateralized and carries with it a schedule of payments of principal and interest according to market rates. If the loan comes from a long-time business associate who definitely expects repayment, collateral may not be required and interest may be charged at a lower rate. The loan also could have been obtained from a long-time friend who charges no interest and simply asks for repayment "when conditions permit." And finally, it may have been granted by a loving parent who expects no money back, just the affection and respect of a child in need.

Similar variations occur with regard to business advice, the letting out of contracts, the hiring of employees, and a host of other economic transactions. In each of them there is room for transactions that appear to involve the exchange of "something for nothing." The ability to obtain such gifts (social capital) does not inhere in the individual, as the possession of money (material capital) or education (human capital) does, but instead is a property of the individual's set of relationships with others. Social capital is a product of embeddedness.

We can distinguish two types of motivation on the part of donors of such gifts. Social capital may arise because donors feel that granting these resources is the right thing to do either to fulfill moral obligations or out of emergent solidarity with a particular individual or group. A Christian may give alms to the poor because she learned in childhood that charity is a good thing. The same person may also contribute to a college fund to support students of her own ethnic group out of solidarity with their needs. Such "principled" sources of social capital are conceptually distinct from those based on the second type of motivation, donors' self-interest. Gifts may be granted to others in the same organization or community because donors fully expect something in return, either in the form of commensurate economic resources or nonmaterial rewards such as social standing and approval.

In a dyadic or triadic situation (relational embeddedness), expectations of reciprocity are based exclusively on past knowledge of other actors and the ability of each individual to withhold resources or apply sanctions if expectations are not satisfied. As we have seen (Figure 1.1), this is a weaker basis for the fulfillment of expectations than exists when both actors are part of a broader network of relationships (structural embeddedness). In the latter situation, economic transfers can proceed with confidence that others will fulfill their obligations lest they be subjected to the full weight of collective sanctions.

The mechanism at play in this case may be labeled "enforceable trust," insofar as the ease with which transactions, concessions, and gifts are made among members of the same community is undergirded by certainty that no one will shirk their eventual repayment.[30] Clearly the configuration of the social networks involved and the position of individuals within them affect the strength of this mechanism. Drawing upon the discussion in the preceding section, we can conclude that the greater the density and multiplexity of the networks involved and the less central the position of an obligated member, the greater the trust in her/his fulfillment of reciprocity expectations.[31]

Figure 1.3 summarizes this discussion and illustrates it with some examples. The concept of social capital represents a shorthand for the positive economic effects stemming from social structures. It is important, however, not to lose sight of the fact that the same social dynamics that produce altruistic gifts and concessionary favors can also constrain individual economic pursuits. Sociability is a two-way street and the resources gained from fellow community members and social network members, although in appearance "free," do carry hidden costs. Two of these will be described as illustrations of this seldom-noted facet of social capital.

Group membership commonly entails the expectation that those who are successful in their business pursuits should, to some extent, "share the wealth" with others. This is especially true if social capital in the form of subsidized loans, business information, buyer loyalty, and the like contributed to that success. In such cases, less fortunate members of the group can avail themselves of the same normative expectations originally used by the successful to press their own claims. At the extreme, as in the case of the ethnic enterprises studied by Geertz in Bali, such expectations may end by turning promising business ventures into welfare hotels, blocking any possibility of accumulation.[32]

In the indigenous villages surrounding the town of Otavalo in the Ecuadorean Andes, male owners of garment and leather artisan shops are often Protestants (or "Evangelicals," as they are known locally) rather than Catholics. The reason is not that the Protestant ethic spurred them to greater entrepreneurial achievement or that they found evangelical doctrine more compatible with their own beliefs, but something rather more instrumental. By shifting religious allegiance, these entrepreneurs remove themselves from the host of social obligations for male family heads associated with the Catholic Church and its local organizations. The Evangelical becomes, in a

Figure 1.3   Social Capital and Its Types

Definition	Sources	Donor's Motivation	Effects	Examples
Ability to command scarce means by virtue of membership in social structures	Values	Altruistic	Transferring resources to others because of general moral imperatives.	Parents' gifts to children
	Bounded Solidarity	Altruistic	Transferring resources to others because of identification with in-group needs and goals.	Gifts to co-ethnics; members of the same religious community
	Reciprocity	Instrumental	Transferring resources to others on the expectation of commensurate returns by beneficiaries.	Market tips and other favors to business associates
	Enforceable Trust	Instrumental	Transferring resources to others on the expectation of higher community status and commensurate returns by beneficiaries subject to collective sanctions.	Concessionary loans; waiving of contractual guarantees for members of the same ethnic or religious community

sense, a "stranger" in his own community, which insulates him from free-riding by others on the strength of Catholic-inspired norms.[33]

A second hidden cost of sociability is the constraint that community norms place on individual conduct and capacity for innovation. This is an expression of the age-old conflict between traditional solidarity and modern freedom, analyzed by Tönnies and Simmel.[34] The greater the density and multiplexity of social networks, the more closely individual conduct is regulated in terms of its observance of general moral precepts and conformity with established patterns of economic conduct. Tightly knit groups stand or fall together and while their solidarity contributes resources to individual entrepreneurship, it also imposes definite limits on personal initiative. This is why ethnic entrepreneurial communities tend to specialize in a few niches of economic activity and remain there across generations.[35]

Nee and Nee cite the example of San Francisco's Chinatown, a highly entrepreneurial community where, until recently, the family clans and the Chinese Six Companies reigned supreme. These powerful groups regulated the business and social life of the community, guaranteeing its normative order and ensuring privileged access to resources for Chinese entrepreneurs. Such assets came at the cost of extensive restrictions on members' scope of action and contacts with the outside world. What put teeth in the clans' demand for conformity was their control of land and business opportunities in Chinatown and their readiness to punish and even hound from the community anyone who adopted too "progressive" a stand.[36]

Long ago, Weber noted that community restrictions on individual initiative and particularistic obligations were precisely the features of traditional economic organization that would be superseded by rational modern capitalism. He thought the spread of its universalistic norms would do away with these and other obstacles to economic efficiency and sustained accumulation.[37] While Weber never claimed that such norms would come to dominate every sphere of economic action, we can assert with the benefit of hindsight that they are far from doing so. Social ties and their attendant obligations pervade every aspect of economic life, even the most "rationalized." We have noted negative consequences of embeddedness by way of cautioning against too rosy a picture of its benefits (social capital). But the benefits are also real. The balance between universalistic and particularistic criteria—what Weber labeled the contest between formal and substantive rationality—varies with the situation and is a matter for empirical scrutiny. The same can be said of the balance between the benefits and costs of sociability. In one setting, social capital may propel individuals and groups forward in a spiral of accumulation and innovation grounded in mutual support; elsewhere, similar social structures may foster conformity and undermine attempts at creative entrepreneurship.

Cumulative and Unintended Effects

Path-dependence is an economic concept used to denote the influence of past states on present conditions. For example, past spells of unemployment may lead to greater chances of present unemployment, even after controlling for individual traits. In sociology, the same notion was introduced by Becker under the label "cumulative causation." He sought to demonstrate how past events and decisions progressively lock individuals into a given career path, increasing the costs and decreasing the probability of shifting to others.[38] In economic sociology, cumulative causation is frequently used as an explanation; unlike the notion of path-dependence in economics, however, the emphasis here is on the social contexts that make such spiraling possible.

An example is Granovetter's analysis of determinants of finding a job. Past spells of unemployment and lack of early employment reduce the probability of finding a job because they cut off the individual from social networks through which job information is diffused. Unemployment thus leads to a downward spiral of removal from labor market opportunities, since the longer people are unemployed, the smaller and more remote their association becomes with the networks in which job-relevant information circulates.[39] The same process also occurs across generations. Lower employment rates among working-class black teenagers as compared with their white peers is partly explained by the weaker capacity of poor black families to insert their offspring in the labor market. As Granovetter explains, teenagers seldom secure jobs; instead, the jobs "come to them." White parents are usually in a better position to make this happen. Lack of early job experience handicaps black teenagers as they later seek adult employment. For many, this represents the beginning of the downward spiral.[40]

A second example comes from Roger Waldinger's study of ethnic occupational niches. The concentration of certain ethnic groups in particular industries, such as construction and retail trade, or in certain public bureaucracies, such as the police or sanitation departments, occurs through a process that is in a sense the opposite of that described by Granovetter. Cumulative causation operates in this case through the entry and successful performance of "pioneers" in certain branches of employment and their subsequent referral of kin and co-ethnics for other job openings. Later arrivals are compelled to work diligently not only to fulfill personal obligations to those who found them jobs but also because they are being monitored by the entire ethnic community (enforceable trust). These employees open the way for others until the ambiance of the workplace acquires the cultural tones of the group. Once this happens, outsiders find it increasingly difficult to overcome entry barriers, while those in co-ethnic networks are granted privileged access. Waldinger illustrates the process with white ethnic control of the New York construction industry and with the experiences of Indian and Egyptian engineers and other professionals in New York's civil service. Originally excluded from public employment because of their foreign status, these immigrant professionals have managed to carve a large niche in the City's bureaucracy and today represent a major force in various departments.[41]

A final type of cumulative effect is that which arises as the unanticipated and unintended consequence of purposive individual action. Over fifty years ago, Merton highlighted the significance of unintended consequences for social theory and the concept has since been applied to a number of research areas in sociology.[42] Recently, Coleman turned it into a centerpiece of his version of rational action theory. Coleman endorses the neoclassical postulate of individuals as independent maximizers, but notes that when a number of actors pursue their goals without institutional restraints, their actions often lead to cumulative consequences that are exactly the opposite of those intended.[43] He offers market "bubbles," "stampedes," and panics as illustrations of this process and argues that the role of sociologists is to study the dynamics of such episodes as well as the development of institutional authority to prevent them. This line of thinking does not, of course, differ greatly from that of neo-Marxists who argue that the "relative autonomy" of the state is a consequence of the functional need for an agency that reins in the self-destructive consequences of capitalism.[44] In both arguments, state authority represents the ultimate answer to the institutional need for control of the irrational collective consequences of individual rationality.

Economic sociologists have noted, however, that unintended consequences can follow not only from self-seeking pursuits, but from altruistic and group-oriented behavior as well. For example, the social capital that accounts for the economic success of members of a particular ethnic community often sets back those who do not belong to it. The substantive advantages gained by collectivities where bounded solidarity and trust are abundant detract from individual freedom and the observance of universalistic rules.[45] The complexity of these interactions sometimes makes sociological analyses of economic life appear hopelessly imprecise. Yet full awareness of these complexities represents a more defensible point of departure for theory building than simpler but thoroughly unrealistic assumptions. Within circumscribed settings, the concepts discussed in this section lead to valid predictions as well as richer explanations of economic outcomes. The field of immigration is such a setting and research findings in it have produced significant conceptual convergencies.

Four from the Sociology of Immigration

Since its beginnings early in the twentieth century, the sociology of immigration developed an autonomous theoretical tradition that sought to explain such things as the higher ratio of mental illness among the foreign-born and the various stages of their integration into the host society. Concepts like marginality, acculturative stress, "eth-class," assimilation, and amalgamation emerged as the field evolved during the first half of the century.[46] Closely allied to the functionalist paradigm by the end of this period, the sociology of immigration underwent a significant transformation during the 1970s and 1980s as its earlier conceptual apparatus was found insufficient to cope with the realities of the new foreign waves. The increasing complexity of modern immigration and the ethnic groups it spawned posed one kind of challenge, while another was posed by the need to come to terms with propositions advanced by the neoclassical school to explain the same processes. The concepts reviewed in this section evolved in the course of a sustained dialogue with both the earlier tradition of the field and modern neoclassical views.

Core-Periphery Influence and Structural Imbalancing

Mainstream economic thinking offers a straightforward analysis of the origins of migration as a result of international differences in the demand and supply of labor. Countries with large labor supplies and small amounts of capital produce low equilibrium wages. The opposite is the case for countries where labor is scarce and capital abundant. The result is migration of the factors until wages decline sufficiently in capital-rich countries and rise sufficiently in labor-rich nations to produce a new international equilibrium. At the individual level, migration stems from a cost-benefit calculation of the differential productivity and returns to human capital in different national settings.

Borjas has introduced the notion of a "global migration market," where individuals rationally calculate the relative benefits of staying put as opposed to moving to one or another foreign destination.[47]

People migrate to places where the expected net returns over a given time period are greatest. Net returns are calculated by multiplying the productivity of human capital in the destination country times the probability of finding employment there and subtracting the material, social, and psychological costs of the journey. If expected benefits exceed costs, people move.

Sociologists of immigration have noted a number of empirical anomalies that systematically contradict these predictions. International labor migration largely originates in countries at an intermediate level of development rather than in countries where wages are lowest. Furthermore, in these intermediate countries, the very poor and the unemployed are not the first to migrate and are generally underrepresented in the outbound flow. Instead, it is people with some resources—small rural proprietors, urban artisans, and skilled workers—who most commonly initiate and sustain the movement. But of course, not all of them leave. Migration is a highly selective process in which certain urban areas and rural communities become prime sources of the movement, while other areas of comparable socioeconomic makeup are not touched by it.

These anomalies have led sociologists to voice dissatisfaction with the predictions of neoclassical theory and to advance an alternative conceptualization. It operates on two levels, one macrostructural and pertaining to differences between nations as sources of outmigration, and one microstructural and focused on intranational community differences.

At the first level, the sociological approach notes the close affinity that exists between a history of contact, colonization, and intervention by powerful "core" nations over weaker ones and the onset of migration flows from the latter. International migration patterns tend to reflect with notable precision the character of past hegemonic actions by global powers. An example is the series of immigration flows that consolidated the present Latin-origin communities in the United States. These flows reflect, mirrorlike, the history of North American expansion into its immediate periphery. The countries that supplied the major contingents giving rise to today's ethnic communities—Mexico, Puerto Rico, Cuba, and the Dominican Republic—were each, in turn, targets of this expansionist pattern. The economic, political, and cultural penetration that followed altered the makeup of these peripheral societies to the point where many would-be migrants were acculturated into North American ways even before setting foot abroad.[48]

The concepts of influence in the core-periphery system and of structural imbalancing were coined to reflect this alternative explanation. According to these concepts the emergence of regular labor outflows of stable size and known destination depends largely on the prior expansion of stronger nation-states into peripheral sending areas. The social, economic, and cultural institutions of the sending areas are then remolded until migration to the hegemonic center emerges as a plausible option. This process has taken several different forms during the history of capitalism, ranging from coerced labor extraction (slavery) beginning in the sixteenth century to the present self-initiated labor flows.[49] Migrant recruitment through deliberate inducements, identified by Piore as a key factor in producing labor flows from peripheral countries, represents the midpoint in the evolution of labor migration in the core-periphery structure. Deliberate migrant recruitment was responsible for the onset of Irish labor migration to the northeast of the United States in the mid-nineteenth century; for rural Italian migration to the same region as well as to Brazil and Argentina later in the century; and for the start of labor migration from the interior of Mexico to the southwestern and midwestern United States in the same period.[50]

Spontaneous migration, when people move without any coercion or without inducement by their future employers, is mostly a twentieth century phenomenon. It corresponds to the increasing integration of peripheral societies into the global economy and their populations' growing awareness of opportunities abroad. The fulfillment of normative consumption expectations imported from the advanced countries becomes increasingly difficult under conditions of economic scarcity, while growing cross-national ties make it easier to seek a solution through migration. Sassen has developed a variant of this argument that links the industrial restructuring and deindustrialization of core countries to the acceleration of labor outmigration from the periphery.[51] In her view, the movement of industrial capital to peripheral locations in search of cheaper labor produces new dislocations in the host societies. Workers in Third World "runaway" industries are exposed to the modes of production and cultural patterns of the advanced West. Their employment is short-lived, however, leaving them with new skills and consumption aspirations but without the means to implement them. Furthermore, runaway industries tend to prefer female workers who are regarded as more pliant and less costly. This preference forces unemployed males to search for alternative forms of employment, both for survival and for preservation of their traditional family status. Emigration emerges as a solution to these multiple disruptions. Sassen, Fernández Kelly, and other authors have studied the experience of the Mexican Border Industrialization Program, highlighting it as a poignant example of the social dislocations created by international industrial restructuring.[52]

In its successive historical variants, the concepts of influence in the core-periphery structure and of imbalancing thus offer a consistent macrosociological explanation of the origins of migrant flows. Wage differentials per se are insufficient to trigger large-scale international migration in the absence of prior contact, economic penetration, and social reorganization of sending societies. This theoretical argument is interpretable as a particular manifestation of *structural embeddedness*. Decisions to migrate do not occur in a vacuum; the "costs" and "benefits" that enter into such individual calculations are themselves conditioned by an institutional structure reflecting external hegemony. Resulting transformations in the economy, society, and culture of peripheral regions provide the contexts in which migration abroad becomes a plausible, even a necessary option for their populations.

At the microstructural level, the sociology of immigration has not developed a similar set of concepts to account for intranational differences in propensities for migration between individuals and communities. Instead it has made full use of the concept of social networks. Migration is defined as a network-creating process because it develops an increasingly dense web of contacts between places of origin and destination. Once established, such networks allow the migration process to become self-sustaining and impervious to short-term changes in economic incentives. Costs and risks of moving abroad are reduced by the operation of these social bridges across national frontiers, allowing women and children to join male family heads abroad. People begin to move for reasons other than the original economic incentives—to join family members, for example, or to fulfill normative expectations as to "proper" behavior for young workers.[53]

The notion that international migration is simultaneously a network-creating and network-dependent process has been well established in sociology by a string of empirical studies dating back to such classics in the field as *The Polish Peasant*. More recent research has been able to determine quantitatively the importance of such ties. In a study of 822 adult male Mexican migrants arriving in two Texas ports of entry during 1973–1974, Portes and Bach found that over 90 percent of their respondents had obtained legal residence through family and employer connections in the United States. Seventy percent of these men had already traveled and lived in the North, mostly as unauthorized immigrants. They had been able to secure their legal papers primarily through family and work ties established during this period. The remainder, with few exceptions, obtained legal status by making use of the family reunification provisions of the United States immigration law.[54]

Massey used the concept of social networks to account for the differential migration propensities of thirteen Mexican communities. He classified these communities into four stages, from one at which migration was still incipient to one at which it reached a mass level. The key differentiating factor was the timing of the first trips abroad by "pioneers" from each community. Once some adult males were recruited to work in the United States or went there on their own, their successful return triggered additional trips and the gradual consolidation of cross-national networks facilitating the movement of new migrants.[55] This portrait of a self-sustaining migration process and the imperviousness of well-established flows to changes in economic incentives contrasts markedly with the views advanced by neoclassical theory, based on individual utility calculations. From the perspective of the sociology of immigration, migration by isolated individuals is an exceptional event. For the most part, the process is group-mediated and its organization and destination determined by social ties established across national borders over time.

Modes of Incorporation

According to the neoclassical model, the economic success of immigrants—as measured by their average earnings—is determined by the education, work experience, and other elements of human capital that they bring along, discounted by these skills' foreign origin. Chiswick pioneered the application of the concept of human capital to immigrant economic attainment. According to him, length of residence in the United States leads to a rapid increase in immigrant earnings due to greater fluency in English and the accumulation of workplace-specific skills. The effect of time-since-migration is so strong as to produce average immigrant earnings that surpass those of comparable native-born workers.[56] This assertion has been hotly contested by other neoclassical economists, but such disagreements nonetheless occur within a theoretical context in which individual skills are paramount.[57]

As in the case of the origins of immigration, sociologists have voiced dissatisfaction with this approach. Clearly education, knowledge of English, and work experience are important factors affecting newcomers' employment prospects, but they do not suffice to fully explain occupational mobility and earnings. Chiswick himself noted that Mexicans failed to obtain returns on their human capital equivalent to those of the native-born or even of other immigrant groups. He attributed this shortfall to a "Mexican ethnic group effect." In her analysis of the 1976 Survey of Income and Education, Reimers confirmed this finding and reported that, in contrast to Mexicans, Cuban immigrants seemed to receive a higher-than-average return on their human capital. She concluded that diversity among Latin-origin groups was so great as to render meaningless any attempt to subsume them under the same ethnic label.[58]

These and other anomalies have led sociologists of immigration to approach the question of long-term economic adaptation from a different perspective. Immigrants are viewed not simply as individuals who come clutching a bundle of personal skills, but rather as members of groups and participants in broader social structures that affect in multiple ways their economic mobility. The concept of modes of incorporation refers to the process of insertion of immigrants into these various social contexts. Contextual effects interact with human capital brought from abroad, determining the extent to which it can be productively used and increased.[59]

Modes of incorporation encompass three different levels of reception. The first is the government's policy toward different immigrant groups. During the last two decades, some groups arriving in the United States—such as refugees—have been granted special resettlement assistance; others have gained legal entry and access to the same social programs available to the native-born; still others have been actively persecuted, their claims for asylum routinely denied or granted with an inferior legal status.

The second reception level involves civic society and public opinion. For various historical reasons, a few immigrant minorities have been greeted with open arms in the United States; others have arrived with little fanfare and their presence has been mostly a matter of public indifference; still others have been unpopular and their arrival has been actively resisted by host communities.[60] Immigrants from Britain and northwestern Europe have typically experienced the least amount of resistance, while those of phenotypically or culturally distinct backgrounds have endured much greater social prejudice. Note that this second level of reception is not necessarily dependent on the first. For example, the large number of unauthorized Irish immigrants in New England have been accorded a favorable public reception, despite their illegal status. By contrast, perfectly legal Iranian and Ethiopian refugees and Jamaican immigrants have suffered much discrimination.[61]

The third reception level is the ethnic community. Some immigrants belong to nationalities too small to form distinct communities and hence find themselves dispersed among the native-born population. Others join communities composed primarily of manual workers. These communities offer some protection against outside prejudice and the shock of acculturation, but even when sizable, they provide few economic opportunities. Still other immigrants are lucky enough to join communities where their co-nationals have managed to create a substantial entrepreneurial and professional presence. These settings offer new arrivals opportunities for economic mobility unavailable to immigrants who join purely working-class communities.[62]

The combination of these three reception levels constitutes the overall mode of incorporation of a particular immigrant group. Assuming that governmental reception is defined by a continuum from active resettlement assistance to active opposition and that societal reception is conditioned by the phenotypical and cultural characteristics of each immigrant group, it is possible to classify immigrant groups in a "tree-like" typology of modes of incorporation. This is done in Figure 1.4. Immigrant groups identified in the bottom row (all relatively recent arrivals in the United States) approximate the characteristics of each ideal type.

The effects of modes of incorporation on individual economic action can also be interpreted as a form of embeddedness. The limits and possibilities offered by the polity and the society at large can be interpreted as the *structural embeddedness* of the process of immigrant settlement; the assistance and constraints offered by the co-ethnic community, mediated through social networks, can be defined as instances of *relational embeddedness*. Empirical findings that appear anomalous when seen from an individualistic perspective (such as the above- or below-average returns on human capital experienced by different nationalities and the different rates of entrepreneurship among immigrants of comparable education levels and work experience) may be explained through this alternative conceptualization.

Middleman Groups and Ethnic Enclaves

Since Ivan Light noted the fact for the first time, specialists in immigration have emphasized the greater propensity for self-employment among the foreign-born. Immigrant entrepreneurship was originally attributed to the discrimination faced by newcomers in the American labor market, forcing many to seek alternative but marginal niches for survival. Subsequent research has shown, however, that the motivations for engaging in independent enterprise are manifold and the results are not limited to a simple escape from destitution.

Figure 1.4 Modes of Incorporation: A Typology

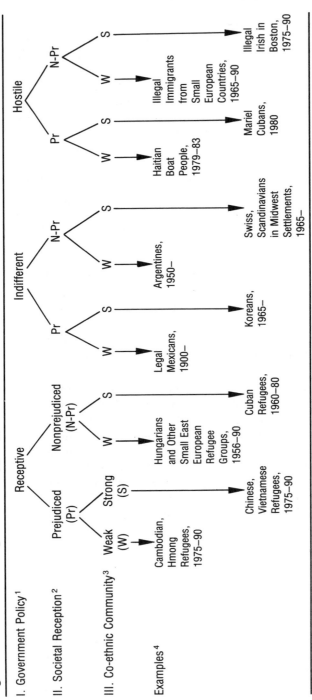

Source: Adapted from Alejandro Portes and Rubén G. Rumbaut, *Immigrant America: A Portrait* (Berkeley: University of California Press, 1990), p. 91.

[1] Receptive policy is defined as legal entry with resettlement assistance; Indifferent as legal entry without resettlement assistance; Hostile as active opposition to the group's entry or permanence in the country.

[2] Prejudiced reception is defined as that accorded to nonwhite groups; Nonprejudiced is that accorded to European and European-origin whites.

[3] Weak co-ethnic communities are either small in numbers or composed primarily of manual workers; Strong communities feature sizable numerical concentrations and a diversified occupational structure including entrepreneurs and professionals.

[4] Examples include immigrant groups arriving from the start of the century to the present. Dates of migration are approximate. Groups reflect broadly but not perfectly the characteristics of each ideal type.

26

Within contemporary ethnic groups created by immigration, the self-employed consistently surpass the average earnings of salaried workers. Within the most entrepreneurial foreign minorities, such as the Chinese, Cubans, Japanese, and Koreans, the income advantage of entrepreneurs remains significant even after equalizing statistically for differences in human capital.[63]

The forms adopted by immigrant enterprise are not homogeneous, and several distinct types have been described and classified by researchers in this field. Bonacich employed the term "middleman minorities" to refer to those groups that specialize in commercial and financial services among a numerically larger but impoverished population. Middlemen are distinct in nationality, culture, and sometimes race from the dominant and subordinate groups to whom they relate. They occupy economic spaces abandoned or disdained in mainstream businesses and simultaneously provide a buffer between these businesses and the poor population they serve.

Middlemen accept the considerable risks involved in conducting transactions in marginal areas in exchange for the opportunity to share in the benefits of such instruments as higher retail prices and usury. In the United States, Jewish and Italian immigrant merchants long acted as middlemen in blighted inner-city areas.[64] During the last two decades, they have been replaced rapidly by Asian immigrants, primarily Chinese and Koreans. Confrontations pitting black inner-city youth against Korean shopowners during the 1992 Los Angeles riot, which led to the destruction of a number of Korean-owned businesses, accord well with Bonacich's description of the buffer role played by middleman groups.

Enclaves are spatially clustered networks of businesses owned by members of the same minority. They are not dispersed among other populations, as middleman groups are, but emerge in close proximity to the areas settled by their own group. Enclave businesses arise at first to serve the culturally defined needs of their co-ethnics and only gradually branch out to supply the broader market. Their success in doing so and their growth depend on three factors: the size of the co-ethnic population that provides their core market and key source of labor; the level of entrepreneurial skills among the immigrants; and the availability of capital resources.[65] All immigrant groups create a few businesses to serve their own cultural needs, but the rise of full-fledged enclaves represents an exceptional phenomenon.

The instances of enclave formation that accompanied accelerated immigration in the first decades of the century and those observed today share several notable characteristics. First, their emergence is signaled by the transformation of certain urban areas, which acquire a "foreign" look that is complete with commercial signs in the immigrants' language and a physical layout of businesses that accords with the group's cultural practices. Second, unlike middleman enterprises which are concentrated in the area of petty financial services and retail trade, enclaves are economically diversified. In addition to trade, they commonly encompass industrial production and specialized services both for the ethnic and external markets. Third, at some point in their development, enclaves become "institutionally complete," allowing newcomers to lead their lives entirely within the confines of the ethnic community.[66]

The institutional completeness of immigrant enclaves is short-lived, seldom lasting longer than one or two generations. Yet while they exist, enclaves create numerous economic opportunities for newcomers that are unavailable in the external labor market. Within the enclave, newcomers can utilize culturally specific skills brought from abroad and learn the ropes of a business through apprenticeship in co-ethnic firms. The Jewish Lower East Side of Manhattan during the first decades of the twentieth century and the cluster of Japanese small firms in Los Angeles that emerged at about the same time are instances of this entrepreneurial form; neither enclave exists today. The Cuban business concentration in Miami, originally dubbed Little Havana; the Chinatowns of San Francisco and New York; the Koreatown area of Los Angeles; and the cluster of Dominican businesses in the Washington Heights area of New York City are contemporary examples.[67]

A third form of ethnic entrepreneurship is the colonization of selected occupational niches, illustrated by the recent transformation of parts of the New York City civil service, as described by Waldinger. Occupational niches are entrepreneurial only *latu sensu* since they do not involve independently owned firms. Instead they consist of the activities initiated by already-employed individuals to bring others of the same national origin to work with them and the gradual transformation of the workplace into an ethnic "enterprise," even if formal ownership lies elsewhere. Use of the immigrants' language for communication at work and the implementation of distinct cultural practices in the performance of tasks are indicators of this transformation, which simultaneously reduces the power of formal managers and owners.

Although differing in structure and modes of operation, middleman minorities, enclaves, and ethnic occupational niches have in common a dependence on *social networks* and *social capital* for their emergence and success. Ethnic networks are the key source of tips for suitable business sites for middleman merchants and for employment opportunities in a developing occupational niche. Networks are equally important as a source of start-up capital for middleman shops as well as enclave firms. Bounded solidarity underlies the common preference that immigrants manifest for their fellows in business transactions. Although buying from co-ethnic firms, hiring other immigrants, or bringing them into the same employment site may still be motivated by self-interest, each such instance also possesses a clear altruistic component based on solidarity with one's in-group.[68]

Similarly, the relative ease with which business is transacted and deals closed within the ethnic economy has its roots in trust in the enforcement capacity of the community. Although middleman merchants are known to take elaborate precautions in their dealing with outsiders, that is not the case in dealing with their fellows. Confidence that agreements will be honored is supported by an awareness that a violator will face ostracism from the ethnic business networks, outside of which there are precious few economic opportunities.[69] Because they have less need for written documents and lawyers to guarantee the observance of contracts, ethnic enterprises have a flexibility not found among firms in the open market and, hence, a significant competitive advantage.[70]

Bounded solidarity and trust enable employers in ethnic enclaves to demand greater discipline and effort from their workers. As we have seen, however, the obligations generated by social structures cut both ways. For employees of such firms, *their* social capital consists of the ability to demand preferential treatment from owners when it comes to promotions and business training. As Bailey and Waldinger have shown, informal training systems are the central mechanism promoting upward mobility within enclaves and facilitating the expansion of enclaves over time.[71]

The Informal Economy

The informal economy is defined as the sum total of income-earning activities that are unregulated by legal codes in an environment where similar activities are regulated. Informal activities are distinguished from criminal ones in that they encompass goods and services that are legal, but whose production and marketing is unregulated. Drugs and prostitution are criminal activities in the United States, while production of garments in clandestine sweatshops and unlicensed street vending are informal.[72] The sociology of immigration has noted a close connection between its subject and the informal economy in the sense that immigrants are overrepresented in those unregulated activities. In her study of the burgeoning informal economy of New York City, Sassen observes:

> There is a strong tendency for such operations to be located in densely populated areas with very high shares of immigrants, mostly Hispanic. Chinese are also prominent, however, as are Koreans and certain European nationalities. Brighton Beach, an area with an almost exclusively Russian emigré population, was found to have an extremely diversified informal economy.[73]

Immigrant overrepresentation in informal activities is closely related to their overrepresentation in small entrepreneurship. For some immigrants, the informal economy is a means for survival in a strange social environment; for others, it is a vehicle for rapid economic ascent. For still others, it is a way of reconciling economic needs with culturally defined obligations. Immigrants whose mode of incorporation is highly unfavorable are commonly found in survival activities. In his study of the Haitian informal economy of Miami, for example, Stepick notes how discrimination, official hostility, and lack of resources have forced Haitians into informal, menial, and badly-paid activities as an alternative to complete destitution. Most informal services in this community (such as auto and home repairs, unlicensed restaurants, and gypsy cabs) cater to other Haitians whose very low incomes limit the possibility of accumulation.[74]

Informal activities thrive within well-developed enclaves. Many of the businesses at the core of these entrepreneurial communities start as informal ventures and only gradually move above ground. Stepick observes, for example, that many of the sizable Cuban residential construction firms in Miami began as "back-of-the-truck," informal home repair businesses. The same is true of many established shops in New York's Chinatown, where Sassen documented the proliferation of clandestine garment sweatshops working under contract for larger manufacturers and wholesalers in the City's fashion district. Informality allows incipient ethnic businesses to bypass costly tax and labor regulations and thus to compete with better-capitalized firms. As we shall see, however, their tenuous legal position also exposes them to certain risks. Successful informal businesses in ethnic enclaves move above ground (that is, become formal) but are usually replaced by new underground ventures initiated by more recent immigrant arrivals.[75]

Informal employment is also a way of reconciling material needs with family and cultural imperatives. In their study of industrial homework among Latin American immigrant women in California and Florida, Fernández Kelly and García observe that pregnancy is a frequent incentive to abandon factory employment and seek homework in garment or electronic production. Unmarried mothers are overrepresented among informal homeworkers since this kind of employment, while yielding low pay, allows them to combine work with infant care. In Miami, however, a massive shift in women's employment from garment factories to homework had less to do with need than with cultural norms stemming from traditional Latin family norms. Fernández Kelly and García quote a prominent South Florida manufacturer on this point:

> Cuban workers were willing to do anything to survive. When they became prosperous, the women saw the advantage of staying at home and still earn some income. Because they had the skill, owners couldn't take them for granted. Eventually, owners couldn't get factory operators anymore. The most skilled would tell a manager, "My husband doesn't let me work outside of the home." That was the worker's initiative based on the values of the culture. I would put ads in the paper and forty people would call and everyone would say, "I only do homework." That's how we got this problem of labor shortages.[76]

By their very character, informal activities are rife with possibilities for fraud. Since no legal framework governs their behavior, parties to a transaction may easily default on verbal commitments. This happens frequently in the informal economy, as when street vendors sell defective merchandise or when contractors change verbally agreed-upon wages in daily labor markets. Immigrant laborers who cluster on certain street corners waiting for a day's work are frequently robbed of their pay by unscrupulous contractors or made to work under much harsher conditions than initially promised.[77]

On the other hand, various types of informal enterprises, particularly within ethnic enclaves, manage to function smoothly over extended periods and to prosper even against the risks of discovery by the authorities and malfeasance by suppliers and buyers. The viability of such firms is predicated on their being embedded in a milieu where *social capital* stemming from solidarity and trust compensates for illegality and the lack of formal means of redress. Bounded solidarity within enclaves shields such firms from the risk of official detection. Enforceable trust cemented by the sanctioning capacity of the community not only increases flexibility of transactions, as we have seen, but allows them to occur entirely outside the pale of state regulation. In its outer appearance, the informal economy represents the operation of an unconstrained free market and indeed has been described in these terms by some economists. In reality, immigrant informal activities can be as regulated as those in the formal sector, except that the courts and the police are replaced by normative enforcement through ethnic networks.

Conclusion

Economists and sociologists alike have attempted in the past to rescue the study of economic action from the exclusive sway of an individualistic perspective. Joseph Schumpeter, in particular, saw economic sociology as a helpful corrective to the neoclassical penchant for transforming people into "mere clotheslines on which to hang propositions of economic logic."[78] North American institutional economists—Veblen, Commons, Slichter, and Dunlop in particular—labored mightily toward the same goal. Although he did not line up with the institutionalists and in fact sharply criticized them, Parsons's intellectual project also represented an attempt to carve out a field for sociology distinct from the academic space occupied by neoclassical economics.[79]

Such early efforts foundered for two reasons. First, the institutionalists and their successors and sympathizers were able to provide tightly reasoned critiques of the neoclassical model, but did not offer an alternative theory in its place. Veblen and his contemporaries produced brilliant case studies of upper-class consumption patterns, labor economics, and comparative development, but these studies were based on ad hoc empirical material and did not cumulate theoretically. The same was true of subsequent sociological studies of labor relations, managerial behavior, and interlocking directorates.[80]

Parsons's project to carve out a distinct academic space for sociology was first elaborated in *The Structure of Social Action* (1937) and culminated, in terms of its applications to economic action, in *Economy and Society* (1956), which Parsons wrote with Neil J. Smelser.[81] This was indeed highly systematic theory, but it suffered from shortcomings exactly opposite to those that plagued the institutionalist camp. Whereas institutionalists were closely attuned to historically specific events, Parsons's categories were almost timeless in their abstraction. And while selfish and opportunistic behavior occupied an important place in the institutionalists' analyses of economic life, it was almost ruled out of existence in Parsons's social system.

The project's emphasis on moral imperatives and value introjection did provide sociology with a distinct analytic core, but one which was patently at variance with the everyday behavior of individual and corporate actors. Some neoclassical economists lost no time in poking fun at the "sociological approach," but most dismissed the project altogether. Economic sociology bifurcated into abstract discussions of a quasi-philosophical character and sound but noncumulative empirical investigations.[82] This rudderless condition prompted the contemporary reaction. As distinct from earlier developments, the new economic sociology employs a theoretical framework that incorporates self-seeking and opportunistic behavior along with altruistic forms of conduct, and aims explicitly at synthesis and cumulation of knowledge.

As an empirically grounded field, the sociology of immigration remained for a long time blissfully indifferent to these theoretical controversies. The field had its own analytic core dating back to the North American origins of the discipline and modified, in recent years, through dialogue with the classics. Convergence with recent developments in economic sociology resulted from the need to correct neoclassical analyses of the origins of immigration and the economic adaptation of immigrants and their descendants. In this sense, there is a clear parallel between the conceptual apparatuses that have developed in both fields. As our discussion indicates, the notions of core-periphery influence and structural imbalancing, modes of incorporation, occupational niches, ethnic enclaves, middleman minorities, and the informal economy can be interpreted as specific manifestations of more general processes, which are captured in the conceptual categories of economic sociology. That so many empirically derived hypotheses in the sociology of immigration "fit" independently developed general concepts attests to these concepts' utility.

However, the task at hand does not consist exclusively of pigeonholing empirical findings and lower-level propositions into more general conceptual categories but also of continuing to mine the factual material in search of results that refine and advance theory. As Merton noted long ago, the defining trait of such "strategic research material" is that it "exhibits the phenomena to be explained or interpreted to such advantage and in such accessible form that it enables the fruitful investigation of previously stubborn problems."[83] Apart from its intrinsic interest, the study of immigration can play a significant role in the present theoretical conjuncture because of the importance of social structures in determining the origins, size, and economic adaptation of the ethnic populations immigration creates.

This chapter was written while I was in residence at the Russell Sage Foundation. I acknowledge gratefully the comments on earlier versions by the authors of other chapters in this volume and, in particular, the comments of Robert K. Merton, the Foundation's scholar-in-residence, whose suggestions proved most helpful. The contents are the author's sole responsibility.

Notes

1. On the reemergence of economic sociology, see Roger Friedland and A. F. Robertson, "Beyond the Marketplace," in R. Friedland and A. F. Robertson, eds., *Beyond the Marketplace: Rethinking Economy and Society* (New York: Aldine de Gruyter, 1990), pp. 3–49; and Richard Swedberg, "Markets as Social Structures," in N. J. Smelser and R. Swedberg, eds., *Handbook of Economic Sociology* (Princeton: Princeton University Press, 1994), pp. 255–282.

2. For recent reviews of sociological theories of immigration, see Alejandro Portes and Rubén G. Rumbaut, *Immigrant America: A Portrait* (Berkeley: University of California Press, 1990); and Charles Tilly, "Transplanted Networks," in V. Yans-McLaughlin, ed., *Immigration Reconsidered: History, Sociology, and Politics* (New York: Oxford University Press, 1990), pp. 79–95.

3. See William I. Thomas and Florian Znaniecki, *The Polish Peasant in Europe and America*, ed. and abr. E. Zaretsky (1918–1920; reprint, Chicago: University of Illinois Press, 1984). See also Robert E. Park, "Human Migration and the Marginal Man," *American Journal of Sociology* 33 (May 1928):881–893; and Everett V. Stonequist, *The Marginal Man: A Study in Personality and Culture Conflict* (1937; reprint, New York: Russell & Russell, 1961).

4. Robert K. Merton, "Three Fragments from a Sociologist's Notebook: Establishing the Phenomenon, Specified Ignorance, and Strategic Research Materials," *Annual Review of Sociology* 13 (1987):1–28.

5. Max Weber, *Economy and Society: An Outline of Interpretive Sociology* (1922 reprint, Berkeley: University of California Press, 1978). Karl Polanyi, "The Economy as Instituted Process," in M. Granovetter and R. Swedberg, eds., *The Sociology of Economic Life* (Boulder, Colo.: Westview Press, 1992), pp. 29–51. Published originally in Karl Polanyi, Conrad M. Arensberg, and Harry W. Pearson, *Trade Market in the Early Empires* (New York: Free Press, 1957).

6. Anthony Downs, *An Economic Theory of Democracy* (New York: Harper, 1957). Paul Samuelson, "Wages and Interest: A Modern Dissection of Marxian Economic Models," *American Economic Review* 47(1957):884–912. Gary Becker, *The Economic Approach to Human Behavior* (Chicago: University of Chicago Press, 1976). Amartya Sen, "Rational Fools: A

Critique of the Behavioral Foundations of Economic Theory," *Philosophy and Public Affairs* 6(1977):317–344.

7. Sen, "Rational Fools." Robert H. Frank, "Rethinking Rational Choice," in R. Friedland and A. F. Robertson, eds., *Beyond the Marketplace: Rethinking Economy and Society* (New York: Aldine de Gruyter, 1990), pp. 53–87.

8. Richard Swedberg, *Economic Sociology: Past and Present* (Newbury Park, Calif.: Sage, 1987). Chris Tilly and Charles Tilly, "Capitalist Work and Labor Markets," Working Paper Series #153, Center for Studies of Social Change, New School for Social Research, New York, 1993.

9. Max Weber, *The Theory of Social and Economic Organization*, trans. A. M. Henderson and T. Parsons (1922; reprint, New York: The Free Press, 1965), Pt. I, pp. 88–115. Originally published as *Wirtschaft und Gesellschaft*.

10. Ibid.

11. Gary Becker, *A Treatise on the Family* (Cambridge: Harvard University Press, 1981). Richard Swedberg, "Major Traditions of Economic Sociology," *Annual Review of Sociology* 17(1991):251–276. Dennis Wrong, "The Oversocialized Conception of Man in Modern Sociology," *American Sociological Review* 26(1961):183–193.

12. Weber, *The Theory of Social and Economic Organization*, pp. 324–329. See also Keith Hart, "The Idea of Economy: Six Modern Dissenters," in R. Friedland and A. F. Robertson, eds., *Beyond the Marketplace: Rethinking Economy and Society* (New York: Aldine de Gruyter, 1990), pp. 137–160.

13. Peter M. Blau, *Exchange and Power in Social Life* (New York: Wiley, 1964). Alvin Gouldner, "The Norm of Reciprocity: A Preliminary Statement," *American Sociological Review* 25(1960):161–179. See also Alejandro Portes and Julia Sensenbrenner, "Embeddedness and Immigration: Notes on the Social Determinants of Economic Action," *American Journal of Sociology* 98 (May 1993):1320–1350.

14. Talcott Parsons and Neil J. Smelser, *Economy and Society* (New York: Free Press, 1956).

15. Donald McCloskey and Lars Sandberg, "From Damnation to Redemption: Judgments on the Late Victorian Entrepreneur," *Explorations in Economic History* 9(1971):89–108. Mark Granovetter, "The Old and the New Economic Sociology: A History and an Agenda," in R. Friedland and A. F. Robertson, eds., *Beyond the Marketplace: Rethinking Economy and Society* (New York: Aldine de Gruyter, 1990), pp. 89–112.

16. Polanyi, "The Economy as Instituted Process." Karl Polanyi, *The Great Transformation* (1944; reprint, Boston: Beacon Press, 1957).

17. Mark Granovetter, "Economic Action and Social Structure: The Problem of Embeddedness," *American Journal of Sociology* 91(1985):481–510.

18. Granovetter, "The Old and the New Economic Sociology."

19. Ronald Dore, "Goodwill and the Spirit of Capitalism," in M. Granovetter and R. Swedberg, eds., *The Sociology of Economic Life* (Boulder, Colo.: Westview Press, 1992), pp. 159–180. Published originally in *British Journal of Sociology* 34 (1983):459–482.

20. Ibid.

21. Calvin Morrill, "Conflict Management, Honor, and Organizational Change," *American Journal of Sociology* 97 (1991):585–621.

22. Ibid., p. 600.

23. Melville Dalton, "Men Who Manage," in M. Granovetter and R. Swedberg, eds., *The Sociology of Economic Life* (Boulder, Colo.: Westview Press, 1992), p. 334. Published originally as *Men Who Manage: Fusions of Feeling and Theory in Administration* (New York: Wiley, 1959).

24. Fritz J. Roethlisberger and William J. Dickson, *Management and the Worker* (Cambridge: Harvard University Press, 1939). Stanley Mathewson, *Restriction of Output among Unorganized Workers* (New York: Viking Press, 1931). William Finlay, "One Occupation, Two Labor Markets: The Case of Longshore Crane Operators," *American Sociological Review* 48 (1983):306–315. Michael Burawoy, "Between the Labor Process and the State: The Changing Face of Factory Regimes under Advanced Capitalism," *American Sociological Review* 48 (1983):587–605. David Stark, "Rethinking Internal Labor Markets: New Insights from a Comparative Perspective," *American Sociological Review* 51 (1986):492–504.

25. Jeremy Boissevain, *Friends of Friends: Networks, Manipulators, and Coalitions* (New York: St. Martin's Press, 1974).

26. Morrill, "Conflict Management." Dalton, "Men Who Manage."

27. Boissevain, *Friends of Friends*, pp. 31–33.

28. Several definitions of the term exist. James Coleman defines it as a variety of entities with two characteristics in common: "They all consist of some aspect of social structures and they facilitate actions within that structure." See James S. Coleman, "Social Capital in the Creation of Human Capital," Supplement, *American Journal of Sociology* 94 (1988):S95–121. In an earlier publication, we defined the concept as "expectations for action within a collectivity that affect the economic goals and goal-seeking behavior of its members, even if these expectations are not oriented toward the economic sphere." See Portes and Sensenbrenner, "Embeddedness and Immigration," p. 1323.

29. James S. Coleman, *Foundations of Social Theory* (Cambridge: The Belknap Press of Harvard University Press, 1990), Ch. 12.

30. Portes and Sensenbrenner, "Embeddedness and Immigration," pp. 1332–1338.

31. This is indeed the pattern observed by Boissevain in his Maltese studies. Other examples include the operation of rotating credit associations among Asian immigrants, as described by Light, and the payment of noncollateralized debts among Cuban and Dominican entrepreneurs, described by Portes and Zhou. See Ivan Light, *Ethnic Enterprise in America: Business and Welfare among Chinese, Japanese, and Blacks* (Berkeley: University of California Press, 1972); and Alejandro Portes and Min Zhou, "Gaining the Upper Hand: Economic Mobility among Immigrant and Domestic Minorities," *Ethnic and Racial Studies* 15 (October 1992):491–522.

32. Clifford Geertz, *Peddlers and Princes* (Chicago: University of Chicago Press, 1963). See also Clifford Geertz, *The Social History of an Indonesian Town* (Cambridge: MIT Press, 1965); and Mark Granovetter, "The Economic Sociology of Firms and Entrepreneurs," Chapter 4, this volume.

33. Portes and Sensenbrenner, "Embeddedness and Immigration," p. 1339.

34. Ferdinand Tönnies, *Community and Society* (East Lansing: Michigan State University Press, 1957), originally published as *Gemeinshaft und Gesellschaft* (Leipzig, 1887). Georg Simmel, "The Metropolis and Mental Life," trans. K. H. Wolff, in K. H. Wolff, ed., *The Sociology of Georg Simmel* (New York: The Free Press, 1964), pp. 409–424. And Georg Simmel, *Über Soziale Differenzierung* (Leipzig, 1890). See also Richard Sennett, ed., "Introduction," in *Classic Essays on the Culture of Cities* (New York: Appleton-Century-Crofts, 1969), pp. 3–19.

35. For recent empirical evidence on this point see Roger Waldinger, Howard Aldrich, and Robin Ward, eds., *Ethnic Entrepreneurs: Immigrant Business in Industrial Societies* (Newbury Park, Calif.: Sage, 1990). John R. Logan, Richard D. Alba, and Thomas McNulty, "Ethnic Economies in Metropolitan Regions: Miami and Beyond," *Social Forces* 72 (March 1994):691–724. Min Zhou, *New York's Chinatown: The Socioeconomic Potential of an Urban Enclave* (Philadelphia: Temple University Press, 1992).

36. Victor Nee and Brett de Bary Nee, *Longtime Californ': A Documentary Study of an American Chinatown* (New York: Pantheon Books, 1973).

37. Max Weber, *The Protestant Ethic and the Spirit of Capitalism*, trans. T. Parsons (Boston: Unwin, 1985), originally published as a two-part article in *Archiv für Sozialwissenschaft und Sozialpolitik* (1904–1905).

38. Howard Becker, *Outsiders: Studies in the Sociology of Deviance* (New York: The Free Press, 1963).

39. Mark S. Granovetter, *Getting a Job: A Study of Contacts and Careers* (Cambridge: Harvard University Press, 1974).

40. Ibid. See also Mark Granovetter, "The Sociological and Economic Approaches to Labor Market Analysis: A Social Structural View," in M.

Granovetter and R. Swedberg, eds., *The Sociology of Economic Life* (Boulder, Colo.: Westview Press, 1992), pp. 233–263.

41. Roger Waldinger, "The Making of an Immigrant Niche," (manuscript, Department of Sociology, University of California-Los Angeles, 1992). See also Thomas Bailey and Roger Waldinger, "Primary, Secondary, and Enclave Labor Markets: A Training System Approach," *American Sociological Review* 56 (August 1991):432–445.

42. Robert K. Merton, "The Unanticipated Consequences of Purposive Social Action," *American Sociological Review* 1 (1936): 894–904. Merton developed the concept further in his "Manifest and Latent Functions," in *Social Theory and Social Structure*, 3rd ed. (New York: The Free Press, 1968), pp. 73–138; see also R. K. Merton, "Unanticipated Consequences and Kindred Sociological Ideas," in *L'Opera di R. K. Merton e La Sociologia Contemporanea*, ed. C. Mongardini and S. Tabbioni (Genoa: ECIG, 1989), pp. 13–29.

43. James S. Coleman, "A Rational Choice Perspective on Economic Sociology," in N. J. Smelser and R. Swedberg, eds., *Handbook of Economic Sociology* (Princeton: Princeton University Press, 1994), pp. 166–180.

44. Portes and Sensenbrenner, "Embeddedness and Immigration." Waldinger, "The Making of an Immigrant Niche."

45. This is the point emphasized by Weber in his analysis of the origins of modern capitalism. Particularistic accumulation and substantive rationality represented the norm in economic life prior to the modern era. Unique to modern capitalism is the diffusion of universalistic norms and formal rationality, which Weber saw as associated with Puritan religious ideology. The clash between formal and substantive criteria of economic action did not disappear, however, but remained a constant tension under contemporary (that is, post-Puritan) capitalism. See H. H. Gerth and C. Wright Mills, trans. and ed., *From Max Weber: Essays in Sociology* (New York: Oxford University Press, 1958), pp. 267–322. Weber, *The Theory of Social and Economic Organization* p. 165.

46. Park, "Human Migration." Stonequist, *The Marginal Man*. Thomas and Znaniecki, *The Polish Peasant*. Milton M. Gordon, *Assimilation in American Life: The Role of Race, Religion, and National Origins* (New York: Oxford University Press, 1964).

47. George J. Borjas, *Friends or Strangers: The Impact of Immigrants on the U.S. Economy* (New York: Basic Books, 1990).

48. Alejandro Portes, "From South of the Border: Hispanic Minorities in the United States," in V. Yans-McLaughlin, ed., *Immigration Reconsidered: History, Sociology, and Politics* (New York: Oxford University Press, 1990), pp. 160–184.

49. Ibid. See also Alejandro Portes, "Migration and Underdevelopment," *Politics and Society* 8 (1978):1–48.

50. Ibid. Michael Piore, *Birds of Passage* (New York: Cambridge University Press, 1979).

51. Saskia Sassen, *The Mobility of Labor and Capital: A Study in International Investment and Labor Flow* (New York: Cambridge University Press, 1988).

52. Ibid. M. Patricia Fernández Kelly, *For We Are Sold, I and My People: Women and Industry in Mexico's Frontier* (Albany, N.Y.: SUNY Press, 1983).

53. Tilly, "Transplanted Networks." Portes, "Migration and Underdevelopment." Douglas S. Massey, "Understanding Mexican Migration to the United States," *American Journal of Sociology* 92 (May 1987):1372–1403.

54. Alejandro Portes and Robert L. Bach, *Latin Journey: Cuban and Mexican Immigrants in the United States* (Berkeley: University of California Press, 1985), pp. 92–93, 125–127.

55. Douglas S. Massey and Luis Goldring, "Continuities in Transnational Migration: An Analysis of Thirteen Mexican Communities" (paper presented at the Workshop on U.S. Immigration Research: An Assessment of Data Needs for Future Research, sponsored by the National Research Council, Washington, D.C., September 17–18, 1992). See also Douglas S. Massey and Felipe Garcia España, "The Social Process of International Migration," *Science* 237 (1987):733–738.

56. Barry R. Chiswick, "The Effect of Americanization on the Earnings of Foreign-Born Men," *Journal of Political Economy* 86 (October 1978):897–921.

57. See George J. Borjas, "Self-Selection and the Earnings of Immigrants," *American Economic Review* 77 (1987):531–553.

58. Cordelia W. Reimers, "A Comparative Analysis of the Wages of Hispanics, Blacks, and Non-Hispanic Whites," in G. J. Borjas and M. Tienda, eds., *Hispanics in the U.S. Economy* (New York: Academic Press, 1985), pp. 27–75.

59. Portes and Rumbaut, *Immigrant America*, Chap. 3. Zhou, *New York's Chinatown*. Rubén G. Rumbaut, "The Structure of Refuge: Southeast Asian Refugees in the United States, 1975–85," *International Review of Comparative Social Research* 1 (Winter 1990):95–127.

60. The latter case is best exemplified among recent immigrants by the experiences of Haitian asylum claimants. See Alex Stepick, "Haitian Refugees in the U.S.," Report #52, Minority Rights Group, London, 1982; and Jake C. Miller, *The Plight of Haitian Refugees* (New York: Praeger, 1984). For a more detailed discussion of different types of governmental reception, see Portes and Rumbaut, *Immigrant America*.

61. See Karen Tumulty, "When Irish Eyes are Hiding . . . ," *Los Angeles Times,* January 29, 1989. Georges Sabagh and Mehdi Bozorgmehr, "Are the Characteristics of Exiles Different from Immigrants? The Case of Iranians in Los Angeles," *Sociology and Social Research* 71 (1987):77–84. Donald J. Cichon, Elzbieta M. Gozdziak and Jane G. Grover, "The Economic and Social Adjustment of Non-Southeast Asian Refugees" (report to the Office of Refugee Resettlement, Department of Health and Human Services, Washington, D.C., 1986, mimeographed).

62. Portes and Zhou, "Gaining the Upper Hand." Bailey and Waldinger, "Primary, Secondary, and Enclave Labor Markets."

63. Light, *Ethnic Enterprise in America.* Alejandro Portes and Min Zhou, "Divergent Destinies: Immigration, Poverty, and Entrepreneurship" in R. Lawson, K. McFate, and W. J. Wilson, eds., *Poverty, Inequality, and the Future of Social Policy* (New York: Russell Sage Foundation, 1995).

64. Light, *Ethnic Enterprise in America.* Edna Bonacich, "A Theory of Middleman Minorities," *American Sociological Review* 38 (October 1973):583–594. Ivan Light and Edna Bonacich, *Immigrant Entrepreneurs: Koreans in Los Angeles 1965–1982* (Berkeley: University of California Press, 1988).

65. Portes and Bach, *Latin Journey,* Chaps. 6, 9. Alejandro Portes, "The Social Origins of the Cuban Enclave Economy of Miami," *Sociological Perspectives* 30 (October 1987):340–372. Logan, Alba, and McNulty, "Ethnic Enclaves."

66. Zhou, *New York's Chinatown.* Bailey and Waldinger, "Primary, Secondary, and Enclave Labor Markets."

67. Bailey and Waldinger, "Primary, Secondary, and Enclave Labor Markets." Luis E. Guarnizo, "One Country in Two: Dominican-Owned Firms in New York and the Dominican Republic" (Ph.D. diss., Department of Sociology, The Johns Hopkins University, 1992). Light and Bonacich, *Immigrant Entrepreneurs.* Portes and Zhou, "Gaining the Upper Hand."

68. Waldinger, "The Making of an Immigrant Niche." Granovetter, "Entrepreneurship." Portes and Sensenbrenner, "Embeddedness and Immigration."

69. Granovetter, "Entrepreneurship." See also Coleman, "Social Capital." Ivan Light, "Immigrant and Ethnic Enterprise in North America," *Ethnic and Racial Studies* 7 (April 1984):195–216.

70. Light and Bonacich, *Immigrant Entrepreneurs.* Zhou, *New York's Chinatown.* Portes and Sensenbrenner, "Embeddedness and Immigration."

71. Bailey and Waldinger, "Primary, Secondary, and Enclave Labor Markets."

72. Edgar L. Feige, "Defining and Estimating Underground and Informal Economies: The New Institutional Economics Approach," *World Development* 18, no. 7 (1990):989–1002.

73. Saskia Sassen, "New York City's Informal Economy," in A. Portes, M. Castells, and L. A. Benton, eds., *The Informal Economy: Studies in Advanced and Less Developed Countries* (Baltimore: The Johns Hopkins University Press, 1989), p. 63.

74. Alex Stepick, "Miami's Two Informal Sectors," in A. Portes, M. Castells, and L. A. Benton, eds., *The Informal Economy: Studies in Advanced and Less Developed Countries* (Baltimore: The Johns Hopkins University Press, 1989), pp. 111–134.

75. Stepick, "Miami's Two Informal Sectors." Sassen, "New York City's Informal Economy." Alejandro Portes and Saskia Sassen, "Making It Underground: Comparative Materials on the Informal Sector in Western Market Economies," *American Journal of Sociology* 93 (1987):30–61.

76. M. Patricia Fernández Kelly and Anna M. García, "Informalization at the Core: Hispanic Women, Homework, and the Advanced Capitalist State," in A. Portes, M. Castells, and L. A. Benton, eds., *The Informal Economy: Studies in Advanced and Less Developed Countries* (Baltimore: The Johns Hopkins University Press, 1989), p. 262.

77. Saskia Sassen and Robert C. Smith, "Post-Industrial Growth and Economic Reorganization: Their Impact on Immigrant Employment," in J. Bustamante, C. W. Reynolds, and R. A. Hinojosa, eds., *U.S.-Mexico Relations: Labor Market Interdependence* (Stanford: Stanford University Press, 1992), pp. 372–393. Joel Millman, "New Mex City," *New York* 7 (September 1992):37–42. Stepick, "Miami's Two Informal Sectors."

78. Joseph A. Schumpeter, *History of Economic Analysis* (London: Allen and Unwin, 1954), pp. 885–887. See also Swedberg, "Major Traditions."

79. Swedberg, "Major Traditions." Charles Camic, "*Structure* after 50 Years: The Anatomy of a Charter," *American Journal of Sociology* 95 (1989):38–107. Granovetter, "The Old and the New Economic Sociology."

80. Granovetter, "The Old and the New." See also Paul Hirsch, Stuart Michaels, and Ray Friedman, "Clean Models *vs.* Dirty Hands: Why Economics is Different from Sociology," in S. Zukin and P. DiMaggio, eds., *Structures of Capital: The Social Organization of the Economy* (New York: Cambridge University Press, 1990), pp. 39–51.

81. Camic, "*Structure* after 50 Years." Parsons and Smelser, *Economy and Society.*

82. Granovetter, "The Old and the New Economic Sociology." Tilly and Tilly, "Capitalist Work."

83. Merton, "Three Fragments," p. 10.

2

Socially Expected Durations and the Economic Adjustment of Immigrants

BRYAN R. ROBERTS

IMMIGRANTS of different national or ethnic origins vary widely in their economic adjustment in the United States. First-generation immigrants and, at times, their descendants have differed in their occupations, in their propensity to be self-employed, and in their average incomes or levels of education.[1] Some explanations of these variations, such as those of neoclassical economists, attribute them to the individual endowments of immigrant groups in terms of education, work skills, or values. However, explanations that only consider individual endowments are inevitably partial, since the usefulness of endowments depends not only on the economic context but on a supportive social environment. Thus, co-ethnics can find well-paid work for an unskilled immigrant while the skilled immigrant remains unemployed for want of such social support. Moreover, immigrant groups differ widely in the strength and nature of their social ties and these differences are likely to affect the pattern of their economic adjustment.

This chapter seeks to extend this sociological understanding of immigrant adjustment in the United States by exploring the temporal expectations of immigrant groups, particularly their expectations of the duration of the immigrant experience. The temporal perspective adds an additional dimension to economic sociology's focus on the way the structure of social relationships shapes economic transactions. Economic transactions are not only embedded in social relationships, but expectations of duration give this embeddness a temporal as well as a spatial dimension.[2] This, as we will see, is the essence of the difference between short- and long-term economic planning at the individual and family level. By fostering short- or long-term planning among immigrant groups, temporal expectations can thus constitute social capital, both positive and negative.[3]

Immigration is a process as much concerned with time as it is with space. People move at particular times in their lives and in those of their families. And their movements occur at certain times in their country's development and in that of the country of destination. Various studies of immigration have used the intersection of these demographic and historical variables to explain variation in the economic adjustment of immigrants.[4] However, the temporal expectations that accompany these particular timings have been neglected. Despite the apparently irreversible nature of the decision to migrate to a new country, immigration is an uncertain move. Those who immigrate cannot know with assurance what the future holds for them and, for many, immigration is provisional and expected to be of temporary duration. An immigrant's career has, to be sure, some clear stages that include naturalization and the birth of children in the new country. Yet many immigrants do not pass through these stages and those who do vary widely in the length of time it takes.

When goals are in the future and their attainment uncertain, then expectations of how long it normally takes to attain these goals are particularly important in determining behavior. Thus, immigrants who come intending to stay temporarily are less likely to make long-term investments such as purchasing a house or to apply for naturalization than are those who come intending to stay permanently. These intentions rarely arise from individual impulse, but are usually based on and enforced by group expectations of the likely duration of immigration. Immigrant networks in country of origin and country of destination are the carriers of these expectations. Recent immigrants are likely to use the experiences of their co-ethnics as a guide to their own career decisions. Officials, employers, or shopkeepers are also likely to see individual immigrants as similar in their commitments to others of their national origin, thus reinforcing the immigrant group's own expectations.

Decisions made in anticipation of career outcomes are likely to ensure that those outcomes are realized. Because of the force of group and institutional pressures, this reality may be imposed even on those who wish to deviate. Nina Toren uses the example of women's academic careers.[5] There are widely held expectations as to the normal length of time that it takes men and women to complete the different stages of an academic career. These expectations are often correct in practice. But this outcome, argues Toren, may result from the climate of expectations that develops within a particular organizational milieu. It is not simply the product of the individual handicaps that women face, such as family responsibilities and family-work role conflicts. Expectations may lead women to decide to delay their careers before events force them to do so. Also, promotional timetables may assume that all women are subject to career delay, thus foreclosing the possibility of exceptions.

Temporal expectations affect immigrant groups in similar but more extensive ways. Immigrants are making a new life that calls into question their collective identity. From being Poles, Italians, or Mexicans, they are transformed into Americans of a particular ethnic background. The new life requires a rethinking of family goals and relationships. In this way, the temporal expectations surrounding immigration affect not simply the time it takes to pass through the formal stages of an immigrant career, but also the cohesion of ethnic and family groups.

The various kinds of temporal expectation are interconnected. For instance, immigrants' expectations of whether or not they will take up citizenship or eventually return to their place of origin will affect their readiness to enter into long-term relationships in their place of destination. Conversely, enduring personal commitments, such as family, entered into in the place of destination are likely to incline immigrants to see their move as a permanent one. The result is that expectations are often mutually reinforcing. Having the right "timings" benefits some immigrant groups, while disadvantage accumulates for those immigrant groups that do not fulfill prescriptions and cannot rely on the long-term support of family and co-ethnic community.

Merton's concept of "socially expected durations" (SEDs) will provide the means to analyze these temporal expectations.[6] SEDs are particularly relevant to understanding immigrant adjustment because immigrants are potentially exposed to multiple, and often conflicting, expectations of the duration of their migration. For instance, expectations that derive from communities of origin may clash with those present in communities of destination. Both types of expectations may conflict with the formal expectations of duration embedded in government restrictions on immigration and emigration. We will consider the official prescriptions of duration contained in United States immigration policy and the persistence of identities based on country of origin. Some immigrant groups make more effective use of their entitlements than do others by fitting in with expectations. Strongly shared temporal expectations can strengthen group identity. Also, temporal expectations and the uncertainties that beset them help explain why family cohesion is important in the adjustment of some immigrant groups but not others.

Temporal expectations have their basis in experiences. These experiences are reflected in the customary migration patterns between sending and receiving country. There are systematic differences between immigrant groups in the balance of temporary and permanent immigration and in the historical duration of migration. We thus need to explore these differences as a prelude to the analysis of temporal expectations. Also, the impact of socially expected durations on immigrant behavior rests on the assumption that immigration is a collective and not just an individual movement. The first section of this chapter thus explores the observed differences in migration patterns among immigrant groups and the conditions that make temporary and permanent migration group attributes and not simply individual attributes. We then explore the characteristics of SEDs that make them a crucial aspect of immigrant adjustment. Finally we consider their impact on three key areas of immigrant experience: citizenship, ethnic identity, and family integration.

This chapter's purpose is mainly theoretical, aiming to extend our understanding of the significance of temporal expectations for social and economic behavior. The temporal culture of an immigrant group can, I suggest, be as significant in influencing economic behavior as are the other aspects of immigrant culture and social structure that will be explored in this volume. The data in this chapter serve to illustrate, not to prove. To analyze properly the impact of temporal expectations would require data collected for that specific purpose. Such data collection must await future research. I shall, instead, be limited to reinterpreting existing data from the perspective of temporal expectations. Mexican immigrants, in particular, will serve as an example of an immigrant group that has been strongly, and adversely, affected by temporal expectations.

Immigration as a Group Process

Immigration is a group and not an individual process because decisions to migrate are usually made within a collective context that includes the family and local community. Immigration flows through social networks uniting places of origin and destination.[7] Furthermore, the overall economic "climate" that affects the local group is likely to influence an individual's decision to migrate even when that individual is not affected in the same way as are others.[8] Tilly puts the issue succinctly: "Individuals do not migrate, networks do."[9] People migrate together from particular places and settle together in particular destinations. It is only within the context of a network of social relationships that individual calculations become useful predictors of the direction and flow of migration.[10]

The general significance of the social context for the temporalities of migration can be captured analytically through the concept of a migration system. I distinguish between two types of collective migration, a temporary labor migration system and a permanent labor migration system. It is the general, group-based expectations of duration that differentiate the two systems. Individuals may deviate from the group norm, but social pressures are likely to make most conform.

In a temporary labor migration system, the community of origin has become organized around the temporary export of labor because of two mutually reinforcing pressures. Local resources are insufficient to provide an adequate subsistence, thus encouraging outmigration to secure additional income. There are, however, enough local resources, usually land, to sustain most of the family in the migrant's absence and to provide (limited) investment incentives to attract the migrants back. Family commitments encourage the return of the migrant. It is, after all, difficult to take the leap into the dark of an unfamiliar culture, and most people are likely to prefer to return when they have opportunities at home.

A permanent labor migration system comes into being when local resources begin to fail a population absolutely so that even partial subsistence is not possible and there are no opportunities for investment. A combination of lack of opportunity and persecution is the condition that is likely to make immigration a permanent move and a collective experience. The group characteristics that make these emigrants an object of persecution at home are likely to be a source of in-group solidarity in the country of destination. Discrimination by other groups in the new country may reinforce this solidarity. Examples are Jewish emigration from Central and Eastern Europe and contemporary refugee groups, such as those from Indochina.

In order for either temporary or permanent labor migration to be considered analytically as a system, these movements must be part of a group response to conditions in places of origin and destination. Shared experiences of deprivation at home and discrimination abroad create incentives for people to help each other with the immigration process. These shared experiences are most likely to be characteristic of homogeneous communities, usually rural, that have low population turnover. Cross-cutting relationships of kinship and friendship reinforce the incentives to help and provide the social contacts needed for adjusting to life in the place of destination. Thus immigrant labor markets, as Sassen shows in this volume, are not circumscribed to specific localities but have an international dimension based on the particular spatial pattern of contacts and on the times at which the contacts were made.

Individuals can of course migrate without being part of a group response, and this possibility gives rise to a third migration type, individualized migration. This can happen when conditions in home communities are heterogeneous, community ties are weak, and people are affected diversely by economic change. This is often the case in urban communities. In towns and cities, size, residential mobility, and a highly differentiated occupational structure are likely to weaken social cohesion. In this situation, people may not know or trust each other well enough to provide information or money to aid fellow community members to migrate. Without the contacts such information provides, adjustment in the place of destination may depend on an individual's unaided efforts, not on networks of people from the same place of origin. Naturally, difficulties with the language of the new country and discrimination may throw immigrants together with others from the same region or culture even when they have no prior ties.

Individualized migration has always been present in the history of immigration to the United States and has considerable weight in the immigrant flows from some countries. It is likely to have become more important in the contemporary period even among groups, such as Mexicans, whose past migration has been heavily based on networks. Individualized migration and its consequences for expectations of duration will only be discussed in passing, however, since their full analysis requires more attention than is possible within the scope of this chapter.

Permanent and Temporary Migration

The evidence shows that most immigration to the United States has been part of a group process in which conditions in sending and receiving communities reinforce the ties among the immigrants.[11] However, the relative weight of temporary and permanent migration has differed among sending countries. We can use the history of immigration to the United States to illustrate the conditions that produce these different types of migration flow. The Irish case of permanent immigration is considered first, followed by the Polish and Italian cases, which display a mix of permanent and temporary immigration, and finally by the case of temporary immigration from Mexico.

The earliest historical example of a permanent migration system is that of the Irish. During the period from 1899 to 1924, only Jewish immigrants surpassed the Irish in their low propensity to emigrate from the United States. Thus, only 4.3 percent of Jewish immigrants in this period and 8.9 percent of Irish immigrants had emigrated by 1924.[12] Faced by poverty and political, religious, and economic persecution at home, the Irish aimed at starting a new life in the United States.

In the late nineteenth century and early in the twentieth, lower transport costs and reductions in journey time led many Europeans to come to the United States as temporary labor migrants.[13] As the urbanization and industrialization of Europe undermined existing agrarian structures, new opportunities emerged at home in both town and countryside, though these new opportunities were often geographically far from the place of birth. Since there were enough resources in the place of origin to sustain at least part of a family or of the wider kinship group, and since new investment opportunities were also being created locally or in the nearby cities, many emigrants were drawn back to their place of origin. Such temporary migrations were characteristic of both Poland and Italy. By 1924, emigrants amounted to 45.6 percent of the Italians and 33.0 percent of the Poles who had immigrated between 1899 and 1924.

But only part of Polish and Italian migration represented a temporary migration system since ties with the home community were weak for many migrants. The loosening of community bonds contributed to permanent migration by making the emigrant more ready to enter long-term commitments in the destination country. In Poland, for instance, farm inheritance usually passed to one child, so the other children had no opportunities in their place of origin, reducing their commitments there.

The most persistent example of a temporary migration system is that which linked the United States to Mexico from the end of the nineteenth century. By the end of the century, a regionally uneven pattern of economic growth in Mexico based on mining, commercial agriculture, and railroads provided alternatives to traditional agricultural subsistence. Many in the center-west and north of the country took up seasonal or longer-term labor migration to destinations elsewhere in Mexico and in the United States. Mexican industry and the country's urban centers offered few new permanent work opportunities and the internal market remained poorly developed. The village remained the main source of livelihood for the vast majority of the Mexican population, so that remittances and the return of migrants were essential to the survival of those at home. The volume of remittances sent back from the United States to Mexico was high.[14] Unlike the situation in Britain or even Poland or Italy, the poverty of Mexican provincial life meant that, for instance, aged parents left behind could not support themselves or depend on other local kin for their survival.

Migration to the United States increased in response to the chaos brought by the Mexican Revolution of 1910 and the subsequent internal conflicts, such as the Catholic counterrevolution, the *Cristiada*, which did not end until the late 1920s. Some of these migrants, particularly those from the middle class, saw their move as permanent. But the majority did not. Taylor's surveys of Mexican labor in California, Colorado, Texas, and the cities of Bethlehem (Pennsylvania) and Chicago show that Mexican immigrants generally believed that they would one day return to their country, especially if conditions improved.[15] This was especially true of areas of recent settlement, such as the Imperial Valley (in California), Bethlehem, or Chicago.[16]

The short-term nature of much Mexican immigrant employment meant that even in cities such as Los Angeles, where distinct Mexican American communities were beginning to settle, there was a high degree of geographical mobility. Less than one third of the Mexicans present in Los Angeles in 1917–1918 were still there a decade later.[17] Taylor reports that Mexicans in Chicago had low rates of property ownership because they expected to return to Mexico.[18]

However, the true consolidation of a temporary migration system between Mexico and the United States came later, with the forced repatriations of the Depression years and stricter controls on Mexican immigration. In 1942, the United States and Mexico entered a contract labor agreement (the *bracero* program) that lasted until 1965.[19] The post-1930 flows have been mainly flows of migrants whose intention is to reside temporarily in the United States.[20] From the 1980s, there is some evidence that the characteristics of Mexican migrants are changing, with higher proportions of women and with migrants more likely to intend to reside permanently in the United States.[21]

But data on remittances show the persistence of a temporary migration system between Mexico and the United States. From at least the 1930s, Mexican migrants have sent regular remittances back to Mexico. Gamio calculates that the average remittance sent by postal money order in 1926 was U.S. $24, with a total of some 100,000 remittances sent.[22] At that time (1926), the average daily wage for a farm laborer was 50 cents in Mexico and some $4 in the United States, making the average remittance six times the daily salary in the United States. Data from the late 1980s and early 1990s show that the average amount sent back by money order has not declined, once inflation is taken into account.[23] The Banco de México estimates that migrants remitted an average money order of U.S. $250 between 1989 and 1991.[24] This was at a time when the average daily wage for farm labor in Mexico was about U.S. $4 and about $32 in the United States, making the average remittance over seven times daily wages in the United States. The number of orders received in Mexico average five million annually.

The Relative Persistence of Immigration

Immigrant groups have also differed in the length of time that their immigration has continued. The persistence of immigration is likely to influence expectations of duration because it refreshes the immigrant culture with new members from the country of origin. In subsequent sections, we will explore the contradictory implications of continuing immigration for immigrant ethnic identity. In this section, four immigrant groups provide examples of immigration of different historical lengths: the Irish, Poles, Italians, and Mexicans.

The Irish were the first of these groups to come in substantial numbers, with large-scale immigration from Ireland beginning in the 1830s and reaching its peak in the later 1840s and early 1850s. In 1850, there were just over 960,000 foreign-born Irish and, by 1860, 39 percent of the foreign-born population in the United States was Irish.[25] The number of foreign-born Irish peaked in 1870 at 1,855,000. After that, numbers declined as new arrivals failed to compensate for the mortality of earlier immigrants. Yet by 1910, there were still approximately 1,300,000 foreign-born Irish in the United States. This number was 29 percent of the total of first- and second-generation Irish. Large-scale Irish immigration was, then, of long duration, starting early and continuing up to the Depression with some 220,000 immigrating in the 1920s.[26]

In the new century, only the Mexicans would immigrate in large numbers over such a long period. Table 2.1 contrasts Mexican immigration with that from Italy and Poland, two countries that contributed large numbers of immigrants but over a shorter period. In 1910, at the height of the new continental European immigration of the turn of the century, there were some 938,000 Poles and 1,343,000 Italians in the United States. Mexican immigration was also beginning on a large scale, and by 1910, there were 220,000 foreign-born

Table 2.1 Foreign-Born Percentage of Two Generations, 1910–1970

Country of Origin	Mexico		Poland		Italy	
Year of Census	Percent Foreign-Born[a]	Rate of Growth FB[b]	Percent Foreign-Born	Rate of Growth FB	Percent Foreign-Born	Rate of Growth FB
1910	58	NA	56	8.9	64	10.2
1920	66	7.8	47	2.0	48	1.8
1930	52	2.8	38	1.1	39	1.1
1950	34	–1.7	31	–1.9	31	–1.1
1960	33	2.4	27	–1.4	28	–1.3
1970	32	2.8	23	–3.1	24	–2.2
1980[c]	28.6	10.6	5.1	–2.7	6.8	–1.9
1990[c]	38.4	7.0	4.2	–0.5	4.4	–2.6

Sources: U.S. Bureau of the Census, *Historical Statistics of the United States*, Part I, Series C195–227, C228–295. Bureau of the Census, 1980 and 1990 Census Special Tabulations.

[a]Through 1970, this is the proportion of the group that is foreign-born (first-generation) of the total population that was either born in the country of origin or whose parents were born in that country. From 1980, the proportion is the proportion foreign-born of the total population that considers itself of that ancestry.

[b]This is the annual rate of growth of foreign-born since previous census year.

[c]The 1980 and 1990 censuses ceased to ask for birthplace of the respondent's parents and, for the first time, contained an ancestry question, asking for the nationality group with which the person identifies (Lieberson and Waters, 1988: 6–9).

Mexicans.[27] The three immigrant groups were similar in that the majority were still first-generation (Table 2.1). The Mexican group has a high rate of growth of the foreign-born between 1910 and 1920. This group records its highest proportion of foreign-born in that year (1920). In the same year, the other two groups begin a steady decline in the percentage of foreign-born. The years after the Depression and during World War II show substantial declines in immigration and, in all three groups, the foreign-born fall to about a third of the first- and second-generation total. In the Mexican case, however, the rate of growth of the foreign-born population picks up again after 1950 and reaches its highest growth rate between 1970 and 1980. That growth rate is higher even than the Italian growth rate between 1900 and 1910, which reflects the peak years of European immigration.

Even when the foreign-born are calculated as a percentage of the ancestry group that includes the grandparent and previous generations, foreign-born Mexicans remain a high proportion of their group. Indeed the 1990 proportion, 38 percent, is higher than the proportions for 1950, 1960, and 1970, although these earlier proportions were based on just the foreign-born and their parents. In contrast, among the two European groups, the foreign-born are small fractions of the ancestry group because of the combined processes of mortality and the decline in the numbers of new immigrants.

Large-scale Mexican and Irish immigration continued long enough to span the generations. Both ethnic groups would include substantial numbers of recent arrivals as well as second and subsequent generations. Neither Italians nor Poles, in contrast, had continuing migration to provide this additional basis for the temporal continuity of ethnic identity. These two groups had a brief period of large-scale immigration, which began at the turn of the century and was over by the 1920s (first because of quota restrictions, then the Depression, and finally the outbreak of war). Second-generation Italian Americans and second-generation Polish Americans would not be faced with substantial numbers of their recently arrived peers and, thus, would neither renew their contacts with their country of origin nor with the ethnic language.

There is evidence, then, that immigrant groups have differed in the duration of the immigration process and the relative significance of temporary migration compared with permanent migration. These two factors provide one basis for differentiating temporal expectations. Thus, whereas the Irish and the Mexicans are similar in the duration of their migration, they contrast in the greater weight of permanent migration among the Irish and of temporary migration among the Mexicans. The significance of this difference in the temporalities of immigrant groups for their temporal cultures will be explored in a later section.

The Significance of Expected Durations

Expectations of duration influence immigrant adjustment because of their significance for coordinating activities. The precision we attribute to time and our reliance on timing are essentially products of the need for coordination in a complex and interdependent society.[28] Coordination requires knowing how long it will take to do something, and for many purposeful activities, including many in the sphere of economics, this knowledge cannot be certain. It will be an estimate—that is to say, an expected duration. Some expected durations may prove more reliable than others in terms of their accuracy as predictions, but without some estimate of the likely duration of an activity planning becomes difficult.

For individual immigrants this task involves, at the minimum, an estimate of the length of time needed to gather the resources to make the journey. Immigrants must also estimate the time needed in their place of destination before they can earn their own living. These personal expectations of duration influence the durations they predict since, as Merton points out, they lead to patterns of behavior that make the expected outcome more likely. People who intend to move are less likely to make local social or economic commitments, especially if the "payoff" is a long-term one, than those who intend to stay.[29]

These assessments are guided by social time, which Elder defines as the widely shared sense that there is an appropriate and likely timing for life events that involve transitions from one role status to another, such as the transition between being unmarried and being married or between being employed and being in retirement.[30] Among Canadian women, for example, there are clear and consistent opinions as to the "right" timing of life course events such as age at marriage, age at birth of first child, and age of becoming a grandmother.[31]

Personal estimates of duration are only part of the picture, however, since any planning depends on others and the timings of others. It is the information and trust present in social relationships that facilitates economic coordination.[32] Strong social networks can produce enforceable trust, as Portes points out in this volume, but enforcement also depends on a shared sense of timing. A shared sense of timing is basic to coordination not simply because those involved can rely on the accuracy of the timings. People also derive a sense of value and self-worth from following appropriate timings. Fernández Kelly shows in this volume that a shared sense of timing creates a temporal culture in the African American ghetto that values the early attainment by adolescents of statuses, such as motherhood, that are achieved later among their more affluent peers outside the ghetto. As she puts it: "Poverty and exclusion flatten and compress temporal rhythms." Temporal cultures, then, can promote short-term as well as longer-term planning.

SEDs are an important source of these expectations, easing coordination with potentially idiosyncratic others. In Merton's use of the concept, SEDs are properties of social structure with various degrees of precision and authority, as we will see. Merton identifies three major types of group expectations of duration: socially prescribed, collectively expected, and patterned temporal expectations.[33] These different types of socially expected durations provide guidelines that enable individuals and groups to coordinate their expectations. Their group and normative nature mean that they are less subject to contingencies than are individual expectations. Their force derives from their being general, that is to say, shared expectations of behavior. The expectation is not about actual durations—how long person X will stay and what person X will contribute to the household. It is about normative durations—how long a person in X's role as son, daughter, or temporary migrant *should* stay and what they *should* contribute. A single unexpected event, such as a change of job, may modify an individual's expectation of stay and capacity to contribute to a household. But it takes many unexpected events to modify or change a group expectation of how long an individual in that particular role position should stay or what he or she should contribute. One implication of this line of reasoning is that the absence of clear and authoritative SEDs to guide immigrant decision making may result in a lack of coordination within the immigrant group.[34]

SEDs facilitate coordination because the migrant roles with which they are associated—that of temporary or permanent migrant—include defined expectations of the behavior normal to the role. Consider the expectations that are present in the letters between Polish families and their emigrant members written at the beginning of this century. The letters make clear that the role of the temporary migrant in the United States is to economize, saving money both to send to family back home and with an eye to acquiring property on eventual return.[35] Emigrants are not expected to spend money on themselves but to send back what they can.

The migrant role belongs, then, to that particular class of roles that Zerubavel calls "temporal roles."[36] Zerubavel's examples are drawn from the hospital services and pertain to people who fill particular time slots, such as day nurses or night nurses. Though the migrant role is less precisely anchored in the rhythms of clock time, it shares with other temporal roles a special sensitivity to changes in expected durations. Changing a nurse's shift from midnight to 4 p.m. has immediate consequences for both his or her own and others' expectations of what is an appropriate routine. And for migrants, even more consequentially, the difference between the status of temporary migrant and that of permanent migrant affects behavior and the expectations of others.

Socially Expected Durations and Immigration

Immigration is a total life experience, necessitating changes that affect relations with family and community and with state and private agencies. Thus, the socially expected durations to which immigrants are subject arise from a wide range of sources. In this section, we consider the main types of SEDs that affect immigrants and suggest what each is likely to contribute, positively or negatively, to immigrant adjustment. Merton's three types of SEDs serve our purposes since they correspond to the three main arenas in which immigrants are involved. Socially prescribed durations arise from the practices of formal institutions, such as government agencies. Collectively expected durations emerge among groups that are formed by exceptional events, as are ethnic groups by immigration. Patterned temporal expectations emerge from the routine of family and community life.

Socially Prescribed Durations

Expectations based on social prescription are the least subject to contingent change. Merton's examples are tenures associated with office holding or term enlistments. Immigration law is our example. Socially prescribed durations are inherent in bureaucratic organizations because they ease the impersonal coordination of activities within circumscribed locations. They are high in precision and are formal, typically written down and protected in law. Their merits and flaws as resources lie in their certainty. People can count on prescribed durations and, consequently, use them to enter long-term commitments. Equally, they are inflexible, locking individuals and organizations into commitments they may later regret.

Although these durations are codified, their consequences derive as much from the normative expectations they engender as from an impersonal interpretation of rules and regulations. Immigration law in the United States, for instance, includes a set of assumptions about the moral obligations attending immigration. In particular, the assumption is that immigration should lead to naturalization, abandoning any commitments to the country of origin and becoming fully committed to the new country. Socially prescribed durations consequently have an intrinsically dual character.

On the one hand, they offer a secure temporal framework that can facilitate planning and engender trust. Thus immigrant groups that naturalize are likely to see themselves as having long-term commitments to the new country, and others are likely to see them in the same light. When personal ties are not present, those who naturalize will be seen by others as safer bets than unnaturalized immigrants for loans for housing or for business, or as partners in economic enterprises. On the other hand, by their very existence socially prescribed durations create disadvantages for those who do not conform to their prescriptions. Not only do nonconformers not derive the direct advantages of socially prescribed durations, but they also are likely to be stigmatized by others because they do not behave as is normatively expected.[37] In the United States, the organization of immigration has been based on the notion of permanence, so groups that conform to expectations profit both from the concrete advantages of citizenship and from becoming publicly trustworthy. Those who come to stay only temporarily are doubly disadvantaged by exclusion from the benefits of citizenship and by the distrust that is engendered by their having violated public expectations. When we examine the impact of immigration law, then, we will be looking for two things. One is the type of resource that immigrant groups derive from following the social prescription to naturalize. Secondly, we will need to examine whether any immigrant groups have attitudes and sentiments that are likely to preclude their naturalization. When this occurs, I suggest, that group is marginalized in the eyes of the rest of the society as inherently temporary.

I further suggest that the "temporariness" of a group in society's eyes may imply their economic marginality as well, since they are seen as people incapable of entering into long-term economic commitments. This temporariness in the eyes of others may, of course, bring economic opportunities of a limited kind as when employers operate with a strategy of recruiting a poorly paid, casual workforce. Indeed, temporal expectations are generally crucial factors in structuring labor markets.[38] Thus, employers' expectations of the likely permanence of different groups of workers are important factors in their employment strategies and, consequently, in the ethnic and gender segmentation of labor markets.

Collectively Expected Durations

The second type of SED is collectively expected duration. This type of expected duration can arise within national communities, as with expectations of the duration of a war; among members of social movements, such as millenarian ones, or in the context of such phenomena as crazes, panics, or riots. What distinguishes these durations from socially prescribed durations is that they tend to be imprecise (or uncertain), are rarely formalized and, we can infer, depend on frequent, nonroutine, group interaction. If we ask those involved in this type of duration, "How long will it last?" their likely reply would be, "As long as it takes."

This type of expected duration puts a group out of phase with others. It creates a distinctive time referent that sets priorities and orders activities. In this way, collectively expected durations become a major component of identity. The identity that is particularly relevant to immigration is ethnic identity based on retaining the culture of the country of origin in the new country. We have noted how immigrant identity is shaped both by collective experiences in the country of origin and in the place of destination, including discrimination. The temporal dimension of ethnic identity is the extent to which it endures among new generations. Thus, the children of first-generation immigrants may see behavior that reveals an ethnic identity as inappropriate for themselves, but not for their parents; among other ethnic groups, ethnic attributes may be a source of pride for second and subsequent generations.

It is likely that the more ethnic identity bridges the generations the more cohesive the co-ethnic community is likely to be. However, this bridging is hard to achieve and sustain. Since a collectively expected duration is imprecise, it is subject to ambivalence and to an accumulation of ambivalences over time that may abbreviate the expected duration.[39] Members of a group cannot completely isolate themselves from others in a society; individually and/or collectively they must enter economic and social exchanges with those around them. Immigrants can create "enclaves" in which they speak their native language, shop in stores owned by co-ethnics, and even be employed by co-ethnics. But many good employment opportunities will lie with employers who are not co-ethnics, while a whole range of government services, including education, are likely to be run by people of a different ethnic origin. The social pressures to "assimilate" to the behavior of others will be considerable since they include rewards for conformity and punishments for nonconformity, as Child shows for second-generation Italian immigrants in the 1930s.[40] Consequently, social and economic exchanges between an immigrant group and the wider society may lead, over time, to a cumulative ambivalence that may erode ethnic identity.

Only a continuing collective experience is likely to sustain an ethnic identity. Thus, it is not the events of a war but working together in the war effort that strengthens collective priorities during wartime. Merton's examples of millenarian movements and wars suggest that the strongest sources of such temporal continuity are desired goals that have yet to be realized. We will use this perspective, in a subsequent section, to understand why some ethnic identities are more susceptible to erosion than others.

Patterned Temporal Expectations

The third type of SED is patterned temporal expectations. These arise from the everyday experiences and needs of people bound together by various kinds of interpersonal and social relations. Merton cites friendship and marriage as cases in point.[41] Patterned temporal expectations are the basis of "family" time: the set of understandings shared by family members about the appropriate timings of individual life course events, such as staying in school, seeking employment, or leaving the household.[42] Patterned temporal expectations are also the basis of family strategies since they facilitate planning. They are essential to the role that the family plays in immigrant adjustment because they identify which relationships family members can count on, for what purposes, and over what period. Their normatively binding character makes economic planning possible when formal contracts are inappropriate, such as when family members are prepared to make sacrifices without expectation of immediate return.

Like other SEDs, patterned temporal expectations derive their strength from the social structure of which they are a part. This circumstance reminds us that family time exists only when supported by the expectations of the wider community. Otherwise, there are likely to be social pressures on individual family members to pursue their own courses independently, pressures that may be reinforced by the structure of employment and housing opportunities. When the prospects of wives and husbands differ or children see more of a future outside the family than within it, family cohesion is less likely to protect its members against negative influences in the immediate environment.

There is a second significant way in which patterned temporal expectations affect immigrant adjustment, and that is through the ambivalences that are inherent in the immigrant role. We have noted the significance of these ambivalences at the collective level, and they are also present in the personal relationships of immigrants, particularly their family relationships. Seeing immigration as temporary is likely to increase these ambivalences. For example, temporary immigration is often associated with the separation of family members, as when the husband migrates and leaves the wife and children behind. Even when husband and wife move together, there are still likely to be ambivalences about responsibilities toward parents left behind and the extent to which the immigrant should, or needs to, keep in touch.[43]

The accumulation of ambivalences over time may reduce the effectiveness of the family and of family networks as a resource in immigrant adjustment in two ways. First, it may disperse immigrant resources, inhibiting investments in their place of destination. Second, it may "dilute" the strength of family relationships through the grievances and lack of confidence in each other that ambivalent relationships bring. We will need to examine the circumstances under which these outcomes are most likely to occur.

This emphasis on temporal expectations focuses on the social structural sources of immigrant family cohesion over time. Thus, some families live in communities whose expectations enhance their capacity to work together and others do not. Individual choice plays only a partial role in this outcome.[44] We will be looking, then, at how structural changes in the opportunities available to immigrant family members are likely to affect expectations of family unity.

Immigration Law and Policy and Socially Prescribed Durations

In this section I look at immigration law and examine some unintended consequences that arise because of its characteristic as a socially prescribed duration. Immigration law in the United States includes assumptions about the moral obligations attending immigration, particularly that it should lead to naturalization, a giving up of all commitments to the country of origin. The formal prescriptions of immigration law generate normative assumptions that are likely to stigmatize those who do not naturalize. Hull provides an example of this process, quoting from the 1924 decision of the Rhode Island state court concerning the rights of legally resident aliens: "Aliens as a class are naturally less interested in the state, the safety of its citizens, and the public welfare."[45]

Consider also this excerpt from a 1930 report written by Enrique Santibañez, a Mexican consul in the United States:[46]

> Whoever registers at the American ports of entry, presenting the documents that the law demands and paying the required taxes, has the right to live in the United States indefinitely. But with the passage of time, the pressure begins on the recently arrived, not on the part of the authorities, but on the part of the American people with whom they are in contact that they naturalize as an American citizen. It is, consequently, the people, in their legitimate right to live as they wish, who do not desire that there are individuals who live indefinitely in the American union as foreigners. In the previous chapter, we showed how this invitation is made to Mexicans and we must add that they [Mexican immigrants], with the rarest of exceptions, present an absolute resistance to changing their nationality.

The temporal expectations associated with immigration law and policy have negative implications, Santibañez implies, for the Mexican immigrant of his day. The prescriptions of immigration law in the United States, as we shall see, have had important positive consequences for the adjustment of certain immigrant groups, while for others they have had negative consequences.

The Rationale of United States Immigration Policy

My starting point is the observation that any formal regulation of entries and exits into a country or from it necessarily creates socially prescribed expectations of duration. Governments seek, at the least, to distinguish between those for whom they have a permanent responsibility, their citizens or prospective citizens, and those for whom their responsibility is limited and temporary, citizens of another state. Immigration law and policy thus give formal prescriptive force to the expected duration of the relationships of those who enter a country. Those who enter temporarily cannot easily enter long-term local commitments. In contrast, permanent immigrants who become citizens can avoid whimsical removal and enter long-term commitments with others.

Immigration policy differs widely among countries in terms of the relative balance permitted between temporary migration (nonimmigrant) and permanent immigration leading to citizenship. Immigration policy in the United States—in contrast, say, to policy in Germany—is one of the most liberal in encouraging immigrants to become citizens through a series of steps, each with prescribed periods.[47] Resident aliens must not absent themselves from the United States for longer than six months, with similar restrictions applying in the first five years of naturalization. The resident alien has a right to apply for citizenship after a period of five years, or three years if close kin to an American citizen.

The restrictions attending resident alien status show that the society does not regard it as a normal status for someone who has come to make the United States their home. As we saw in the excerpts from the report by the Mexican consul, Enrique Santibañez, popular sentiment echoes and enforces this view. There is no legal bar to remaining a resident alien for life, but resident aliens are subject to certain regulations and fiscal penalties that do not apply to citizens.

The United States authorities, then, see immigration as a formally prescribed duration. They expect immigration to end, in normal circumstances, with citizenship—when immigrants become, for most legal purposes, indistinguishable from native-born citizens.[48] The emphasis on family reunification in United States immigration policy underlines this commitment to permanent settlement. In the visa allocation system current at the end of the 1980s, the spouse and unmarried children of the immigrant who has permanent residence status receive a high preference under the worldwide quota.[49] Once the immigrant becomes a citizen, his or her spouse and unmarried children enter free of quota and other family members receive preferential quotas. Family reunification provisions brought in over 80 percent of the 643,000 immigrants admitted in fiscal year 1988.[50]

United States immigration policy and American public opinion have both persistently resisted accepting the idea of there being large numbers of migrant workers in the United States who do not become citizens. Yet the United States economy, like others, has generated a continuing demand for workers who are willing and able to take on low-pay jobs of an essentially seasonal or temporary nature. These jobs are frequently found in agriculture and in construction. To live off such jobs often requires considerable mobility, as in the case of railroad construction or seasonal agriculture. Employers claim that there is not an adequate supply of resident labor for these jobs, including the unskilled urban service jobs that have been taken by many recent immigrants.[51] A continuing tension thus exists between the social prescriptions attending immigration and the demand for a supply of temporary workers.

The contract farm labor program (the *bracero* program) was an attempt to provide such a supply through official channels. However, it included only Mexican nationals, reinforcing the image of Mexicans as essentially temporary, unskilled workers. Garcia points out that "Operation Wetback" had a significant negative affect on people of Mexican descent in the United States.[52] It targeted only one ethnic group and highlighted their essentially provisional status in the United States. The mass repatriations of people of Mexican origin in the 1930s reinforced this status. Some of those repatriated were legal residents and citizens.[53]

Many United States officials and politicians assumed that Mexicans were in the United States only temporarily, and this view affected second- and third-generation Mexican Americans settled in Los Angeles who suffered discrimination in housing and were treated as a temporary presence incapable of making long-term work commitments.[54] The Los Angeles Chamber of Commerce and the California Development Association depicted Mexicans in the 1920s as essentially a temporary labor force. A member of the local business community described the Mexican as someone who "comes to America primarily to sell his labor for American money that he may return to Mexico and be a landed citizen."[55]

Naturalization statistics provide a clear indication of group differences in temporal expectations of commitment to the United States. Those groups that stayed permanently, such as the Germans or Irish, had high rates of naturalization. Italians and Poles, who had a history of temporary migration, had the lowest European rates of naturalization in 1920—30 percent of the foreign-born Italians and 28 percent of the foreign-born Poles.[56] Mexicans had even lower rates of naturalization. The 1920 Census reported that only 4.8 percent of the foreign-born Mexican-origin population sought naturalization.[57] By the 1980s, Mexicans who were legal residents in the United States continued to have a low propensity to become citizens. Mexico had approximately 4 percent of males and females naturalizing within ten years of admission to the United States in the 1971 immigrant cohort. Only Canada had lower proportions among the top ten countries of origin of immigrants.[58] In contrast, Asian immigrants have a high propensity to naturalize.

These group differences in likelihood of naturalizing will have real consequences for immigrant adjustment. A naturalized citizen has more rights than does the resident alien to sponsor the immigration of kin. This right has been a significant source of family reunification for Asian immigrants and, it can be suggested, a means of consolidating family-based enterprises. Furthermore, low rates of naturalization reduce the political clout of immigrant groups. The historic tendency of Mexican immigrants not to naturalize is likely to have reduced the political involvement even of their American-born descendants.

Immigration prescriptions thus unwittingly create a collective presumption that immigrants from particular countries are suspect with regard to their temporal commitments to the United States. Even officials may treat them as if their presence is suspect, regardless of each individual's right to remain.

The Temporal Basis of Ethnic Identity

The temporalities of the immigrant experience give rise to three types of ethnic identity. We noted that adhering to group goals that are yet to be realized is likely to be the strongest temporal basis for immigrant cohesion over the generations. The first type of identity, then, is that which is present among immigrant groups that see themselves as politically and culturally in exile. Jewish, Irish, and more recently, Cuban immigrations to the United States provide good examples. The expectation of returning to their place of origin may not be realistic, but for these groups, the temporal continuity of their culture is the basis of a group identity, linking future goals with past traditions. The sense of exile derives, in part, from not being culturally "at home," since their collective expectations place "home" in the future, not the present.

I will describe this type of immigrant group as "cultural exiles." I see them as equivalent to Bonacich's category of *sojourners* or *strangers*.[59] The relatively long time horizon of these "exiled" groups enables them to make commitments such as establishing businesses, buying property, and providing local education for their children. Exiles are likely to be particularly effective in the economic sphere. Their expectations may, however, encourage involvement in certain types of business activities in preference to others, such as businesses with assets that can be quickly realized. Their common goals and common time referents create bases for cohesion.

A continuing flow of immigration from the country of origin is another source of ethnic identity, revitalizing the use of the language of origin and renewing relationships with the home country. However, when the continuing flow is based on a temporary migration system, it gives rise to a "transnational ethnic community" whose culture and commitments are neither wholly oriented toward the new country nor toward the old.[60] This is the second type of ethnic identity. For temporary migrants, the immediate prospect of return discourages their making long-term commitments, economic, social and cultural, in their host country. But since migrant income is often an essential factor in the survival of sending communities, the economy, politics, and culture of these communities are inseparably bound to the continuation of migration.

The formation of transnational ethnic cultures is likely to weaken the temporal cohesion of the co-ethnic community since transnational ethnic identity depends on continuing contacts between immigrants and those in the home country, contacts which the second and subsequent generations are unlikely to maintain. Consequently, although transnational ethnic identity is potentially a strong form of immigrant identity, it is also the most disruptive of intergenerational co-ethnic cohesion when the immigrant flow has a long history.

The final type, labeled "ethnic American," includes those groups who neither sustain their identity by continuing immigration nor by unrealized collective goals. The ethnic American identity may provide a sense of roots and a convenient source of fellowship or help in times of need, but there is little to protect it from the disruptive forces of geographical and social mobility. There is, for instance, nothing inherent in Italian or Polish identity that requires Polish Americans or Italian Americans to retain it over the generations.

Cultural Exiles

Irish identity in the United States was not an immediate source of co-ethnic cohesion in the nineteenth century.[61] At the beginning of large-scale Irish immigration there were substantial cleavages between middle-class Irish immigrants and the mass of immigrants who were mainly unskilled laborers and peasant farmers. The following quotation from a working-class Irish immigrant illustrates that these cleavages could be impediments to ethnic solidarity: "An Irishman was the worst boss you could have [in the United States], slave-driving all the time."[62] Over time, however, co-ethnic solidarity was built around the Catholic Church, its parochial schools, and politics. By 1900, the group identities of the Irish on both sides of the Atlantic would be remarkably similar.

The cement here was opposition to English domination in Ireland. Irish in the United States joined with those at home in promoting land reform and, ultimately, Home Rule. These were issues that tended to unite immigrants of all classes, reinforcing the notion that Irish emigration was essentially political exile. The exactions of absentee English landowners and restrictions on Irish trade and business were felt by many types of farmers, artisans, and small-scale merchants. Many had emigrated as a direct result of English exactions and almost all had relatives in Ireland who still suffered from them. Also, the issue of English domination made the Catholic Church an especially active element in Irish ethnic cohesion in the United States. Anti-Catholic prejudice in the United States and restrictions on the Church in Ireland contributed to the cohesion of Irish Catholics on both sides of the ocean. The Catholic Church in Ireland allied itself with the movements opposing English and Protestant rule, and in the United States, helped to organize the Irish community in support of Home Rule. Miller argues that the conservative stance of the Church on family issues and on labor issues helped reconcile middle-class Irish Americans with their working-class co-ethnics to form a cohesive co-ethnic community. Concentrated in a few urban centers and constituting the first major Catholic group in the United States, the Irish dominated the parochial school system. Irish employers and political bosses operated patronage networks that were mutually beneficial and that included many working-class Irish. They also served to incorporate new arrivals.

In practice, as we have seen, few Irish ever returned to Ireland. However, Miller states that "the Irish retained the notion that emigration was exile."[63] Even the granting of Home Rule in 1920 only assuaged in part this culture of exile. The continuation of English rule over Northern Ireland left part of Irish identity unaccomplished.

More recently, it can be suggested, the co-ethnic cohesion of the Cuban immigrant community has also been based on a sense of cultural exile. This immigration began on a large scale in the 1960s, with the rise to power of Castro and the consolidation of communism on the island. The first emigrants were predominantly middle-class who saw themselves as fleeing communism, while retaining the belief that they would return once Castro fell. Immigration from Cuba has continued and the ethnic community is now concentrated in Miami and, to a lesser extent, a few other American cities. The culture of exile is particularly strong among members of the Cuban business community in the United States who have been substantial financial contributors to political campaigns aimed at ending the communist regime in Cuba. The idea of return is used to bind the entire Cuban immigrant community by providing common material and ideological goals.

The culture of exile is likely to provide the second generation with a continuing reason for maintaining Cuban culture in the United States. Though this immigration has not continued over as long a period as did Irish immigration, there is some evidence that second-generation Cuban Americans retain a strong sense of identity with Cuba and its culture. Thus, in this volume, Portes shows how second-generation Cuban high school students retain Spanish to a higher degree than Haitians retain French or Haitian Creole. They also are the least likely to see the United States as a society that discriminates against minorities because, suggests Portes, they are supported by a cohesive ethnic culture.

The Transnational Community

Mexican immigration provides many examples of the persistence of ethnic identity based on transnational communities. We have noted that Mexican immigration has been part of a temporary labor migration system. Studies have reported an ongoing process of back-and-forth migration between specific locations in Mexico and in the United States as far back as 1920.[64] These movements have created an interdependence between immigrant communities in the United States and their home communities in Mexico that neither can do without. The economies of communities in Mexico are sometimes organized around remittances, while consumption patterns reflect the types of goods brought from "the North."[65] In the United States, immigrants from Mexico prefer to join fellow-villagers in the city in which they settle. Once there, new arrivals organize much of their social life around such contacts, which also help with obtaining work and shelter.

The identities emerging within the framework of these transnational communities are distinctive because they provide immigrants with choice and a sense of alternatives. Thus, Rouse's Mexican informants in Redwood City stress the constraints of life in the United States.[66] They talk of the drudgery of wage work, the burden of American cultural expectations, and their preoccupation with the police and the Immigration and Naturalization Service (INS). They were, however, long-term residents and had bought houses in the United States. Their continuing interest in their hometown in Mexico is based not so much on concrete plans to return as on possible alternatives such as setting up an independent business in the hometown or living free of the vices and cultural contamination that they identify with life in the United States.

Research on immigrants in New York from a small township, Ticuani, in the Mexican state of Puebla provides compelling examples of the strength of the transnational migrant identity.[67] Most of New York's Mexican immigrants appear to have originated in this township and others close to it. Like migrants from the center-west of Mexico, the first migrants from the Puebla region helped others join them so that at least thirteen of the local townships "specialized" in sending migrants to New York.[68] Some of these migrants returned after a short absence and some after a longer one. Still others move back and forth between New York and Puebla. In the case of Ticuani, even immigrants who see themselves as settled in New York maintain an active interest in the township. As was true of Rouse's informants, the hometown has become an alternative community for them that increases the life course options open to them.

A transnational migrant identity is likely, however, to be inappropriate for second- and subsequent-generation descendants of immigrants. These descendants are likely to encounter a peculiar problem of temporal identity. In the preceding type of ethnic identity, cultural exile, identity could persist as an idealized view of a common culture that spanned the generations. By their nature, identities that are tied to continuing movement between two countries are unlikely to span the generations. Ties will break as paths diverge between the descendants of those once bound by transnational kinship and friendship networks. Moreover, the transnational identity is based on behavior, such as saving in the United States and sending remittances back home, that nonimmigrant members of the ethnic group may find inappropriate.

Pablo Vila's analyses of ethnic identities on the United States-Mexico border bring out the reactions of the second and subsequent generations of Mexican Americans to the new waves of Mexican immigrants.[69] These new immigrants constantly recreate the image of the Mexican as the economically impoverished, temporary labor migrant. In this situation, Mexican Americans adopted a version of their ethnic identity that puts them out of phase with the new immigrants.

A third-generation Mexican American lawyer, Alfredo, speaks of the temporal break in the identity of Mexicans in the United States, in contrast to what he takes to be the coherence of Jewish identity:

> I think every one of us is left to our own world and the way we interpret, . . . umm, our Mexican American culture, heritage, world, . . . whatever you want to call it. It's a little different because there's really not ties left to Mexico, at least for me . . . so I think it's nothing like the Jewish that have, . . . I mean, it's just one strand period and it runs through history and wherever they are, it's the same and they contact each other, and build a house together.

Mexican immigrants on the border say that they prefer Anglo employers to Mexican Americans, echoing the sentiments of Irish immigrants. Unlike the Irish case, there is no shared set of ethnic attributes and goals to bridge the immigrant and native-born generations. As

Vila puts it, to some immigrants it is the Mexican Americans who are poor without dignity, since it is they who reject Mexico.

Ethnic Americans

Written in 1918, *The Polish Peasant in Europe and America* is too early an account to document fully the direction of Polish ethnicity in the second and subsequent generations. The account makes it clear, however, that Polish American identity was based on the interests of Poles in America, not on a sense of exile from their homeland. Thomas and Znaniecki describe the weakness of Polish political organizations in the United States, such as the Polish National Alliance, when they concerned themselves with Polish issues.[70] This was the case despite the high degree of return migration. They account for this weakness by pointing to the economic motivation of Polish emigration, as opposed to the motive of political persecution. They point to the lack of any coherent political project in Poland that might make return more attractive. Polish clergy used the support of Polish American associations in their attempts to establish parochial schools and parishes, often against a predominantly Irish hierarchy, but took little or no interest in Poland's struggles for independence. Without a compelling nonmaterial reason for the survival of Polish identity in the United States, Thomas and Znaniecki worried that the second generation would not be as constrained as was the first generation by the moral bonds of Polish American society: ". . . the second generation, unless brought in direct and continuous contact with better aspects of American life than those with which the immigrant community is usually acquainted, degenerates further still."[71]

Irvin Child interviewed second-generation Italian Americans in New Haven, Connecticut, in the late 1930s.[72] His account of these interviews provides insight into the social pressures that dilute ethnic identity in the absence of continuing immigration and cultures of exile. He detected three patterns of response to ethnic identity among his informants. One he labels the "rebel reaction," in which the second generation effectively denies their ethnicity, seeing its attributes as inferior to those they see as characterizing mainstream American culture. They recognize the barriers to being accepted as truly American, but they are determined to continue the struggle. The second is the opposite to the first. It is an "in-group reaction" in which the second generation emphasizes the value of being Italian, of speaking Italian, and prefers to associate with others who have the same priority. Finally, there is the "apathetic reaction" in which the second generation is neither particularly for nor against Italian customs or language.

Through the words of Child's informants, a clear picture is given of the circumstances that give rise to these different reactions. Second-generation Italians attend schools that use English as the language of instruction and emphasize American values and customs. They must seek work in businesses and organizations where the bosses and often most of the workers are not Italian. There are thus rewards for rejecting Italian attributes in the approval of teachers, fellow-workers, and employers, and there are punishments for resolutely sticking to ethnic customs. Italian identity survives most strongly among those who confine themselves to the co-ethnic community either because of rejection by the outside or because the nature of their employment allows them to do so. As long, then, as a strong co-ethnic community exists, with its own sources of employment, ethnic identity persists. Among Child's informants, there is a sense that the Italian co-ethnic community is not strong. As an in-group informant put it, "I blame it [discrimination] on the Italians because they don't have any power since they aren't together. . . . They don't vote; or if they do, they don't know what they're voting for. . . ."[73]

Italian immigrants lived, however, alongside other immigrants and usually were not employed by co-ethnics. After World War II, residential mobility dispersed the Italian community, weakening further the neighborhood basis of ethnic identity.[74]

The temporal basis of ethnic identity is, however, only one of the various factors differentiating the cohesion of immigrant groups in the United States. To it would have to be added factors such as migrant networks, the demographic structure of the migrant group, the timing of its arrival, the nature of its human capital, and the regional economies in which immigrants settled. Collective expectations of ethnic identity are significant because they provide the cement that can, at times, mitigate the centrifugal forces of assimilation.

Family Timings and Immigration

The basis of successful immigrant adjustment is often seen to lie with the family. The widespread use among immigrant groups of family-based strategies of economic adjustment occurs because the family may be the only resource available to those who come with few material assets and with low levels of skill.[75] Even for those immigrants with more educational and material resources, various studies have shown that family members are still likely to represent the most trustworthy and the least costly collaborators in business. Family members tolerate sacrifices, like working without pay in a family business, because they contribute to the general welfare and future of the family and because the alternatives may be less attractive.

National cultures differ in their patterns of family organization and in the importance assigned to family cooperation.[76] Thus, having the "right" family values has been suggested as an explanation of why some immigrant groups use family strategies more successfully than do others. Asian families earn praise because children listen to their parents and parents single-mindedly work to advance long-term family welfare. In contrast, commentators see weak family values as producing high rates of family disintegration and persistent poverty among other immigrant groups.

The temporal perspective allows us to see these patterns of family adjustment in a different light. In order for families to use such strategies, members must have a sense of family time—of their mutual interests, persisting over the generations, in taking it in turns to give and to receive. This sense of a common future depends, however, less on abstract values than on the reinforcement that community expectations give to family time. Thus, we turn in this section to the differences among the settlement processes of immigrant groups, considering how these strengthen or weaken community support for family time. Again, the temporal approach is only a partial explanation. It will need to be complemented with a sense of the broader structure of differential opportunities with which individual family members are confronted. As Laurel Cornell points out, families usually act as coalitions of interests that inducements, such as property, keep together and attractive alternatives pull apart.[77]

The Community Basis of Family Cohesion

The history of immigration to the United States provides many examples of the variation in family strategies or life-plans, as Hareven calls them, and of changes in family coalitions.[78] The examples of successful family strategies are those where expectations of family time and the realities of community structure reinforce each other. Thus, the family is likely to be strongest when the opportunities available in the wider community are most easily accessed by a collective family strategy and by family-based networks. In the early part of this century, individual timings were often closely dependent on collective family needs and schedules. Among the French Canadian immigrants in Manchester, New Hampshire, there were clear expectations of the timing of life transitions such as when wives would leave the labor force or when children should leave home, and these were dependent on other timings such as when daughters reach work age, or when younger children are old enough to substitute in domestic tasks or to take over money contributions from their elder siblings. As Hareven puts it, family members could "count on each other."[79]

The uses to which such coordination were put ranged from implementing defensive life-plans to implementing long-term plans aiming at attaining middle-class status, and a family's choice depended, largely, on economic circumstances.[80] Also, the same immigrant group might marshal family resources differently depending on the socioeconomic context. For example, Di Leonardo shows that Italian immigrant families in California, in contrast to those on the East coast, were more likely to have family economies in which husbands, wives, and children worked together in truck farming, stores, and bakeries.[81] Italians in California found less prejudice against them and many more opportunities for self-employment than did Italians on the East Coast.

There have, however, been fundamental changes in the relationship of the family economy to the labor market and these have affected family time as a coping strategy. The major change is the increase in employment opportunities for married women, and the decrease in employment opportunities for dependent children. In contrast to the early part of this century, children are now encouraged to stay in school. Previously, the preference was to start a work career at an early age either as a means to future social mobility through apprenticeship or as a useful source of family income. Employment prospects for those without a high school diploma have become increasingly poor, and even the young who have completed high school or more may face unemployment. In this situation, the primary family economic strategy changes from that of working children to that of working wives. This is a basic finding of a study of changes in a New England mill town that contrasts Polish, Italian, and Irish immigrants at the turn of the century with Portuguese and Colombian immigrants in the 1970s.[82]

The "working wives" strategy is likely to undermine the importance of family time. First there is the problem of child care when both parents are at work. Secondly, absent parents are less likely to be able to supervise their children's conduct and education. For immigrants at the turn of the century, child care was not an issue since mothers tended not to work outside the home. This meant that in the early years of the family cycle, households depended on the wage of the male breadwinner. This could be supplemented by the wife taking in boarders or taking in work to do at home. Thus, family strategies based on working children are likely to have a centripetal effect, strengthening family cohesion. In contrast, those based on working wives are likely to be more centrifugal in their effects, making family members more independent of each other.

Other kin may substitute for the working wife, but this depends on the immigrant group being mature enough demographically to have grandparents and other kin present. For instance, Lamphere shows that the longer-settled Portuguese could more readily count on kin for child care than could the more recently arrived Colombians.[83] Thus, the change to working wives poses particular difficulties for immigrant groups that have just begun their settlement in the United States or for those, like the Mexicans, whose immigration has mainly been temporary. In the latter case, some or all other family members are likely to remain in the country of origin. In contrast, refugees are more likely to have a balanced demographic structure and contain three-generational families (often, of course, in two households). Since their reasons for leaving are not work-motivated, refugees are more likely than labor migrants to be of any age and to come as whole families.

Compare, for instance, Cuban and recent Mexican immigration. Both ethnic groups have similar family values, emphasizing the importance of family cohesion and the duties of children to their parents. However, as a refugee group, Cubans have an older age structure since many immigrated when they were over thirty. In contrast, the Mexican age structure is younger with very few immigrants likely to have first migrated after age thirty.[84] Cubans are the least likely of the Hispanic-origin groups to have single-parent families.[85] An analysis of a large sample of legal and illegal Mexican immigrants living in San Diego county shows that the family living arrangements that accompany Mexican immigration are diverse.[86] The single-parent category among the legal migrants makes up approximately 20 percent of households containing children, a much higher proportion than is the case among the turn-of-the-century immigrants studied by Lamphere.[87] Browning and Rodríguez stress the turnover in household composition among their Mexican immigrant informants that adds to the uncertainties attending family calculations of income and planned expenditures.[88]

The strategy of working wives also poses less of a problem for family cohesion when the family and the co-ethnic group control their own economic and residential environment. In this respect too,

Cubans have the advantage over Mexicans. Cubans control more employment opportunities than do Mexicans both because they are much more likely to be self-employed and because co-ethnic employment is more likely than among the Mexicans.[89] It is, then, more likely that Cubans can operate family strategies than can the Mexican immigrant group. The Cubans are more likely to have kin, particularly grandparents, living close by who can care for children if both husband and wife are working. They are also more likely to be self-employed, a condition that makes the family and family relationships key to economic survival and advancement.

Ambivalence and Immigration

Where immigrant groups have been involved in temporary migration systems, then there are likely to be severe ambivalences undermining family cohesion in the place of destination. These ambivalences can arise because family members differ in their expectations of whether to stay or to return. Thus, husbands may have different expectations from their wives, and children from their parents. Also, ambivalences are likely to arise because immigrants are often exposed to conflicting expectations of family time that reflect differences in family norms between community of origin and community of destination.

A recent illustration of these ambivalences is provided by Hagan's case study of a group of Guatemalan Indians who had immigrated illegally, settling in an apartment complex in Houston in the late 1970s and 1980s.[90] The research took place when the provisions of the Immigration Reform and Control Act of 1986 made it possible for this group to apply for amnesty and legal residence. Members of the community helped each other find jobs and housing. They also maintained frequent contact with the home village in Guatemala. Seventy-eight percent of the adults in the community are under thirty years of age. Women make up almost one-half of the group; many of them are single and had come unaccompanied to join relatives who were already established in Houston. Most of these immigrants wish to return eventually to Guatemala. Though this return is constantly being postponed, it does have the effect, Hagan argues, of discouraging long-term plans, such as house purchase.

However, the women are less ready to countenance return to Guatemala than are the men. They work as domestic employees, living during the week with their employers and returning to the apartment complex only at weekends. Their social isolation frustrates them, but they also comment on the difficulty of returning to the circumscribed life that they would live in a traditional Guatemalan Indian village. They value the greater independence of life in the United States, free from community controls and free to spend what they earn. The men, too, value the high wages of the United States compared with Guatemala and the consumption that these wages make possible. However, they are unhappy about women's greater independence in the United States. They also see themselves as having opportunities to use their savings to invest in small-scale business in Guatemala.

Hagan argues that relations between men and women are under strain because of the time that often elapses between the arrival of males and that of their wives and children.[91] The men become accustomed to the greater amount of time and disposable income that they have when they live alone and resent the restraints that a cohabitating family places upon them. When a family has immigrated together then the ambivalence over residence is likely to be less pronounced. Among the Guatemalan sample, those who were firmest in their desire to legalize were married couples with children.

The contrast in the residence intentions of male and female immigrants is also documented in Grasmuck and Pessar's analysis of Dominican immigration to New York.[92] Dominican women, in contrast to men, were more ready to postpone the return since they objected to the patriarchal constraints of Dominican society. They valued the independence brought by working outside the home for pay. Some of them came to resent boarding immigrant kin free, and one woman was explicit in refusing to be either a slave to the family or to the employer of her husband's relative. The accumulation of ambivalences in these relationships often results in marital breakup: of the fifty-five female heads of household in the Dominican sample, eighteen were separated from their husbands while in the United States.

The Existence of Alternatives

Ambivalence makes alternatives to family time more attractive. We have already noted the significance of women's employment opportunities in providing a source of independence from family constraints, particularly those of the husband. Remember, however, that the alternative is only likely to be attractive when the immigrant group has low expectations of family-based mobility. When group support for family-based mobility is greater, as is the case of the Cuban immigrant community, then women may prefer to stay at home.[93]

The attraction of alternatives to family time can be particularly strong for immigrant children and particularly for the native-born offspring of immigrants. The children are being educated in American schools and taught that the path to social mobility is through educational achievement, not family cohesion. Moreover, these children go to school with co-ethnics whose native-born parents are economically unsuccessful. The available ethnic role models in the United States may thus be children who have developed an anti-school culture because of poor prospects of social mobility.

We can take the case of Mexicans. New immigrants have tended to seek out the places to which previous migrants went, residing in or close to neighborhoods—the *barrios*—where the Mexican-origin population has previously settled.[94] Long-established Mexican American neighborhoods in cities such as Los Angeles, San Antonio, and Chicago provide homes to recent immigrants or are so close to new immigrant neighborhoods as to be almost indistinguishable from them in the public eye.

The history of discrimination against Mexicans in the United States and their concentration in low-paying jobs have contributed to an anti-educational culture among children brought up in the *barrios*.[95] This is based on their perception of the lack of opportunities for people like themselves. Recent immigrant children and those with a strong sense of attachment to Mexican culture escape, to some extent, this anti-school culture, and are often viewed as "good" students by teachers.[96]

The previous history of immigrant success or failure affects the chances of the new generations. Families can counter negative peer influences on their children where a degree of social and geographical isolation reinforces the links between the generations.[97] Despite discrimination in school from the white majority, a California study shows that Sikh children retain enough confidence in the system to achieve academically.[98] In this case, parental pressures on children to achieve are supported by the relative economic success of the immigrant group. Also, geographical distance protects the Sikh children from peer group alternatives. There are no poor minorities nearby with whom they might identify and whose lack of success might undermine confidence in the school system.

Conclusion

This chapter argues for the advantages of analyzing immigration from the perspective of socially expected durations. It has also made, more indirectly, a case for using temporal perspectives in economic sociology. Expectations of duration can, indeed, be factors in determining behavior in any field of activity that requires persistence over time, whether in coordination with others or in pursuit of individual goals. Expectations of duration anticipate outcomes and thus help determine them. They do so at the level of the individual and even more strongly when the expectations are shared and enforced by a group.

Socially expected durations, however, only partially explain immigrant cohesion or the success or failure of immigrant groups. Social expectations will, after all, only be present when immigrants share a common culture and transmit it through interaction. Even when a common culture is present, the force of socially expected durations will depend, as we have seen, on their continuing relevance to the situation of the immigrant group. Indeed, the influence of socially expected durations will be limited by the ambiguities and exceptions that attend any socially transmitted set of norms. This is particularly likely to be true when the community relationships of immigrant groups are not multiplex.

Focusing on socially expected durations is a complement to other approaches to explaining immigrant success and failure, not a substitute for them. Thus it would be wrong to suppose that socially expected durations are more significant than immigrant human capital in determining the jobs immigrants obtain or their individual economic success. However, the "right" socially expected durations are likely to help immigrants maximize the capital they bring, while the "wrong" temporal expectations may deter them from putting their capital to full use.

Moreover, the focus on socially expected durations requires a careful analysis of the sociostructural determinants of immigrant success or failure. Immigrants are likely to settle together and develop a certain in-group solidarity. This solidarity will be affected by the social structure of the group and by the structure of economic opportunities in the host society. Cities and regions differ in the opportunities they provide and in the degree of immigrant concentration that residential patterns permit. As other chapters of this book demonstrate, these factors mediate the strength of immigrant social relationships and are crucial to the understanding of the types of trust and social capital that immigrant communities develop. Temporal expectations can transcend, however, the restrictions imposed by a group's present situation. They thus enable us to take account of group traditions and culture. When they are present, they interact with the other elements of social structure, at times reinforcing their effects, at times weakening them.

This perspective contributes to understanding the differences in entrepreneurship among immigrant groups discussed by Ivan Light in this volume. In particular, it enables us to resolve the puzzle of the lack of entrepreneurship among Mexican immigrants when compared to groups of other national origins. It is a puzzle because Mexicans are highly entrepreneurial in their own country. Also, most Mexican immigrants have originated in vibrant centers of small-scale entrepreneurship, namely the center-west of Mexico.

The lack of resources among the predominantly poor Mexican immigrants is part of the explanation, but it is not a sufficient one. The Japanese were highly entrepreneurial in the initial stages of their immigration and were similar to the Mexicans in their human and material capital. They also faced discrimination by the dominant groups. The major difference between the two groups is that the Japanese intended to stay, and given the long distance home, had little alternative to staying. Mexicans always had the alternative of returning and few, as we have seen, imagined that they would spend their lives in the United States.

Temporal expectations interact in similar ways with the other sociostructural determinants of ethnic cohesion. Though a common language, customs, and values are part of ethnic identity, the pressures to abandon them increase with settlement. The ethnic identity of immigrants can be sustained by the continuing flow of immigration, but only at a certain cost. This cost is the rupture between the identities of new immigrants and those of previous generations. The transnational migrant community is a strong source of identity for the first-generation immigrant, but it is likely to weaken their ties with American-born co-ethnics. This again is a source of disadvantage in terms of Mexican adjustment to the United States.

Mexican Americans and Mexican immigrants are a sizeable share of the United States population, and in certain regions and cities they are numerically dominant, for example in the border region with its multiple opportunities for trade with Mexico. Yet there is little evidence of a social and economic cohesion among the two Mexican-origin groups that would work to the advantage of both immigrants and the American-born. When ethnic identity is based on unfulfilled goals, however, rupture is less likely to occur. Thus groups such as the Cubans, with "cultures of exile," are notoriously more cohesive, to their considerable economic advantage.

Finally there is the immigrant family, and here too, temporal expectations can make a difference. The family values of immigrant groups are often similar, but their application in the new country varies widely. Immigrants who come expecting to stay temporarily are unlikely to have the expectations of family unity that can be the basis of social mobility strategies in the new country. Again, Mexican immigrants are likely to be at a disadvantage. Their culture places a strong emphasis on family cohesion, but in the United States, their temporariness has often meant divided family commitments and has contributed to family breakup.

There is, in fact, a sense in which Mexican immigration to the United States has gotten all its timings wrong. The country *par excellence* of temporary migration had the misfortune to share a border with the country *par excellence* of permanent immigration. The collective expectations that helped enforce the temporary nature of Mexican migration contributed to the gulf between immigrants and the settled Mexican American population. And thus instead of reinforcing immigrant identity and family cohesion, these expectations contributed ambivalences that weakened the family as a resource for adjusting to life in the United States.

Mexican immigration has been predominantly made up of people with low endowments of capital. Yet the persistence of poverty among large sectors of the Mexican-origin population requires explanation. One explanation is offered in this paper. It is that group mobility depends on mutually reinforcing expectations of duration between both immigrant families and their co-ethnic communities. Confidence in the future and long-term planning can be a group property. Individual immigrants or even their families, particularly when poor and unskilled, may not easily sustain it in isolation.

This chapter was written while I was in residence at the Russell Sage Foundation, whose support is gratefully acknowledged. I owe a special debt to Robert Merton for his guidance in the uses of time in the analysis of immigration. My colleagues in the Immigration Working Group at the Foundation, Patricia Fernández Kelly, Mark Granovetter, Alex Portes, and Saskia Sassen, were an invaluable source of continuing intellectual stimulation and comments on the task at hand.

Notes

1. See Alejandro Portes and Rubén G. Rumbaut, *Immigrant America* (Berkeley: University of California Press, 1990); George J. Borjas, *Friends or Strangers: The Impact of Immigrants on the U.S. Economy* (New York: Basic Books, 1990); Stanley Lieberson, *A Piece of the Pie* (Berkeley: University of California Press, 1980); Stanley Lieberson, "Socioeconomic Attainment," in Donald Horowitz and Gérard Noiriel, eds., *Immigrants in Two Democracies* (New York: New York University Press, 1992), pp. 301–330; and Stanley Lieberson and Mary C. Waters, *From*

Many Strands: Ethnic and Racial Groups in Contemporary America (New York: Russell Sage Foundation, 1988).

2. See Mark Granovetter, "Economic Action and Social Structure: The Problem of Embeddedness," *American Journal of Sociology* 91 (1985):481–510.

3. For a discussion of social capital, see Alejandro Portes in Chapter 1 of this volume. As Patricia Fernández Kelly argues in this volume, the formation of social capital depends, in part, on shared understandings about temporal demarcations that vary across groups.

4. See Harley L. Browning and Nestor Rodríguez, "The Migration of Mexican Indocumentados as a Settlement Process," in George Borjas and Marta Tienda, eds., *Hispanics in the U.S. Economy* (Orlando, Fla.: Academic Press, 1985), pp. 277–297); Tamara K. Hareven, *Family Time and Industrial Time: The Relationship between the Family and Work in a New England Industrial Community* (Cambridge: Cambridge University Press, 1982); Micaela Di Leonardo, *The Varieties of Ethnic Experience: Kinship, Class, and Gender among California Italian-Americans* (Ithaca: Cornell University Press, 1984); and Portes and Rumbaut, *Immigrant America*.

5. See Nina Toren, "The Temporal Dimension of Gender Inequality in Academia," *Higher Education* 25 (1993):439–455.

6. Robert K. Merton, "Socially Expected Durations: A Case Study of Concept Formation in Sociology," in W. W. Powell and Richard Robbins, eds., *Conflict and Consensus: A Festschrift for Lewis A. Coser* (New York: The Free Press, 1984), pp. 262–286.

7. Jorge Durand and Douglas S. Massey, "Mexican Migration to the United States: A Critical Review," *Latin American Research Review* 27 (1988):3–42.

8. Douglas Massey, "Social Structure, Household Strategies, and the Cumulative Causation of Migration," *Population Index* 56, no. 1:3–26 (1990).

9. Charles Tilly, "Transplanted Networks," in Virginia Yans-McLaughlin, ed., *Immigration Reconsidered* (New York: Oxford University Press, 1990), p. 84.

10. For the analysis of these individual calculations, see George Borjas and Marta Tienda, "The Economic Consequences of Immigration," *Science* 235 (February 6, 1987):645–651; Lieberson, *A Piece of the Pie;* Lieberson, "Socioeconomic Attainment," and the discussion of the settlement process in Browning and Rodríguez, "The Migration of Mexican Indocumentados." Even in the years of high rates of Italian migration to the United States, there was little or no international migration from some provinces which exhibited high rates of internal migration. See David I. Kertzer and Dennis P. Hogan, *Family, Political Economy, and Demographic Change: The Transformation of Life in Casalecchio, Italy, 1861–1921* (Madison: University of Wisconsin Press, 1989).

11. John Bodnar, *The Transplanted: A History of Immigrants in Urban America* (Bloomington: Indiana University Press, 1985). The country where individualized emigration appears to have dominated is nineteenth century Britain. Britain did not have local communities that were stable enough or sufficiently based on interlocking interests to sustain strong emigrant networks. See Alan Macfarlane, "The Myth of the Peasantry: Family and Economy in a Northern Parish," in Richard M. Smith, ed., *Land, Kinship and Life-Cycle*, (Cambridge: Cambridge University Press, 1984), pp. 333–349. British immigrants were usually dependent workers, either farm laborers, tenant farmers, or unskilled and semiskilled industrial workers, seeking independence in the United States, often as farmers. See the immigrant letters collected by Charlotte Erickson, *Invisible Immigrants: The Adaptation of English and Scottish Immigrants in Nineteenth-Century America* (Coral Gables, Fla: University of Miami Press, 1972).

12. See Thomas J. Archdeacon, *Becoming American: An Ethnic History* (New York: The Free Press, 1983), Table V-3.

13. Michael Piore, *Birds of Passage* (Cambridge: Cambridge University Press, 1979), pp. 149–154.

14. This is reported by both Paul S. Taylor, *A Spanish-Mexican Peasant Community: Arandas in Jalisco, Mexico* (Berkeley: University of California Press, 1932) and Manuel Gamio, *Mexican Inmigration to the United States* (Chicago: University of Chicago Press, 1930).

15. Paul S. Taylor, *Mexican Labor in the United States*, Vols. I and II (1930, 1932; reprint, New York: Arno Press, 1970).

16. Ibid.: I:71; II:18, 218.

17. Ricardo Romo, *East Los Angeles: History of a Barrio* (Austin: University of Texas Press, 1983), pp. 124–128.

18. Taylor, *Mexican Labor in the United States*, II:165.

19. J. R. Garcia, *Operation Wetback* (Westport, Conn.: Greenwood Press, 1980), pp. 18–61.

20. Durand and Massey, "Mexican Migration to the United States: A Critical Review."

21. In the 1980s, a more permanent pattern of settlement became evident as a consequence of Mexico's economic crisis, the amnesty offered illegal immigrants by the Immigration Reform and Control Act of 1986, and an increase in female migration and that of dependent children. See Wayne Cornelius, "*Los Migrantes de la Crisis:* The Changing Profile of Mexican Migration to the United States," in Mercedes González de la Rocha and Austín Escobar, eds., *Social Responses to Mexico's Economic Crisis of the 1980s* (La Jolla, Calif.: Center for US-Mexican Studies, 1991), pp. 155–193.

22. Gamio, *Mexican Inmigration to the United States*, pp. 30–32. See the discussion of remittances to the village of Arandas in Jalisco, Mexico, in Taylor, *A Spanish-Mexican Peasant Community: Arandas in Jalisco, Mexico*, pp. 32–34. The average money order appears to be higher than in Gamio's figures, approximately U.S. $40 for 1926, when the average daily wage for a farm laborer in Mexico was around fifty cents U.S. In 1926 there were 1,033 remittances to a population of probably 5,000 households. Taylor shows evidence that the remittances sent by registered mail (and thus not counted in Gamio's money order figures) may have been greater in number than those sent by money order, and may have been for more money.

23. Undocumented Mexican immigrants reported in a survey of those seeking legalization that they sent back approximately 7 percent of their U.S. income in 1987, with an average yearly remittance of $1,304. Immigration and Naturalization Service (INS), *Immigration Reform and Control Act: Report on the Legalized Alien Population* (Washington, D.C.: U.S. Department of Justice, Immigration and Naturalization Service, 1992), Tables 25 and 26.

24. Fernando Lozano, *Bringing it Back Home: Remittances to Mexico from Migrant Workers in the United States*, Monograph Series #37, Center for U.S.-Mexican Studies, University of California, San Diego, 1993, Table 4.

25. Archdeacon, *Becoming American*, p. 47.

26. U.S. Bureau of the Census, *Historical Statistics of the United States: Colonial Times to 1970* (Washington D.C.: U.S. Department of Commerce, 1975), Part 1, C195–295, C89–119.

27. Ibid., 1:C228–295.

28. See Norbert Elias, *Time: An Essay* (Oxford: Basil Blackwell, 1992), pp. 93–107.

29. Merton, "Socially Expected Durations," p. 277.

30. Glen H. Elder, Jr., "Age Differentiation and the Life Course," *Annual Review of Sociology* 1 (1975):165–190.

31. Ellen M. Gee, "Preferred Timing of Women's Life Events: A Canadian Study." *International Journal of Aging and Human Development* 31, no. 4 (1990):279–294.

32. See Granovetter's discussion of successful entrepreneurship in this volume. Also Mark Granovetter, "Economic Action and Social Structure."

33. Merton, "Socially Expected Durations," p. 280.

34. Individuals within a group may, of course, use their personal expectations of duration as the basis of planning. Where these are congruent with those of the wider society, they may be a more effective basis of economic strategies than group expectations of duration that limit

individual initiative. In this case, the group expectations are examples of "negative social capital." See Alejandro Portes and Julia Sensenbrenner, "Embeddedness and Immigration: Notes on the Social Determinants of Economic Action," *American Journal of Sociology* 98 (May 1993):1320–1350.

35. Examples are Thomas and Znaniecki, *The Polish Peasant in Europe and America*, Vol. 1, p. 500, 508 n. 1, p. 841.

36. Eviatar Zerubavel, *Patterns of Time in Hospital Life* (Chicago: University of Chicago Press, 1979), p. 110.

37. See the analysis of organizationally expected durations in a New Jersey township. R. K. Merton, Patricia S. West, and Marie Jahoda, *Patterns of Social Life: Explorations in the Sociology and Social Psychology of Housing* (New York: Columbia University Bureau of Applied Social Research, 1949), Chap. 3, pp. 39–40.

38. Charles Tilly makes this point in a personal communication.

39. Vanessa Merton, Robert K. Merton, and Elinor Barber, "Client Ambivalence in Professional Relationships: The Problem of Seeking Help from Strangers," in B. DePaulo, A. Nadler, and J. Fisher, eds., *New Directions in Helping* (New York: Academic Press, 1983), Vol. 2, pp. 13–44.

40. Irving L. Child, *Italian or American? The Second Generation in Conflict* (1943; reprint, New York: Russell & Russell, 1970).

41. Merton, "Socially Expected Durations."

42. Hareven, *Family Time and Industrial Time*.

43. Di Leonardo cites the case of an Italian migrant in California who continued to send remittances to his mother in Italy for many years after his temporary (and originally seasonal) migration became converted into a more permanent one with the formation of a family in the United States and the establishment of a business there. He only stopped during the Depression when he needed every penny to keep himself and his immediate family afloat. See Di Leonardo, *Kinship, Class, and Gender*, pp. 879–880.

44. This is the essential difference between my position and rational choice approaches to family strategies such as Gary Becker, *Treatise on the Family* (Cambridge: Harvard University Press, 1981), p. 299, and John Hoddinott, "Rotten Kids or Manipulative Parents: Are Children Old Age Security in Western Kenya?" *Economic Development and Cultural Change* 40 (1992):545–565.

45. Elizabeth Hull, *Without Justice for All: The Constitutional Rights of Aliens* (Westport, Conn.: Greenwood Press, 1985), p. 40.

46. Jorge Durand, ed., *Migración México-Estados Unidos. Años Veinte* (Mex-

ico, D. F.: Consejo Nacional para la Cultura y las Artes, 1991), p. 99, p. 101 [my translation].

47. See William Rogers Brubaker, "Introduction" and "Citizenship and Naturalization: Policies and Politics," in W. R. Brubaker, ed., *Immigration and the Politics of Citizenship in Europe and North America* (Lanham, Va.: University Press of America, 1989), pp. 1–27 and pp. 99–127.

48. Naturalized citizens are not quite of equal status with native-born citizens. Certain high offices of state are barred to them and they can lose citizenship under certain conditions.

49. Guillermina Jasso and Mark R. Rosenzweig, *The New Chosen People: Immigrants in the United States* (New York: Russell Sage Foundation, 1990), Table 1.4.

50. Ibid., Table 1.6.

51. Take the case of the Nebraska Meat Packers reported in the *Chicago Tribune* of October 16, 1992. The plants are located in small towns without a reservoir of labor and have a high turnover, estimated at twenty-four new workers a week for a plant of 1,500 employees. Faced with this problem, management recruited workers from Laredo, Texas, and also encouraged workers to refer others to the company. Managers complained about INS raids which, in one case, resulted in the deportation of 300 illegal workers, saying that the job of management was to get labor, not to investigate credentials.

52. Garcia, *Operation Wetback*.

53. Rosemary Rogers, "Migration Theory and Practice," in Walker Connor, ed., *Mexican-Americans in Comparative Perspective* (Washington D.C.: Urban Institute, 1985), pp. 185–190. Also see Abraham Hoffman, "Mexican Repatriation Statistics: Some Suggested Alternatives to Carey McWilliams," *Western Historical Quarterly* 3 (1972):391–404; and Romo, *East Los Angeles*, p. 113.

54. See Romo, *East Los Angeles*, pp. 86–87.

55. Ibid., p. 87.

56. Archdeacon, *Becoming American*, p. 157.

57. Gamio, *Mexican Inmigration to the United States*, p. 129 n. 1.

58. Jasso and Rosenzweig, *The New Chosen People*, Table 2.1.

59. Edna Bonacich, "A Theory of Middleman Minorities," *American Sociological Review* 38 (1973):583–594. In Bonacich's concept, *sojourners* take up entrepreneurial activities that allow for the easy transfer of any wealth accumulated to the country of origin. The activities may, of course, involve fairly long-term commitments in the host country such as are required to build up a business, and success, as Bonacich points out, may lead to settlement not return.

60. Roger Rouse, "Making Sense of Settlement: Class Transformation, Cultural Struggle, and Transnationalism among Mexican Migrants in the United States," *Annals of the New York Academy of Sciences* 645 (1992):25–52.

61. See Miller, "Class, Culture, and Immigrant Group Identity in the U.S."

62. Ibid., p. 110.

63. Ibid., p. 101.

64. Massey et al., *Return to Atzlan* (Berkeley: University of California Press, 1987); Durand and Massey, "Mexican Migration to the United States."

65. See German Vega, "Tradición migratoria y legislación: el impact de la ley Simpson-Rodino en cuatro localidades del estado de Jalisco," *Frontera y Migraciones* III (1992):151–169 (Mexico: El Colegio de la Frontera Norte/Universidad Autónoma de Ciudad Juarez). Vega notes that even the municipal police cars in the Mexican *municipio* that he studied have California license plates.

66. Rouse, "Making Sense of Settlement."

67. Smith, *Los Ausentes Siempre Presentes.*

68. The transnational networks of Mexican communities in the states of Jalisco, Michoacan, and Guanajuato are reported in Massey et. al., *Return to Aztlan* and in Douglas Massey, Luis Goldring, and Jorge Durand, "Continuities in Transnational Migration: An Analysis of Thirteen Mexican Communities," working paper, Population Research Center, University of Chicago, 1992.

69. This is the conclusion of Vila's analysis of focused group interviews that included Mexican immigrants and Mexican Americans in El Paso, Texas. See Pablo Vila, "Visiones a Traves de la Frontera," *Colef II* (El Colegio de la Frontera Norte, Tijuana, October 1992) and "Ethnic Identity and the 'Invention' of a Heritage," working paper, Department of Sociology, University of Texas, El Paso, May 1993.

70. Thomas and Znaniecki, *The Polish Peasant,* pp. 1581–1623.

71. Ibid., p. 1650.

72. Child, *Italian or American?*

73. Ibid., p. 124.

74. Di Leonardo provides an account of the gradual dilution of Italian ethnic identity with time in *Kinship, Class, and Gender.*

75. The family is equally important in internal migration. Family networks in places of origin and destination and joining the two have been important mechanisms in facilitating the mass rural-urban movements of population in the nineteenth century urbanization of the developed world, and in the contemporary urbanization of the developing world. See Michael Anderson, *Family Structure in Nineteenth Century Lancashire*

(Cambridge: Cambridge University Press, 1971); Larissa Lomnitz, *Networks and Marginality: Life in a Mexican Shantytown* (New York: Academic Press, 1977); and Bryan R. Roberts, "The Interrelationships of City and Provinces in Peru and Guatemala," *Latin American Urban Research* 4 (1974):207–235.

76. L. L. Cornell, "Taking Reproduction Seriously: An Essay on the Modern Family in China, Japan, and the United States" (paper presented at 81st Annual Meeting of the American Sociological Association, New York, N.Y., August 30–September 2, 1986).

77. L. L. Cornell, "Where Can Family Strategies Exist?" *Historical Methods* 20, no. 3 (1987):120–123.

78. See Hareven, *Family Time and Industrial Time*, pp. 361–362.

79. Ibid:, pp. 6–7, 189–217.

80. Ibid., pp. 361–362.

81. Di Leonardo, *Kinship, Class, and Gender*, p. 103.

82. See Louise Lamphere, *From Working Daughters to Working Mothers: Immigrant Women in a New England Industrial Community* (Ithaca, N.Y.: Cornell University Press, 1987), pp. 257–258.

83. Ibid., Tables 20–21.

84. See Frank Bean and Marta Tienda, *The Hispanic Population of the United States* (New York: Russell Sage Foundation, 1987), Figs. 3.5, 3.7.

85. Ibid., Table 6.8.

86. See Chavez, "Households, Migration and Labor Market Participation."

87. In Lamphere's table, the single-parent category is that of widows, which in the French-Canadian case includes approximately 8 percent of households containing children. See Lamphere, *From Working Daughters to Working Mothers*.

88. See their discussion of the adjustment of immigrant families and the problems caused by these uncertainties in Browning and Rodríguez, "Migration of Mexican Indocumentados."

89. See Portes and Bach, *Latin Journey*.

90. Jacqueline M. Hagan, "The Legalization Experience of a Mayan Community in Houston" (Ph.D. diss., Department of Sociology, University of Texas at Austin, 1990). See also Jacqueline M. Hagan, *Deciding To Be Legal* (Philadelphia: Temple University Press, 1995).

91. A similar situation is reported by Hondagneu-Sotelo, who describes the lesser readiness of the younger generation of wives of absent Mexican immigrants to tolerate long absences by their husbands. Pierrette Hondagneu-Sotelo, "Overcoming Patriarchal Constraints: The Reconstruction of Gender Relations among Mexican Immigrant Women and Men," *Gender and Society* 6, no. 3 (1992):393–415.

92. Sherri Grasmuck and Patricia Pessar, *Between Two Islands: Dominican International Migration* (Berkeley: University of California Press, 1991), pp. 153–158.

93. M. Patricia Fernández Kelly and Anna García, "Power Surrendered, Power Restored: The Politics of Home and Work among Hispanic Women in Southern Florida," in L. Tilly and P. Gurin, eds., *Women, Politics, and Change* (New York: Russell Sage Foundation, 1990), p. 115. See a similar case, for Colombian immigrants, in Patricia Pessar, "Sweatshop Workers and Domestic Ideologies: Dominican Workers in New York's Apparel Industry," *International Journal of Urban and Regional Research* 18, no. 1 (March 1994):127–143.

94. John H. Ogbu and Maria Eugenia Matute-Bianchi, *Understanding Sociocultural Factors: Knowledge, Identity, and School Adjustment* (Los Angeles: Evaluation, Dissemination and Assessment Center, California State University, 1986).

95. Ogbu and Matute-Bianchi, *Understanding Sociocultural Factors.*

96. See Harriet Romo, "The Mexican Origin Population's Differing Perceptions of Their Children's Schooling," *Social Science Quarterly* 65 (1984):635–649, and Maria Eugenia Matute-Bianchi, "Ethnic Identities and Patterns of School Success and Failure among Mexican-Descent and Japanese-American Students in a California High School," *American Journal of Education* 95 (1986):233–255.

97. See Alejandro Portes and Min Zhou, "The New Second Generation: Segmented Assimilation and Its Variants among Post-1965 Immigrant Youth," Working Paper #34, Russell Sage Foundation, New York, 1992.

98. M. A. Gibson, *Accommodation Without Assimilation: Sikh Immigrants in an American High School* (Ithaca, N.Y.: Cornell University Press, 1989).

3

Immigration and Local Labor Markets

Saskia Sassen

U sing constructs from the new economic sociology and data from the immigration literature, this chapter develops the concept of the local labor market. Going beyond the focus on the moment of exchange typical in neoclassical analyses, the purpose here is to capture the impact of pre- and post-exchange processes. This has the effect of expanding the analytic terrain within which we conceptualize labor market operation. In principle this type of analytic effort can assume several conceptual forms; working with the data on immigration and the concepts in the new economic sociology contributes to a recentering of labor market operation in the workplace-household or workplace-community nexus.

When labor market operation is analyzed in terms of the moment of exchange (that is, the completion of the transaction whereby a worker is offered a job and accepts it), a range of processes that precede and follow that moment of exchange are left unexamined. These are precisely the processes of interest to sociologists. For instance, a focus on the moment of exchange leaves unexamined the transformation of immigrants from a potential to an effective labor supply and the transformation of their demand by employers from a potential to an effective demand; it may be illuminating to view this transformation as problematic rather than taking it for granted. This would involve examining the processes of competition and mobility that precede the exchange transaction. How do immigrants get a chance to compete with long-established groups? How do they gain access to the queue implied by standard models of the labor market? Also, labor markets presuppose a variety of institutional arrangements within which supply and demand forces can meet and materialize into a market. When we use the neoclassical model of the labor market, these issues do not have much relevance since the mere fact that jobs are filled by workers indicates that demand and supply forces are working. But from a sociological perspective, changes in the institutional underpinnings of labor markets do have significance for specifying labor market operation.

Knowledge about such pre- and post-exchange processes may not always alter the overall explanation for labor market *outcomes* offered by the neoclassical model; the kind of job and wages an immigrant has are largely determined by his or her human capital. But it does contribute to an elaboration of how labor markets work. Given the growth of diversity in the workforce by gender, nationality, and race, and given the sharp differentiation in labor market outcomes for these diverse groups, adding to our understanding of how labor markets operate should be of value.

For the analytic elaboration of the concept of the local labor market I make use of the specialized literature in economics and in economic geography. It helps specify in greater detail the existence of patterns within broad, spatially defined labor market areas: the impact of race, gender, income, and nationality on job search patterns; sensitivity to job location; and access to information about jobs. This contributes to the elaboration of a conceptual and analytic apparatus within which to ground concepts such as networks, social capital, and cumulative causation. While the focus here is principally on immigrants, the analysis also contributes to a more general discussion of labor market operation.

The chapter proceeds from the more general conceptualization of local labor markets in the empirical economics literature to the particularities of the immigration literature to conclude with a resynthesis. Given the amount of material covered and the diversity of the literatures involved, this can only be done through the cumulative introduction of new materials. The only constants are the analytic effort of expanding the terrain within which to conceptualize the local labor market and the empirical focus on immigration. What makes this effort compelling in my view is the richness of conceptual developments and empirical findings in these various literatures and the possibility of using the concept of the local labor market as an analytic nexus.

The first section of this chapter briefly discusses the concept of the local labor market and my proposed elaboration. The second section examines several major findings in the empirical economics literature on labor markets and immigrant employment which deviate from the findings theory would predict. They thus invite a more detailed, often qualitative examination of the subject and for that reason can be used to explore alternative explanations of the labor market outcomes found for immigrants. The third section discusses the patterning of labor markets in terms of variables such as sensitivity to job location and information gathering. Of interest here is the growing evidence from economic geography on internal differentiation in metropolitan areas and patterning by race, gender, and income. It invites us to examine whether immigrants also evidence specific sensitivities to job location, information gathering channels, or job search paths. The fourth section uses the new economic sociology and immigration data to propose a partial reconceptualization of the local labor market as centered in the workplace-household or workplace-community nexus.

Local Labor Markets: The Concept and Its Problems

In its origin, the concept of the local labor market was centered on the employing establishment. Today empirical studies about "local" labor markets tend to use regional labor market areas specified in terms of journey-to-work. While the original concept of the local labor market is based on and defined by the behavior of the employing establishment, the central organizing principle in the regional labor market is the functional region itself. The information provided by these concepts is quite different: in one case, the linkages between employing establishments and residential catchment area are described; the other offers an account of the employment and earnings distribution of an area.

Much of the economics literature on local labor markets and immigrants has focused on the second concept, typically in urban-centered regions. Today the concept is frequently used interchangeably with such concepts as the spatial and regional market, described as "a spatially contiguous travel-to-work area, defined by way of commuting patterns," and operationalized in terms of standard metropolitan areas (SMAs) or counties.[1] Similarly, most work on the geographical aspects of labor markets has tended to use metropolitan areas or regions as a whole rather than do intra-area analyses.[2] For these researchers the metropolitan area, or city or county, is the smallest spatially identified labor market. Morrison observes that the notion of a local labor market was not introduced in the economics literature as a conceptual category but as a means for imposing further statistical control on wages; without such controls, wages would reflect high regional variation.[3] The object was to abstract from or control for geography in order to reduce extraneous sources of variations in wages and to test for internal sources.[4]

Here I propose to return to the original notion of the local labor market as centered on the employing establishment, but to elaborate it conceptually and empirically in two ways. First, I want to recenter the concept of the local labor market on the workplace-household nexus rather than centering it exclusively on the former. This recentering maximizes the introduction of information about the extensive margin and the determinants of labor supply formation. Secondly, I would like to free the concept of the local labor market from its narrow geographic definition in terms of "proximity," such as is suggested by the notion of journey-to-work. Local labor markets can be conceived of as socially conditioned activity spaces that may assume nonterritorial forms. The case of immigrants allows us to isolate certain aspects of labor market operation which may in turn contribute to a more general specification of labor market dynamics.

This recentering entails three types of analytic displacement or repositioning in the study of labor markets. These displacements pivot on (a) questions of worker mobility, one of the crucial factors feeding into theoretical propositions about market clearing and equilibrium; (b) questions of proximity, one of the crucial factors in the specification of local labor markets in economics and in economic geography; and (c) questions of competition, one of the crucial factors in the specification of labor market dynamics.

There are at least two ways of interpreting what such analytic displacements might entail. One is that they make endogenous certain aspects that economic models take as given or exogenous. This could then simply represent yet another expansion in the domain covered by standard economic models of the labor market. The other is that these analytic displacements produce a different kind of explanatory model. The approach followed here is of the second type; it may or may not preclude the type of modeling typical of the neoclassical economics literature on the subject.

Immigrants in Local Labor Markets

We know that immigrants are disproportionately concentrated in relatively few cities and that they tend to stay there. What impact, if any, has this been found to have on native employment and mobility patterns? The rapidly growing empirical economic literature on labor markets generally, and on immigrant employment in particular, has produced a number of important findings which have generated questions of a sort that invite a more detailed and qualitative examination.

Among the findings, discussed in greater detail below, the following stand out. First there is the finding that "local" labor market variables, especially unemployment levels, in a region or Standard Metropolitan Statistical Area (SMSA) did not seem to affect immigrants' propensity to settle in an area or, more generally, where they decided to settle. Such variables do explain the decisions of native workers. Other variants of this finding suggest that immigrants and natives, including natives of the same ethnicity as immigrants, do not respond to the same locational criteria. The second notable finding is that the presence of a large resident immigrant population and/or new immigrant arrivals has little if any impact on the levels and growth rates of wages in those areas. Immigrants are disproportionately concentrated in a few regions and they account for a disproportionate share of low-income workers; one could, then, expect a relative decline in wages compared with regions lacking a significant immigrant population. Thirdly, note the finding of disproportionate immigrant job gains not only in growing industries but also in declining ones. National data show that most unemployment growth over the last two decades has been among low-skill and/or low-wage workers; during this same period real average wages have fallen in these jobs. Thus one could expect falling reservation wages among these workers and hence at least somewhat greater difficulty for immigrants in getting these jobs than seems to have been the case. A fourth finding is that blacks in areas with high immigrant populations and/or arrivals show little or no response in terms of their migration behavior, even though their educational and skill levels tend to be somewhat equivalent to those of immigrants. According to standard labor market models, mobility in the form of outmigration could have been expected.

Finally, of particular relevance to the case of immigrant workers is Heckman's observation that a major lesson of the past twenty years is that the strongest empirical effects of wages and nonlabor income on labor supply are to be found at the extensive margin (at the margin of entry and exit) rather than the intensive margin (choices about hours of work or weeks of work for workers).[5] Such effects have also been found to be key determinants in the supply of female labor. There is considerable ethnographic and case study evidence that the decision to enter the labor market may be arrived at differently among immigrants than among natives of similar skill and education.

There follows a more detailed discussion of these findings and of their conceptual implications for our inquiry.

Several studies have analyzed net migration of native workers as a function of variables describing the particular area out of which or into which such migration occurs. The conventional interpretation is that significant measured effects are an indicator of the presence of characteristics found to be attractive by potential migrants. Filer examined foreign immigration into an area as yet another factor that could conceivably explain the mobility patterns of native workers.[6] He found a statistically significant effect mostly for white natives with skill levels similar to those of immigrants. This effect was present both in the sense that they were more likely to move out of an area receiving high levels of foreign immigration and in the sense that they were more likely not to move into such an area.[7] The effect was insignificant on natives in high-level occupations. It is worth noting that Filer found that this negative effect was sufficient to offset population gains through foreign immigration into these areas. As has been observed, this would explain Card's finding that the large Cuban influx into Miami resulting from the Mariel boatlift did not have a long-run effect on the city's population size.[8]

Further, Filer found that the effect of less skilled immigrant arrivals was stronger than that of highly skilled immigrants. The effect was disproportionately concentrated on those with less than a high school education. Yet this effect was mostly concentrated among white natives; the effects on blacks were nil. That is, immigrant arrivals had no effect on the propensity of blacks to move in or out of that area even though they could, in principle, have been competing for the same jobs. There was a smaller-than-proportional effect on college graduates. Filer also found that the effect was larger on those with some college education than on those who finished their education with high school. He infers this may be due in part to the well-known greater propensity of young native workers to move than of older workers. There were particularly large effects on men in crafts and sales occupations, and smaller-than-average effects on men in professional, technical, and service jobs.

Clearly, native migration behavior may indicate that natives leave for reasons built into the characteristics of the local area rather than because of high levels of immigrant arrivals; and those same place-characteristics may be precisely why immigrants are arriving in large numbers. The economic restructuring in major cities over the last decade would be a case in point. There is evidence showing that the most important locational determinant for immigrants was the existence of concentrations of groups of the same national origin.[9]

Most immigrants do not seem to settle in high-wage locations, while natives of the same ethnicity do.[10] These and other studies indicate that immigrants and natives do not respond to the same criteria for locational decisions.

Filer's findings may also shed light on the often-stated finding that immigrants do not have a negative impact on the levels and growth rates of wages, as measured through the impact of high concentrations of immigrants on wages in local labor markets. This would imply that the migration impact on wages is neutralized by the departure of natives from, or failure to go to, such local labor markets and the fact that labor market prices tend to return to equilibrium. It is especially the second half of this proposition that I plan to focus on later. Furthermore, in the case of Filer's findings, we need to raise a question as to the impact of economic restructuring on net migration of natives. Again, I will address this through some of the findings in our study which show that the overall decline of certain industries as reflected in aggregate data obscures the fact of significant growth of new firms in these same industries but under different conditions (in the organization of production and of labor markets, including informalization).[11] Both Filer's and our findings raise questions about how local labor markets are conceived conventionally in the economic literature, but they do so along very different lines of inquiry.

Bronars found an inverse correlation between immigration and native mobility among states in 1980 but not in earlier censuses.[12] Using Current Population Surveys, Butcher and Card found a positive correlation between the inmigration rates of natives to particular cities and immigration flows in the 1980s.[13] The evidence thus suggests that Filer's findings may reflect "the particular historical period of the late 1970s rather than a structural pattern of response."[14] Thus, it could be that Filer's migration response happens in one period, and in other periods, flows of capital or immigrant-induced expansion of demand for goods offset the immigration effect on local labor market areas.

Borjas and Freeman observe that the apparent inconsistency between their finding of a strong negative impact on wage levels of low-skill workers, and studies of SMSAs that find little if any impact, may be smaller than at first reading.[15] First, in the spatial literature many of the point estimates of the effect of immigration on native earnings are statistically insignificant (see, for example, Altonji and Card).[16] Secondly, they argue that the continuing growth of immigrant flows over the latter half of the 1980s relative to native population growth raises the weight of immigration in the late 1980s compared with 1980 Census data. A third reason they give is that local labor markets adjust rapidly to the increased supply of immigrant workers. If markets clear rapidly, so the argument runs, the effects of immigration will be dispersed throughout the economy and thus cannot be captured through spatial analyses.[17] Under these conditions, cross-city comparisons show no difference between cities in correlations between native wage rates and the presence of immigrants in local labor markets. Borjas and Freeman note that both the macrofindings and the spatial correlations are correct.[18] But they address different questions. The spatial correlations correctly tell us that immigrants have no measurable effects on particular markets, but they do not tell us much about the economy-wide effects of immigration. The aggregate analysis indicates that immigration affects economy-wide labor supplies, with a sizeable effect on aggregate economic opportunities of natives. In the last section of the paper we explore a third explanation for these outcomes, one that focuses on the absorption of these effects, or costs, within submarkets.

A second question is how the assumption of rapid market clearing at the local level squares with findings about little sectoral or cross-industry mobility and with findings about the nature of unemployment which show a growing frequency of long-term unemployment and a falling frequency of short-term unemployment. The finding of little sectoral or cross-industrial mobility among the unemployed means that industry changers accounted for a small share of the unemployed. Furthermore, this share has changed little over the last twenty years. This would seem to be yet another reason for obtaining additional insights into the move of immigrants into a growing share of low-skill jobs. Industrial reorganization by itself is not enough to explain it. Most unemployment was due to increases in unemployment *within* labor force groups. There was sharp growth in long-term unemployment and long-term nonparticipation, while the frequency of short-term unemployment actually fell. Notable from the perspective of economic theory was that low-skill workers had both the highest unemployment rates and the sharpest relative fall in wages.[19]

As for the findings on unemployment over the last twenty-five or more years, Topel finds that unemployment and nonparticipation are largely concentrated among the least skilled.[20] The rates for highly skilled men are unchanged since the 1970s. Second, he finds the main reason for the increase in joblessness is a secular decline in the demand for less-skilled workers. Wages are demonstrably flexible in the long run, and they have fallen sharply among the less skilled. Third, unemployment is not a brief event. Much of it is long-term and entails sharp losses. Many of the unemployed were recently highly skilled and suffer a sharp decline in income when their skills become obsolete.

One question raised by these findings is whether the units of analysis used, either the nation or the SMSA, are adequate scales for understanding some of these impacts (that is, the correlations between native migration and immigrant presence, and between immigrant presence and wage levels). Furthermore, the findings about little cross-industry mobility, the long-term nature of unemployment, and the fall in the demand for low-skill workers all raise questions about the mechanisms through which immigrants gained access to a growing share of the low-wage job supply in several industries. Orr found[21] that immigrants are almost 10 percent of workers in twenty industries with the most severe negative shifts in terms of trade (see also Tienda and Bach).[22] Can we just take this replacement for granted, especially if we consider the still rather large numbers of native workers with low educational attainment? High and increasingly long-term unemployment levels among such workers, limited state support, and the fact that many of these workers are in jobs that pay less than in the past—these conditions suggest that the reservation wage of such workers has fallen and hence that they are more competitive with low-wage immigrants. While 25 percent of workers with less than a high school education were immigrants, that still leaves natives in 75 percent of such jobs.

Under these conditions, the growing presence of immigrants in low-wage jobs can be seen as a replacement process (whether as complements or substitutes), at least vis-à-vis the effective native supply for those jobs. We need to focus on the process of competition that leads to this replacement, on how the queues are formed through which immigrants became an effective labor supply and equivalent native workers did not. Further, we need to focus on the labor market implications associated with employed workers securing jobs for their households and/or community. These are among the pre- and post-exchange processes that can be illuminated through some of the concepts of the new economic sociology and the immigration literature.

Next I address some of these questions through a discussion of basic labor market processes such as job search and information gathering. The object is to make these processes problematic, to open them up in order to capture the presence of pre- and post-exchange processes in labor market operation.

Job Location, Job Search, Information Gathering

Here I examine several conceptual and empirical issues that suggest the need for additional qualification of the category "local labor market" and raise the possibility that such elaboration may contribute to a more detailed explanation of labor market operation generally. An organizing question concerns the differentiation of labor supply determinants in terms of variables such as gender, race, and nationality, and how these in turn can shape sensitivity to job location, job search paths, and information gathering. A second organizing question concerns labor market segmentation and the proposition that it produces heterogeneity in the workforce; in other words, that heterogeneity in the workforce is not simply a result of premarket differences, but that there are differences produced through labor market operation as is illustrated by the possibility of more than one earnings function.

Job Location

The definition of "local" labor markets in terms of travel-to-work boundaries or commuting patterns is problematic. It implies internal coherence,[23] and supposes a geographic scale of labor markets which is partial in terms of class and gender.[24] There is now growing evidence of identifiable labor submarkets within metropolitan areas,[25] including spatial segmentation along gender lines.[26]

For certain types of inquiry these assumptions about internal coherence and lack of spatial differentiation may be neutral. But if we want to understand, for example, how supply and demand actually are constituted, how an exchange is produced under conditions of change on both the supply and demand side, then these assumptions are an obstacle. This is evident, for instance, in some of the spatial analyses of immigrant labor market outcomes in the current economic literature discussed above.

Part of the explanation for these "anomalous" findings lies in the fact that most workers operate in far more spatially constrained labor market areas than the SMSA.[27] The evidence is particularly compelling on differences by gender and income. Census data on commuting patterns in large metropolitan areas show that these areas tend to function as a labor market area for male workers in the higher occupational categories. For instance, women clerical workers living in the suburbs of New York City are unlikely to have a job in the city while the opposite holds for men in high-level professional and technical jobs.[28] Journey-to-work distances for women and men differ significantly, with women tending to work closer to home; evidence also shows that women who work in female-dominated occupations have markedly shorter trips to work than women working in other types of jobs.[29] Finally the evidence shows that women's mode of transportation to work is different from men's, with women more likely to use public transportation or go by foot.

This evidence suggests that journey-to-work patterns are gendered and that they contribute to specifying the labor supply in terms of sensitivity to location. We can also see this as an elaboration of Heckman's point about entry into the labor force and labor supply determinants. The typical focus has been on the characteristics of women in terms of their human capital and household constraints. When we introduce sensitivity to job location we reduce the centrality of human capital variables in explaining labor market outcomes.

The above raises at least two questions of interest here. Does a significant share of the immigrant population have job location sensitivities and hence at least some labor supply determinants that distinguish them as a group from native workers with analogous human capital endowments? Secondly, do such different job location sensitivities further clarify the finding that a significant immigrant presence in an SMSA does not appear to have a measurable impact on wage levels, and do they qualify the proposition that this impact is neutralized through the operation of local labor markets and thereby dispersed onto the larger economy?

Job Search and Access to Information

One standard way of analyzing these issues is through job search patterns. Much work on job search in economics rests on the proposition that economic behavior operates in an imperfect environment and that information is costly; thus the relative efficiency in information gathering has consequences for individual outcomes and for the aggregate efficiency of the economy as a whole.[30] Search models seek to theorize information collection and its consequences, based on a number of assumptions about the pertinent markets. In applications to labor markets, it is the neoclassical conception of individual behavior and macroequilibrium-oriented adjustment that dominates, though there are some models with a Keynsian orientation.[31]

It can be argued that the conception of information in these models is rather limited. Clark argues that information should be considered a heterogeneous entity, indeterminate, in part due to the spatial differentiation of those seeking to obtain information. Thus a given piece of information will have different meaning depending on the individual's spatial position. In this sense information is indeterminate, leading to different outcomes, different behaviors in different places.[32] Finally, information is not equally shared or accessible: an employer may not share certain types of information about wages and jobs; an established immigrant may not share such information with a newly arrived one. Information is often a strategic variable.

What is important in this argument for our purposes is that once the notion of imperfect information is replaced by that of indeterminate information, we confront questions of location and power rather than equilibrating tendencies. Hanson's work on gendered commuting patterns can be seen as one form of elaboration of spatial position in terms of location. The evidence on immigrant search and employment patterns may offer yet another differentiating attribute in the specification of how local labor markets operate.

Given search costs and given that the benefits are unknown until wages are actually sampled, Phelps posits that rarely will the search include the most outlying markets from a worker's original location.[33] Outlying in this proposition does not necessarily refer to a geographic dimension. But once we give it empirical content it very easily assumes a geographic dimension and, indeed, its obverse can be seen in the determining impact of proximity on job search and attainment in the conceptualization of the local labor market. The case of immigrants allows us to elaborate on this empirical reformulation of the proposition that the job search rarely includes the most outlying markets. We may ask, for instance, whether such a narrowly geographic correlate of the notion of restrictions in job searches assumes a new meaning when these restrictions hold despite the enormous initial distance traveled by immigrants whose job search takes them to another country?

Some job search models make information received a function of interacting with job offers and not merely a reaction to firms' signals.[34] In such a model the path taken in the search process is a key factor in the exchange moment—when an employment relation materializes. The geographic dimension of this proposition has received considerable attention. Clark notes the possibility of geographic bias in the search path, and Greenwood finds that the geographic mobility of workers follows specific search paths which are a function of initial location and the location of others.[35] The literature on international migration has accumulated an enormous body of evidence, which we will discuss later, showing the centrality of linkages to the pattern and destination of immigrant groups. What matters for our purposes is that one consequence of the centrality of linkages is the formation of distinct geographic trajectories for immigrant groups according to nationality and place of origin.

Of interest here also is MacDonald's information-accumulation search model, which posits that information is collected sequentially through related activities.[36] This represents a considerable elaboration within the neoclassical model. Standard models do not include the possibility of learning through one's activities and hence the possibility that one's reservation wage may change, that better information can be collected through the search process itself. This is interesting because the evidence on low-income immigrants suggests that they spend less on job search and have shorter spells of unemployment between jobs than natives, which could mean that they are collecting lower-quality information. As a result one could interpret lower attainment levels not as a consequence of human capital variables but of the lower quality of the information they obtain.

Curry notes the geographical inefficiency of labor markets.[37] The real world is composed of specialized regions with differing channels for diffusion, contacts, formation of expectations. One aspect distinguishing geographic models is that information is structured by space.[38] Economic models tend to posit information as aspatial and hence as indifferent to spatial differentiation. For geographers the spatial differentiation of the economy is assumed to entail that information on jobs and wages is also spatially differentiated.[39] If there is a distribution of market prices, as opposed to a single market-clearing price, submarkets for labor need not be automatically rationalized in terms of an overreaching aggregate market price. If we add to this that information gathering costs money and hence the search process will be differentiated according to individuals' capacities and dispositions (immigrants may differ from native workers, women from men, high-income professionals from clerical workers), then we can see that the job search process can produce spatial discontinuities. In Phelps it is (imperfect) information about wages that allocates labor to places and creates aggregate outcomes; it is not prices that are the ultimate market signal, but information about prices.[40] All labor market behavior, including job search activities, becomes dependent upon the quantity and quality of price information.[41]

Labor Market Segmentation

Several authors have posited that segmentation theory can be used to specify local labor markets and address some of these kinds of differentiation. In its origins, the segmentation concept was proposed largely in reaction to the assumption of homogeneity of labor embodied in the neoclassical treatment of the labor market. While the latter recognized differentiation of the labor force, it posited that if the labor market worked according to the neoclassical theory, little would be lost if labor was assumed to be homogeneous. The heterogeneity in the workforce is thereby seen as arising because of pre-market differences among people (innate ability, education) and not out of the operation of the labor market itself.[42]

At issue here was not how these differences arise but how the market worked, that is, how well the price mechanism worked to distribute labor. Dispersion in earnings suggests that the wage-setting process is considerably more complicated than the simple rewarding of human capital. Even when very narrowly defined occupations are used, there is wage variation in cross-industrial and cross-regional comparisons.[43] Explanations of interindustry wage differentials often rely on institutional differences between industries. For example, efficiency wage models explain why high-wage firms do not cut wages given unemployment and workers' willingness to take lower wages. These models argue that firms pay higher wages to raise workers' productivity.[44] The fact of limited information on comparative wages can introduce further dispersion; any regional difference in wages for a given occupation contributes to dispersion.

Variables other than human capital need to be included to explain the distribution of job rewards: structural variables as well as workers' characteristics that are not encompassed by human capital.[45] Morrison argues that the specific contribution of dual labor market theory lies in recognizing fundamental differences between two alternative treatments of labor which result not in one but in two, or more, quite different earnings functions; the essential difference is the way in which labor is priced in each segment.[46]

These are some of the labor market mechanisms through which distinct local labor markets are constituted. These conceptual and empirical materials serve to elaborate the category of the local labor market, to take it beyond the notion of the functional region specified in terms of journey-to-work. The main points to be extracted from the above discussion can be summarized as follows. First, both conceptual and empirical materials show or suggest strongly that there are significant differences by gender and income in sensitivity to job location, job search paths, and information gathering. Secondly, these differences contribute to specify the labor supply for a given set of jobs and hence can be seen as contributing to an analytic elaboration of conditions of entry into the labor force (see Heckman). Thirdly, there is conceptual work on job search models suggesting that once we consider information as indeterminate because it is spatially differentiated, the issue is no longer the equilibrating outcomes of information attainment, but rather the geographic restrictions in access to information and the geographic bias in information channels. Fourth, information is also the result of interaction with job offers and therewith contributes to spatial patterning; further, information gathering is enhanced through the job search process itself, and hence the latter will also affect the information gathered. Fifth, information gathering costs money and hence the job search process can produce spatial discontinuities and reproduce existing channels of access, therewith providing the same information over and over, making a switch to another local labor market more difficult.

In brief, competition, mobility, and information gathering do not necessarily clear markets but may on the contrary contribute to the reproduction of existing local labor markets, somewhat impervious to "externally" induced changes. We see here the elements of cumulative causation rather than market clearing.

Recentering the Local Labor Market: The Workplace-Community Nexus

The overall conceptual effort in this section is to expand the analytic terrain within which to locate and explain labor market operation. It means introducing into the discussion of labor market operation not only the types of constraints and specifications found in the economic geography literature on labor markets discussed above, but also key categories from the new economic sociology. Among these are networks, social ties, social capital and cumulative causation, conditions under which the household releases labor to the labor market, channels of information about jobs, and the implications for communities of employers' preference for word-of-mouth recruiting. This should contribute to the specification of local labor markets as activity spaces that are both spatial and institutional and that are centered on the workplace-household and/or workplace-community nexus.

To that end this section examines various findings in the sociological immigration literature which can contribute to specifying pre- and post-exchange variables in local labor market operation. Much of the evidence on immigrant employment and immigrant communities shows that immigrants have very specific job search paths and channels of access to information about jobs. The contributions of much of this literature lie in the detailed accounts of particular cases. Insofar as generalizations have been produced out of these particular cases, they have largely been presented as specifying immigrants and their communities. Here we discuss some aspects of this large array of detailed studies to further a systematic inquiry into some of the questions raised in the preceding section about the nature of local labor markets. This discussion should also contribute to a more in-depth explanation of some of the generalizations and questions coming out of the economic empirical literature about labor markets and immigrants.

Supply Determinants:
The Impact of Community and Household

Most of the evidence on immigrant employment has not necessarily been framed in terms of sensitivity to job location, access to information, and job search patterns. Rather, the key organizing categories in this literature are the concepts of social ties and, more generally, networks. The emphasis in my discussion is not on the importance of social ties or networks per se in job attainment; their importance is already a fairly well-established fact for immigrants and, though this is somewhat more contested, for the population at large. The emphasis will be on what we know about the differential impacts of social ties for different categories of workers and the labor market implications of different types of networks.

There is some evidence showing that sensitivity to job location among low-wage immigrant workers assumes different contents than among native workers with similar characteristics. The fact of moving from one country to another in itself can be construed as low sensitivity to location (distance is not a deterrent) compared with natives, particularly in light of some of the findings discussed earlier about low mobility in some categories of native workers with analogous human capital endowments to those of immigrants. Furthermore, there is growing evidence that shows immigrants in large SMSAs are willing to travel unusually long distances to get to unusually low-paying jobs, often requiring considerable improvisation in terms of transportation. Overall, this tends to be seen as indicating that immigrants are willing to travel longer distances than analogous natives, perhaps even a majority of natives.

But besides indicating a differential propensity in journey-to-work patterns among immigrants compared with natives, it may also be an outcome of the distinct spatial patterns of immigrant social ties, networks, and information channels. This would certainly seem to be the case in the move from country of origin to that of destination. Are the spatial correlates of immigrant networks and information channels inside the United States also different and are they a factor explaining labor market outcomes and, more generally, how the labor market operates for immigrants?

There is considerable general evidence about the importance of networks in the patterning of job searches and outcomes. Much information about jobs flows through informal networks and significant shares of workers obtain their jobs through this type of information.[47] There is also considerable evidence for the case of immigrants.[48] It shows that kinship ties, residential networks, and association with co-ethnics facilitate job search and attainment among immigrants.[49]

It has now become clear that much of the research on the role of informal networks in job searches has focused on men, both in the general and in the immigration literature. It suggests we need to specify the operation and outcomes of networks in terms of group characteristics. Thus, recent evidence shows that informal networks and their job outcomes are gendered. Hanson and Pratt, among others, have shown exhaustively how the social ties of women differ from those of men and lead to different job outcomes; they find that the gendering of social life contributes not only to the sex segregation of jobs, but also entails that workplace-based contacts are less likely to lead to jobs in the case of women than other types of contacts.[50] In their study they found that workplace-based contacts led to only 17 percent of job findings for women, while the family accounted for 37 percent.

The evidence on women's networks also points to the presence of a spatial dimension that has implications for labor market outcomes. Women's networks in general have been found to contain more relatives while men's are more likely to have more coworkers.[51] Thus the location of networks for women is more likely to be in residential areas and that of networks for men outside the neighborhood and at the workplace. Furthermore, women's work contacts will also tend toward gendered outcomes insofar as a significant percentage of women are in jobs where women are in the majority and insofar as the locational distribution of female-dominated jobs is different from that of other jobs because women are more location-sensitive in their journey to work. Women may lack access to information on non-female-dominated jobs insofar as these have a different locational distribution.

One question for us is how this works for immigrant men and women given their concentration in immigrant communities and the centrality of networks in these communities. Is there a distinct spatial patterning in the networks of immigrants, and is it gendered? Does gender override nationality in the spatial patterning of immigrant networks?

Gender and Space in Networks   Also the evidence in the immigration literature shows gendering in the systemic associations between social ties and wages and between ties and job getting.[52] We know that immigrant women and men have diverse occupational patterns and that family and community ties are more important for women's employment patterns and wages than they are for men.

Greenwell and her coauthors examined whether different types of social ties have different impacts on wages among immigrant men and women of two different nationality groups, Filipinos and Salvadoreans.[53] They were particularly interested in seeing what the wage impact was of social ties not apparently connected to the workplace in order to understand whether broader types of networks also play a role in immigrant attainment. They found only partial support for the notion that the wage impact of social ties would be strongest for those with workplace-based ties. They found that men working with relatives earn more than other men, but the opposite was true for women.[54] Overall they did not find the expected progression from lower wages and family-based social ties to higher wages and workplace-based social ties.[55] This is quite interesting given our concern to establish whether the experience of immigrants can contribute new insights into labor market operation.[56]

In the study of Filipinos and Salvadoreans the impact of social ties was found to vary according to gender but not according to nationality of origin. This finding is particularly remarkable because the researchers found few differences in terms of human capital variables between men and women in each nationality group, and great differences between the two nationality groups as a whole. Yet men earned significantly higher wages than women in each group. Men and women had very different patterns of social ties and concentrations of co-nationals in workplaces. This gendered pattern held even though within each gender group, Filipinos had much higher levels of human capital than Salvadoreans. The researchers found that the wages of Filipinos and Salvadoreans were predicted by the same factors, even though the wage levels of the two groups are very different. But they found significant differences in the factors predicting women's and men's wages in each nationality group.

It would seem then that gender can override nationality or culture of origin. This would be further supported by the evidence showing that employers of women are more likely to pay lower wages throughout the economy.[57] This is a structural condition that will override immigrant status, even though such status can exacerbate the negative impact on wages. There is some evidence that family-based ties can lead to better-paying jobs among women with poor English skills, while this has not been found for men.[58] On the other hand, men with good English skills were found to earn more when working with relatives.[59]

Overall it seems that working *with* relatives is associated with higher wages among men, but lower wages among women—even for women in the primary sector. This may be pointing to community stereotypes that devalue women's paid work. Zhou and Logan explain this type of pattern in terms of women's subordination and household-based strategies for economic attainment.[60] Their explanation would give a particular meaning to the finding that poor immigrant women find jobs more easily than poor immigrant men.[61] I have elsewhere described a structural condition underlying these outcomes as the feminization of the *job supply* to distinguish it from another major process, the feminization of the labor force.[62]

Labor Market Segments and Networks   Labor market segment, immigrant status, and social ties interact in ways that point to gendered outcomes. The findings discussed above do not support the general proposition that social ties will compensate for human capital deficiencies and/or raise the returns on limited capital endowments. The interaction between the labor market segment where an immigrant is employed and his or her social ties may explain certain outcomes since labor market segment is an indicator not only of skill level but of institutionalized bargaining power in occupations and industries. Secondary labor market status may override the "negative" impact of immigrant status and the positive impact of social ties. Labor market segmentation can be seen as *producing* heterogeneity in the labor force, and in this sense the presence of an immigrant labor supply is understood as being partly reproduced through the dynamics of the labor market rather than simply resulting from shared human capital deficiencies producing low-wage status.

A central assumption in most models of labor mobility and location decision making is that all market behavior is voluntary. Constraining circumstances or agents are deliberately excluded from consideration, and are likely to be cast aside as premarket differences. While this may be a reasonable proposition for large sectors of the population, particularly the middle strata, it is far less certain that it holds for immigrants, especially if they reside in immigrant communities. Immigrant communities and households can be characterized by the weight of social ties that bind people into relations of trust and mutual obligation, the fact of "enforceable trust" (see Portes, this volume), and the weight of collective rather than individual economic attainment strategies. All of these shape and influence the release and allocation of labor in the immigrant household.

By the time the immigrant is in the queue for a job, a multiplicity of processes have taken place that will tend to influence the exchange moment. Because it is pursuing a collective economic attainment strategy, the immigrant household can release one or more of its members, often women, to very low-wage and unstable jobs that may not cover the social reproduction costs of the individual worker. Furthermore, through the operation of "enforceable trust," members of the household or community may be obliged to take jobs obtained through relatives or friends' ties even when they do not want to take those jobs. These household- and community-based decisions and capacities shape the immigrant labor supply and influence the moment of exchange. One feature of the operation of the local labor market, in the case of immigrants, is the inclusion of household- and community-based labor supply determinants. We know that to some extent this is also the case with gender in the larger population. Thus the detailed information produced in the sociological literature about immigrant household- and community-based constraints and capacities may provide insights into larger questions about labor market operation.

Information, Space, and Networks   This analytic displacement towards the incorporation of household and community characteristics in labor market operation assumes distinct forms in the case of yet another crucial category, information. The assumption in standard models is that information is homogeneous and universal, though its attainment is imperfect. Conceptualizing information as contingent on spatial and social position means it ceases to be homogeneous. And once spatial interaction is recognized as part of the process of gathering information it cannot be assumed that the information gathered is universal. There must then be spatial patterning in the information gathered which is unique to the spatial patterns of contacts and the times at which contacts took place.[63] We can then reconceive information as place-based "knowledge."[64]

Place-based knowledge in this conception of local labor markets replaces analytically the category "information" of neoclassical labor market theory. Such place-based knowledge also recasts the whole matter of information in international migration: it replaces analytically or at least qualifies the utility calculus. If an immigrant has a factory job in New Jersey at a certain wage, this is the information his cousin in Mexico will use to make a decision about emigrating, not some sense of the comparative relative differential in returns to skill in Mexico and the United States.[65] Under these conditions, understanding information becomes a local event. As a local event it is shaped, we can assume, by position in space and time, by gender, race, and nationality.

On Networks and Locational Choices Among Employers

The locational patterns and decisions of firms are, clearly, also a crucial variable in the formation and continuity of local labor markets. Economic geographers particularly have shown that labor markets are spatially segmented and that this segmentation reflects underlying place-to-place differences in the nature of the labor force.[66] What is less clear is how those markets emerge and how the experience-based knowledge of workers and employers is implicated in the segmentation process.[67] Storper and Walker note that there is a spatial division of labor underlying the segmentation of economic life; Clark maintains further that spatial labor market segmentation is partly the result of the use of local criteria by employers and workers in their evaluation of potential workers and job offers, respectively.[68] The demand-side explanation of occupational segregation, typically conceived in terms of jobs available to specific groups of people, is now also being conceptualized in terms of the locational aspect of job availability. For instance, there is now some evidence on how the suburbanization of factory, transportation, and warehousing jobs has made it difficult for inner-city blacks to gain access to those jobs, simply because of transportation problems and distance.[69] In their pioneering work, Hanson and Pratt have shown that the spatial distribution of jobs itself is different for women than for men.

The matter of job location as it feeds the spatial segmentation of labor markets is an issue that goes beyond the question of transportation. It involves forms of job location sensitivity that can operate also when distances are fairly short and transportation is available. Thus barriers that have to do with race and with gender are instances where sensitivity to location is in part also a socially constructed event, and it is as such that it contributes to spatial segmentation of labor markets.[70] Further, where the locational choices of employers primarily involve access to a certain type of worker, such choices are clearly contributing to labor market segmentation.[71] At least some employers who need access to large pools of specific types of female labor make locational decisions accordingly; for example, firms with large clerical workforces will locate in suburban areas where they have access to educated women. The spatial structure of employment opportunities for women and female labor force participation can then be seen as partly interrelated in that they are embedded in the same activity space.

Insofar as costs of production vary across space and are a factor affecting locational outcomes of firms, access to a desirable pool of workers (such as low-wage, educated female workers) is clearly a locational consideration that may contribute to a specific geography of group-typed jobs (in that case, female-typed jobs). This in itself can contribute to occupational segregation and to its reproduction. If we add to this the specific geography of information channels and the fact that they are often group-specific, we have yet other factors contributing to occupational segregation based on distinct labor force groups.

While less studied than the case of women generally, there is some evidence that analogous locational decisions by employers may operate in the case of immigrant workers. Furthermore, a functional equivalent to relocation that is frequently evident in firms employing a large proportion of low-wage immigrant workers is the decision to change, or perhaps more typically, not to change the organization of production in a firm or industry branch. This can also have implications for type of labor supply sought. Thus there is good evidence that the locational patterns and/or choices about technologies of production in certain industries or sectors of industries are related to the availability of large supplies of low-wage immigrant labor.[72]

Yet firms do not simply locate where the "best" (or cheapest) labor supply is found. There is considerable evidence that interfirm linkages—access to suppliers, contractors, subcontractors—are extremely important, especially for small firms. In his study of electronics assembly plants in southern California, Scott found that there were locations in the region with large concentrations of low-wage Hispanic workers and good transportation access, yet no firms had located there even though they had to fill large numbers of low-wage positions; instead he found firms clustering around purchasers of assembly services.[73] In our study, we found a similar importance of interfirm networks in explaining locational patterns: we found fairly dense networks of contractors and suppliers clustering in distinct areas for the electronics and garment industries. Clearly, for some types of firms locational choices respond more to interindustrial linkage structures than to the geographic distribution of potential labor supplies.

The presence of a low-wage immigrant workforce does not necessarily mean that those immigrants will be the labor supply of choice in firms with low-wage jobs and hence replace other labor supplies. That is to say, we cannot assume that replacement will occur just because low-wage immigrant workers are there and they are cheaper than other workers. This is again illustrated by Scott's study described above. We found a similar pattern in our comparison of the employment of Hispanics in the garment and electronics industries in southern California and the New York-New Jersey area. While both areas have very large Hispanic populations, and both industries are known to seek low-wage labor, the incidence of Hispanic employment is quite different. In southern California approximately 72 percent of the workers in the garment industry were of Hispanic origin, compared to under 30 percent in the New York-New Jersey area. In the electronics industry the figures were respectively 64 percent and 16 percent. This pattern of differences contrasts to some extent with the similarity in the figures for women employed, regardless of nationality. In both southern California and the New York-New Jersey regions women make up over 50 percent of the garment labor force in our samples. In the electronics industry, 60 percent of workers in southern California and 34 percent in the New York-New Jersey regions were women. Each area had roughly a 50 percent Hispanic female work force in garment production. But while 35 percent of women workers were Hispanics in southern California, this figure was only 11 percent in the New York-New Jersey area. As is the case with findings of studies discussed in the preceding section, gender frequently overrides nationality in labor market outcomes. There is also the matter of employers' ties to a place. For example, in the New York region we found several employers who had started their own new firms after their former employers, typically large mass-production plants, had moved out of the region. And there is the attachment of employers to their workforce. In his detailed case study, Fernandez finds that once employers develop close ties to a highly localized labor force, they are reluctant to relinquish that labor force even when the need for more space dictates relocation.[74]

Finally, spatial dependencies between employing establishments and communities or households are likely to emerge when the networks used by workers to obtain information about jobs also become recruitment conduits for employers. Networks not only contain information circuits but also screening mechanisms. Employees are likely to know their employer's preferences and will channel what they consider to be appropriate members of their networks into any job openings that arise at their workplace. In the case of the immigrant community, this knowledge about an employer's preferences and expectations may be crucial when it comes to language proficiency, legal status, and "cultural adjustment." We found several cases where employers both encouraged word-of-mouth recruitment and were very supportive of more senior workers coaching "their" recruits on the job and helping them with the language (for example, by translating instructions). Employers often see additional benefits in this, since it strengthens worker cooperation.[75]

Several studies have found that employers say they prefer hiring production workers via word-of-mouth.[76] The figures in these same studies suggest that employers do not always get their way: a good proportion of all jobs were *not* filled via word-of-mouth. Thus we can infer that the immigrant community offers an advantage given the intensity of its networks and the channelling of newly arrived immigrants into immigrant-dominated labor markets. It is probable that a greater share of jobs can be filled via word-of-mouth when immigrants and their communities are involved. Further, in the immigrant community, matters of control and enforceable trust (see Portes) give additional strength to these screening and coaching mechanisms.

If preferences, expectations, and standards differ across labor markets and can be shown to be at least partly place-specific and related to the characteristics of an activity space, then we can argue that they are at least partly endogenous to the economic system.

All of this suggests that the locational distribution of jobs or firms is embedded in multiple spatial dependencies: interfirm linkages, recruitment and information networks binding firms and their workforces, and employers' attachments to a given place. Geographic variables matter not simply because of the relationship between location and costs, but also because spatially constituted activity spaces form specific institutional environments in which employers and workers act.[77] As with our elaboration of the supply determinants, consideration of these spatial dependencies has the effect of extending the analytic terrain within which we may understand employers' decision making about locational and recruitment choices.[78]

The Question of Proximity in Local Labor Markets

Spatial analyses of the labor market by economists and economic geographers have tended to emphasize only one type of spatial correlate for local labor markets: variable degrees of geographic proximity between workplace and home. Proximity to the workplace is assumed to be a key factor in the operation of local labor markets generally and in word-of-mouth recruitment and the residential clustering of workers in particular.

I add a second dimension: the space dependency between employer and employee can assume nonterritorial spatial correlates. This would also mean that we can identify different types of spatial dependency given such different spatial correlates.

The case of immigrant workers suggests that proximity is only one of several spatial correlates in the operation of local labor markets. We can identify alternative patterns which may allow for a broader analytic specification of the spatial dimension in local labor market dynamics. First, in the case of immigrant channels for word-of-mouth recruitment, proximity is not always evident: the actual word-of-mouth recruitment channel may extend into a foreign country—one's friends and relatives back in a particular town in Mexico, the Dominican Republic, or the Philippines. This channel has typically been found to operate through relatives. But it does not have to: Hanson and Pratt found that one of the employers in their study had a recruitment arrangement with a local Polish parish through which they kept replacing Polish workers with newly arrived Poles after what seemed to be three-year stints in the United States. In this case the parish is the labor market nexus. Even over these vast distances, the fundamental pattern of network intensity is crucial, but it is a transterritorial network.

Secondly, the tightness or intensity of the workplace-home nexus is not necessarily related to close proximity. A tight workplace-home network may involve a two-hour carpooling or informal transportation system. The key is the intensity of networks within the particular immigrant community from which the workers come. Thus we found an instance of a factory in New Jersey with a good share of workers living in upper Manhattan, two locations not directly connected by any public transportation whatsoever and quite distant from each other.[79] The workers organized an informal transportation link for themselves—a large old van.

There are other instances where it can be shown that the spatial correlates of local labor markets include nongeographic forms. An instance of a local labor market with a transterritorial spatial correlate is the market of the new international professional and managerial workforce. The latter moves in a local labor market with multiple locations represented by major cities in the world that are international business centers.[80] Further, as was discussed earlier, the introduction of gender leads to a specification of additional spatial correlates for labor market operation—both in terms of women's sensitivity to location and employers' locational decisions.

This systemic quality can also be seen at work in other dimensions of labor market operation. Again, the case of immigration offers perhaps some of the clearest examples of how two very different labor markets in geographic terms can actually be two distinct segments of a single labor market system. Zabin documents how two geographically distinct labor markets—growers in Baja California (Mexico) and growers in California—interact to produce the labor market outcomes typical of each.[81] Because they can't compete with the wages of growers in the United States, the growers in Baja California have become dependent on labor supplies from southern Mexico, where they recruit new migrants and their families. In California, the minimum wage provides a rough floor for wages; this higher wage attracts Mexicans who queue for jobs in California where growers can then select the best workers and extract higher worker effort. Baja growers cannot compete, so they have trouble retaining their workforce. Instead of raising wages or rewarding their high-productivity workers, growers in Baja have adopted a strategy of continually recruiting workers from southern Mexico and promoting their settlement in Baja. They can compete with a labor market 2,000 miles away (Oaxaca), rather than competing with the California market 200 miles away. They use family settlement as an anchor and hence must accept a workforce with a high proportion of women and children, which reduces the productivity of these workers. Zabin shows how the strategies used by employers to manage their workforce and the strategies used by workers and their families to earn a livelihood while operating in different institutional contexts on each side of the border interact to produce the outcomes in each place. The Baja and California labor market areas are interrelated and the two wage regimes must be thought of as integral parts of one labor market system. Workers in Baja accept lower wages because it is part of a package that includes the possibility of eventually going to California. At the same time, Baja's wage levels put downward pressure on wages in California.[82]

Proximity should not be reified as a precondition for local labor markets or for the tightness of a local labor market. Nor does proximity per se explain the formation of local labor markets. What is crucial is the existence and intensity of networks. These networks have spatial patterns, but they are not necessarily characterized by geographic proximity. They may involve distances that go beyond the commuting norm in a SMSA, they may connect distant cities such as New York or Los Angeles, or they may connect two communities in different countries.

Summarizing the Argument

The following key points summarize and organize the evidence from the immigration literature in terms of the categories of the local labor market. First, immigrants have a different sensitivity to job location than natives with analogous characteristics. Yet the longer distances immigrants travel, beginning with the original immigration move, may also be an indication of different spatial patterning in their networks and information channels. Second, the presence/formation of an immigrant labor supply (or of a labor supply that can be marked as immigrant) is partly reproduced through the dynamics of the labor market rather than being a result of shared human capital deficiencies as such. Third, the characteristics of local labor markets for immigrants raise questions about the notion that all market behavior is voluntary; the immigrant community places distinct obligations on its members and has distinct mechanisms for their enforcement. The local labor markets in which many immigrants function reenforce such constraints and are in turn reenforced by them. The inclusion-exclusion dynamic is therewith strengthened. Fourth, the moment of exchange is influenced by a series of pre-exchange processes. Fifth, the operation of the labor market strengthens the place-based nature of the "knowledge" about jobs that immigrants are most likely to have access to. This place-based nature of knowledge also operates transterritorially. The potential emigrant is not likely to be responding to national information about relative returns in the country of destination, as posited by Borjas, but to specific place-based information about specific jobs, most likely jobs within specific local labor markets. Sixth, the experience-based knowledge of employers and workers is implicated in the segmentation process, particularly in the formation of a local labor market. Seventh, the spatial structuring of a job supply for a given group of workers and the labor force participation of that group contribute to reproduce the local labor market. Eighth, the specific geography of information channels is therewith also increasingly embedded in that market. This dynamic is further strengthened when such information channels also become recruitment channels.

These key points can help explain a number of important findings in the empirical analyses of immigrants in the labor market. For instance, the finding that immigrants do not have an impact on wage levels in areas of heavy immigrant presence could be explained in terms of the closure of local labor markets within which immigrants move. Rather than concluding that the negative impact of low wages disperses through the national economy because local labor markets have strong clearing mechanisms (as did Borjas and Freeman), we see that it is the immigrant community which is absorbing a disproportionate share of the impact of any lowering in the wage levels.

Secondly, the particular dynamics of local labor markets discussed above contribute to explaining why and how an immigrant labor supply in a given place is reproduced as a low-wage labor supply (see the discussion above on spatial patterning in information channels and in job search patterns). It is not simply individual human capital deficiencies that determine an individual's labor market outcome, for even if some of these immigrants acquire higher levels of human capital they may well have no upward mobility in their labor market outcomes due to the closure of local labor markets. A parallel argument can be made about women in women-typed jobs. It is frequently quite difficult to jump out of one and into another, more desirable local labor market.

The operation of local labor markets as theorized here would also help explain the repeated finding that there is no competition between African Americans and immigrants with analogous human capital characteristics. Once a nexus between a given set of workplaces and a community (or communities) is established, closure is strengthened and outsiders will have difficulty gaining access to the queue. In this sense, a local labor market is a form of social capital. At the same time, this closure also helps explain why the pronounced geographic mobility of immigrants does not translate into upward occupational or income mobility. For many immigrants the move across the border is actually a move within a transterritorial yet local labor market; the immigrant is responding to specific information coming from the immigrant community of destination, about a particular job or set of jobs. And here we see some of the negative impacts associated with social capital—how the closure of a local labor market that maximizes job access by the network members also operates as an imposed closure or encasement.

Further, the spatial bias in search patterns and information channels helps explain why immigrants do not respond to labor market variables the way theory suggests they should. Immigrants have settled in areas that were not necessarily the areas native workers were drawn to (see Filer), including areas with high unemployment levels.

In brief, the local labor market is a rather pronounced mechanism for inclusion/exclusion and in this regard represents a form of social capital with both positive and negative impacts or attributes. Spatially constituted activity spaces form institutional environments in which employers and workers act. This conceptualization of the labor market posits that the operation of local labor markets leads to cumulative causation rather than market clearing.

Conclusion:
Toward the Concept of Local Labor Market Systems

The multiple dependencies between employers and employees contribute to the formation of distinctive localized labor markets. Such a view displaces the exchange dynamic—a component of all markets—from the center of labor market operation, where it lies in the neoclassical model. The concrete processes that specify this displacement will vary for different types of local labor markets (compare, for example, the local labor markets of the new transnational professional and managerial workforce with the local labor markets of immigrants). Here the focus has been on the dependencies centered on the relationship between workplace and household, and between workplace and community. Conceiving of the local labor market as being centered on this relationship makes individual preferences internal to the economic system, and indeed, makes a series of other community- or household-centered variables endogenous. These processes cannot be reduced to a question of returns to human capital. They bring to the fore how household structure, class, race, gender, and nationality bound and circumscribe "activity spaces," in this case the activity space we call a labor market.

Thinking about labor markets as activity spaces determined or specified in part by the workplace-home link or the spatial dependency of employers and workers introduces a series of variables into the analysis that are typically seen as exogenous. Most important to us are information about the market and formation of preferences. Both information and preferences can be shown to be at least partly—but often in good measure—place-specific, internal to the activity space or "economic subsystem" under consideration. Framing labor markets as activity spaces also allows us to detect or reconstruct how gender, race, and nationality can shape information channels in the labor market and thus shape individual expectations. This can be inferred to have a strong reproductive effect for existing patterns and contributes to explaining labor market segmentation. Local experience or place-based knowledge can be seen as central to the spatial segmentation of labor markets.

The analytic elaboration of proximity frees this category from a narrow geographic specification and introduces it into a more abstract arena of labor market operation. Thus immigrants are specified as a different type of labor supply from native workers with analogous human capital variables *not* because of differences in the distances they are willing to travel, but rather because of differences in the labor market systems within which they are moving. And, we should add, these are labor market systems whose spatial correlates assume different forms from those we have usually assumed to represent the full array of possibilities.

The analytic elaboration of mobility and competition allows us to see that notwithstanding vast distances, immigrants actually engage in a very restricted search when they first migrate. Much of the data suggest the act of migrating involves a move from one particular community in the country of origin to another particular community in the country of destination. We can interpret this as representing movement from one particular local labor market to another. This specific job search pattern has the effect of altering the geographic dimension often implied by job search models, especially among low-wage workers. It also qualifies an important proposition in the economics literature that analyzes immigration in terms of standard neoclassical labor market dynamics—to wit, that immigrants move in response to the better relative returns-to-skill they expect in the country of destination compared with the relative returns in their country of origin. It would seem rather that the decision-making and evaluation processes operate in terms of very specific local labor markets.

The fact of a highly restricted institutional environment appears to continue to operate once immigrants are in the area of destination. But its restrictive character operates rather differently among immigrants from how it seems to operate among native workers, particularly African Americans of analogous skill levels, and from how standard models suggest it operates. Thus while the evidence on distance/proximity to the job, as it relates to job search, may be interpreted as showing that immigrants are willing to try for far more outlying markets than natives, the fact is that immigrants' networks have a different spatial patterning, one that often involves long commuting distances. Notwithstanding the far-ranging area within which many immigrants search for jobs, they are actually moving largely within a very confined institutional setting, even when they must travel long distances and improvise informal transportation systems. This is another way of conceptualizing the role of networks. These networks have spatial patterns, but they are not characterized by geographic proximity. Furthermore, while they may cover immense distances they do not necessarily offer great opportunities for mobility or place immigrants in particularly competitive positions vis-à-vis natives.

This restricted institutional (as opposed to geographic) space within which immigrants move is also suggested by the evidence showing that immigrants have shorter unemployment spells between jobs. Immigrants appear to be more likely to take another job quickly, even if its wage is below that of the prior job. Of interest here is also the finding that men in the general population engage in longer searches than do women. Usually this evidence is seen as an indication of risk adversity (in other words, women and immigrants are more risk-adverse than men and natives respectively). This interpretation treats these differences as premarket differences that will be reflected in the jobs and wages held by each group. An alternative interpretation, however, could see the evidence as a further indication of the confined institutional space within which women and immigrants find themselves searching for jobs—confined partly because there is a spatial segmentation of labor markets (the specific locational distribution of jobs aimed at the female labor supply, discussed earlier) and partly because of the specific ways in which social ties and hence access to information about jobs operate in the case of immigrants and of women. Rather than being a matter of individual attributes such as greater or lesser risk adversity, these differential labor market outcomes are at least in part a result of labor market operation, specifically aspects of labor market operation that can only be captured if we introduce a series of variables having to do with pre- and post-exchange conditions. This is not to exclude other factors, including individual attributes and employers' preferences, but rather to expand the arena within which we interpret labor market outcomes.

This focus on activity spaces and the place-based knowledge they engender may allow us to specify what we could think of as labor market *systems*. Furthermore, the local-ness of these activity spaces allows us to identify class-specific migration systems and class-specific labor market systems. International labor migration and the labor market incorporation of immigrants can then be shown to pivot not on a general and overarching labor market dynamic, but on these local and transnational activity spaces into which immigrants step and within which they move.

This chapter was written while I was in residence at the Russell Sage Foundation, whose support I gratefully acknowledge. I want to thank Mrs. Vivian Kaufman for her precise and intelligent assistance in preparing this manuscript. Last but not least, thanks to our working group at the Foundation for making all the difference through an abundance of comments, suggestions, and laughs.

Notes

1. J. Peck, "Reconceptualizing the Local Labor Market: Space, Segmentation, and the State," *Progress in Human Geography* 13 (1989):42.

2. W. F. Lever, "The Operation of Local Labor Markets in Great Britain," *Papers of the Regional Science Association* 44 (1980):37–55. R. Rosenfeld, "Job Changing and Occupational Sex Segregation: Sex and Race Comparisons," in B. F. Reskin, ed., *Sex Segregation in the Workplace: Trends, Explanations, Remedies* (Washington, D.C.: National Academy Press, 1989); M. Semyonov, "Community Characteristics, Female Employment and Occupational Segregation: Small Towns in a Rural State," *Rural Sociology* 48 (1983):104–119.

3. P. S. Morrison, "Segmentation Theory Applied to Local, Regional, and Spatial Labor Markets," *Progress in Human Geography* 14 (1990):488–528.

4. K. Mayhew, "Earnings Dispersion in Local Labour Markets: Implications for Search Behavior," *Oxford Bulletin of Economics and Statistics* 39, no. 2 (1977):93–107.

5. James J. Heckman, "What Has Been Learned About Labor Supply in the Past Twenty Years?" *AEA Papers and Proceedings: Lessons From Empirical Labor Economics: 1972–1991* (1992):118.

6. Randall K. Filer, "The Effect of Immigrant Arrivals on Migratory Patterns of Native Workers," in George J. Borjas and Richard B. Freeman, eds., *Immigration and the Work Force: Economic Consequences for the United States and Source Areas* (Chicago: University of Chicago Press, 1992).

7. Lagged immigrant arrival rates had stronger effects in reducing native inmigration rates and a smaller effect in raising outmigration rates of natives than contemporaneous immigrant arrivals. Filer, "The Effect of Immigrant Arrivals," p. 262.

8. David Card, "The Impact of the Mariel Boatlift on the Miami Labor Market," *Industrial and Labor Relations Review* 43 (January 1990):245–258.

9. Ann P. Bartel, "Where Do the New U.S. Immigrants Live?" *Journal of Labor Economics* 7 (October 1989):371–391. Frank D. Bean and Lindsay Lowell, "The Illegal Population in the Metropolitan United States: Estimates from the 1980 Census" (transcript, Population Research Center, University of Texas, Austin, Tex., no date).

10. Bartel, "Where Do the New U.S. Immigrants Live?"

11. M. Patricia Fernández Kelly and Saskia Sassen, "Hispanic Women in the Garment and Electronics Industry" (final research report presented to the Ford, Revson, and Tinker Foundations, New York, N.Y., 1992).

12. Stephen G. Bronars, "Immigration, Internal Migration and Economic Growth: 1940–1980" (University of California, Santa Barbara, 1989, mimeographed).

13. Kristen F. Butcher and David Card, "Immigration and Wages: Evidence from the 1980s," *American Economic Review* 81 (May 1991):292–296.

14. George J. Borjas and Richard B. Freeman, "Introduction and Summary," in George J. Borjas and Richard B. Freeman, eds., *Immigration and the Work Force*, pp. 1–15.

15. Ibid., pp. 1–15.

16. Joseph Altonji and David Card, "The Effects of Immigration on the Labor Market Outcomes of Less-Skilled Natives," in John M. Abowd and Richard B. Freeman, eds., *Immigration, Trade, and the Labor Market* (Chicago: University of Chicago Press, 1991).

17. For example, if immigrants are substitutes in production with natives, then immigrant arrivals make wages fall; natives move out in search of markets with higher wages; capital moves into immigrant-heavy areas, and wage levels are (supposedly) restored given expanded labor demand.

18. Borjas and Freeman, "Introduction and Summary."

19. This would seem to go against the market clearing proposition, since the decline in wages should have had the effect of raising their demand; the only way to square this would be to argue that wages didn't fall enough, no matter that they fell sharply. Topel argues that a market clearing model is consistent with these data, but only over the very long run. Robert Topel, "What Have We Learned from Empirical Studies of Unemployment and Turnovers?" *AEA Papers and Proceedings: Lessons from Empirical Labor Economics: 1972–1992* (1992):115–119.

20. Robert Topel, "What Have We Learned from Empirical Studies of Unemployment and Turnover?"

21. James Orr, "Industrial Restructuring: Role of Immigration Policy" (Immigration Policy Group, U.S. Department of Labor, Washington, D.C., 1988, mimeographed).

22. See also Marta Tienda, L. Jensen, and Robert Bach, "Immigration, Gender, and the Process of Occupational Change in the United States, 1970–1980," *International Migration Review* 18 (Winter 1984):1021–1044.

23. A. G. Champion, A. E. Green, D. W. Owen., D. J. Ellin, and M. G. Coombes, *Changing Places: Britain's Demographic Economic and Social*

Complexion (London: Edward Arnold, 1987). R. Santana-Cooney and A. E. Colon-Warren, "Declining Female Participation Among Puerto Rican New Yorkers," *Ethnicity* 6 (1983):281–297.

24.   G. L. Clark and J. Whiteman, "Why Poor People Do Not Move: Job Search Behavior and Disequilibrium Amongst Local Labor Markets," *Environment and Planning A* 15 (1983):85–104. Susan Hanson and Ibipo Johnston, "Gender Differences in Worktrip Length: Explanations and Implications," *Urban Geography* 6 (1985):192–219.

25.   Clark and Whiteman, "Why Poor People Do Not Move."

26.   Hanson and Johnston, "Gender Differences in Worktrip Length." Susan Hanson and Geraldine Pratt, "Dynamic Dependencies: A Geographic Investigation of Local Labor Markets," *Economic Geography* 68, no. 4 (1992):373–405.

27.   Hanson and Pratt, "Dynamic Dependencies."

28.   On the other hand, women in high-income jobs tend to live in the city and have thereby been central to the process of urban gentrification related to the expanded demand for professional workers in the 1980s. See Saskia Sassen, *The Global City: New York, London, Tokyo* (Princeton: Princeton University Press, 1991), Chap. 9.

29.   Hanson and Johnston, "Gender Differences in Worktrip Length." Janice Madden, "Why Women Work Closer to Home," *Urban Studies* 18 (1981):181–194. Larry Singell and Jane Lillydahl, "An Empirical Analysis of the Commute to Work Pattern of Males and Females in Two-Earner Households," *Urban Studies* 23 (1986):119–129.

30.   Phelps shows that workers' expectations of money wages elsewhere will adapt less-than-proportionally to the unforeseen fall of sampled money wage rates. There will be constraints on the number of searches and the geographical pattern of search; no search can completely exhaust all options, and few searches will reach more outlying markets. For Phelps the overall equilibrium clearing-wage of the labor market system will depend on the efficiency of workers' searches and the flow of information between islands—where island is the image used to describe different markets. E. Phelps et al., *Microeconomic Foundations of Employment and Inflation Theory* (New York: W. W. Norton, 1970), p. 7. G. L. Clark, "Toward an Alternative Conception of Job-Search Theory and Policy: Information as an Indeterminate Process," *Environment and Planning A* 18 (1983):804–805. J. J. McCall, "Introduction," in *The Economics of Information and Uncertainty* (Chicago: University of Chicago Press, 1982), pp. xi–xxii.

31.   Clark, in "Toward an Alternative Conception of Job-Search Theory and Policy," develops a critical analysis of spatial labor market models which use job search concepts to explain the allocation of labor between competing regions. A concept such as the cost of obtaining information, which implies the existence of imperfect information, is

used in standard neoclassical manner to explain why there are spatial discontinuities (that is, inefficiencies) in labor allocation between areas of excess labor demand and areas of excess labor supply. Clark and Whiteman, "Why Poor People Do Not Move." See also J. Stiglitz, "Symposium on Economics of Information: Introduction," *Review of Economic Research* 44 (1978):389–391.

32. Clark further argues that since macroefficiency would entail a measure of consistency in behavior across locations with respect to market signals, these characteristics of information (heterogeneity and indeterminacy) suggest that aggregate economic stability is unlikely.

33. E. Phelps et al., *Microeconomic Foundations*. Clark notes that there might be as many wage offers (clearing market prices) as there are locations. Price dispersion and market segmentation will then characterize the spatial economic system. The whole labor market system will be relatively inefficient.

34. There are job search models that posit multiple information channels, as in P. Rogerson, "Spatial Models of Search," *Geographical Analysis* 14 (1982):217–228. P. Rogerson and R. D. MacKinnon, in "Interregional Migration Models with Source and Interaction Information," *Environment and Planning A* 14 (1982):445–454, use information about job vacancies to derive search decisions with the assumption of skill-homogenous workers and homogenous jobs. The attempt is to match jobs and workers given imperfect information about the location of job vacancies.

35. Clark, "Toward an Alternative Conception." Michael J. Greenwood, "Research on Internal Migration in the United States," *Journal of Economic Literature* 13 (June 1975):397–433.

36. G. M. MacDonald, "A Market Equilibrium Theory of Job Assignment and Sequential Accumulation of Information," *American Economic Review* 72 (1982):1038–1055.

37. L. Curry, "Inefficiencies in the Geographical Operation of Labour Markets," *Regional Studies* 19 (1985):203–216.

38. Ibid.; G. Maier, "Cumulative Causation and Selectivity in Labor-Market Oriented Migration Caused by Imperfect Information," *Regional Studies* 19 (1985):231–242.

39. There is a considerable amount of work by economic geographers that seeks to specify the spatial character of wage diffusion. See G. L. Clark, "On Testing the Unemployment Dispersion Hypothesis," *Journal of Regional Science* 20 (1980):483–487; D. W. Jones, "Mechanisms for Geographical Transmission of Economic Fluctuations," *Annals of the Association of American Geographers* 73 (1983):35–50; R. L. Martin, "Wage-Change Interdependence amongst Regional Labor Markets: Conceptual Issues and Some Empirical Evidence for the United States," in R. L. Martin, ed., *Regional Wage Inflation and Unemployment* (London: Pion, 1981), pp. 96–135.

40. E. Phelps et al., *Microeconomic Foundations*. Here we also should note the significance of institutional factors in wage structures (for example, the "stickiness" of wages) and Wietzman's revival of Keynes's theory about this.

41. The differences in the capabilities for information gathering segment searches into different submarkets. Dispersion in prices/wages "splits the markets and charges a higher purchase price to the submarket of inefficient searchers." S. Salop, "The Noisy Monopolist: Imperfect Information, Price Dispersion and Price Discrimination," *Review of Economic Studies* 44 (1978):393–406. Clark adds a geographic dimension and posits that information is to some extent geographically contingent. See also M. Webber, *Impact of Uncertainty on Location* (Cambridge: MIT Press, 1972). There are implications here for immigrant-dominated local markets.

42. P. S. Morrison, "Segmentation Theory Applied to Local, Regional, and Spatial Labor Markets," *Progress In Human Geography* 14 (1990):488–528; Paul Ryan, "Segmentation, Duality, and the Internal Labor Market," in F. Wilkinson, ed., *The Dynamics of Labor Market Segmentation* (Cambridge: Cambridge University Press, 1981), pp. 3–20.

43. W. T. Dickens and L. F. Katz, "The Reemergence of Segmented Labor Market Theory," *American Economic Review* 76 (1988):129–134.

44. An alternative explanation of interindustry wage differentials would focus on the evolution of institutions and social relations as a context within which firms choose labor management practices and workers respond to employment opportunities.

45. Thus, efficiency wages (J. Yellen, "Efficiency Wage Models of Unemployment," *American Economic Review* 74 (1984):200–205), can vary across regions. See S. C. Farber and R. J. Newman, "Regional Wage Differentials and the Spatial Convergence of Worker Characteristic Prices," *The Review of Economics and Statistics* LXXI 2 (1989):224–231. Furthermore, ascriptive traits (sex, race, nationality) can be used as indicators of expected performance. Several authors have noted that these ideas have now been incorporated in human capital theory, and some (Dickens and Katz, 1988) argue that many aspects of segmented labor markets can be included in the neoclassical model. For example, efficiency wage arguments are now being explicitly linked to those of dual labor market theory (L. I. Bulow and J. H. Summers, "A Theory of Dual Labor Markets with Application to Industrial Policy, Discrimination and Keynesian Unemployment," *Journal of Labor Economics* 4 (1986):376–414). There are now competing and often sharply differing models of segmentation (Dickens and Katz, 1988). For instance, recent developments in human capital theory have contributed to our understanding of likely sources of wage variation, but they do not question the underlying relationship between education and job rewards. Dual labor market theory does.

46. Morrison, "Segmentation Theory."

47. Marta Tienda and Jennifer Glass, "Household Structure and Labor Force Participation of Black, Hispanic, and White Mothers," *Demography* 22, no. 3 (1985): 381–394. Howard Wial, "Getting a Good Job: Mobility in a Segmented Labor Market," *Industrial Relations* 30, no. 3 (1991): 396–416. James D. Montgomery, "Job Search and Network Composition: Implicatios of the Strength-of-Weak-Ties Hypothesis," *American Sociological Review* 57, no. 5 (1992):586–596. Peter V. Marsden and Jeanne S. Hurlbert, "Social Resources and Mobility Outcomes: A Replication and Extension," *Social Forces* 66, no. 4 (1988):1038–1059. Mark S. Granovetter, "The Strength of Weak Ties," *American Journal of Sociology* 78 (May 1973):1360–1380. William P. Bridges and Wayne J. Villemez, "Informal Hiring and Income in the Labor Market," *American Sociological Review* 51, no. 4 (1986):574–582.

48. Thomas Bailey and Roger Waldinger, "Primary, Secondary, and Enclave Labor Markets: A Training Systems Approach," *American Sociological Review* 56 (1991):432–445. Monica Boyd, "Family and Personal Networks in International Migration: Recent Developments and New Agendas," *International Migration Review* 23, no. 3 (1989):638–670. Greta A. Gilbertson and Douglas T. Gurak, "Broadening the Enclave Debate: The Labor Market Experiences of Dominican and Colombian Men in New York City," *Sociological Forum* 8, no. 2 (1993):205–220. Tienda and Glass, "Household Structure and Labor Force Participation." Kenneth L. Wilson and Alejandro Portes, "Immigrant Enclaves: An Analysis of the Labor Market Experiences of Cubans in Miami," *American Journal of Sociology* 86 (1980):295–319; Marta Tienda, "Sex, Ethnicity, and Chicano Status Attainment," *International Migration Review* 16, no. 2 (1982):435–472. Also see Portes, this volume; Roberts, this volume.

49. There are several studies showing that social ties work to compensate for the human capital deficiencies of immigrants. A good part of immigrant occupational disadvantage has to do with deficiencies of human capital, particularly the lack of English proficiency. See Cordelia Reimers, "A Comparative Analysis of the Wages of Hispanics, Blacks, and Non-Hispanic Whites," in G. Borjas and M. Tienda, eds., *Hispanics in the U.S. Economy* (Orlando, FL: Academic Press, 1985); C. Hirshman and M. G. Wong, "Socioeconomic Gains of Asian Americans, Blacks and Hispanics 1960–1976," *American Journal of Sociology* 90, no. 3 (1984):584–607; Edwin Meléndez, "Labor Market Structure and Wage Inequality in New York City," in E. Meléndez, C. Rodriguez, and J. Barry-Figueroa, eds., *Hispanics in the Labor Force: Issues and Politics* (New York: Plenum Press, 1991); Tienda, in "Sex and Ethnicity"; George Borjas, "The Intergenerational Mobility of Immigrants," *Journal of Labor Economics* 11 (January 1993). We also know that English knowledge has a greater impact than education on the labor force participation rate of immigrant women; that English is more important for initial wage attainment (at least among Mexican immigrants) than education (Tienda, in "Sex and Ethnicity"). Victor Nee, Jimy M. Sanders, and Scott Sernau, "Job Transitions in an Immigrant Metropolis: Ethnic Boundaries and the Mixed Economy,"

American Sociological Review 59 (1994): 849–872. Other studies have found that social ties can compensate for lack of English: Portes (in "Immigrant Enclaves") found this for immigrants working for co-nationals, though there is evidence that it may work best for men, and much less so for women. See S. Grasmuck and P. Pessar, *Between Two Islands* (Berkeley: University of California Press, 1991); Fernández Kelly and Sassen, "Hispanic Women."

50. Susan Hanson and Geraldine Pratt, "Job Search and the Occupational Segregation of Women," *Annals of the Association of American Geographers* 81, no. 2 (1991):229–253.

51. J. Miller McPherson and Lynn Smith-Lovin, "Women and Weak Ties: Differences by Sex in the Size of Voluntary Organizations," *American Journal of Sociology* 87, no. 4:883–904. Monica Boyd, "Family and Personal Networks in International Migration"; Denise D. Bielby and William T. Bielby, "Work Commitment, Sex-Role Attitudes, and Women's Employment," *American Sociological Review* 49, no. 2 (1984):234–247. Marta Tienda and Patricia Guhleman, "The Occupational Position of Employed Hispanic Women," in George J. Borjas and Marta Tienda, eds., *Hispanics in the U.S. Economy.* Min Zhou and J. R. Logan, "Returns on Human Capital in Ethnic Enclaves: New York City's Chinatown," *American Sociological Review* 54 (1989):809–820.

52. Marta Tienda and Jennifer Glass, "Household Structure and Labor Force Participation of Black, Hispanic, and White Mothers," *Demography* 22, no. 3 (1985):381–394. See also notes 48 and 49.

53. Lisa Greenwell, Julie DaVanzo, and R. Burciaga Valdez, "Social Ties, Wages, and Gender among Salvadorean and Filipino Immigrants in Los Angeles," *RAND* (March 1993).

54. An interesting finding in this study is that women in the secondary sector with relatives in the United States (not the same as working with or for relatives) earn more than others. This may in good part be due to the disproportionate weight in this sample of Salvadorean women who work as household cleaners: since they have relatives in the United States, they have gotten better information about wages and better access to households that will pay that wage.

55. Given the possibility that these findings may be reflecting a selection effect, it is worth noting that in this study the wages of those employed did not differ from the predicted wages of those who were not employed, a finding also produced by other studies (Greenwell, "Social Ties, Wages, and Gender"). Also Reimers in "A Comparative Analysis of the Wages" finds no selection effect either among men or women in her analyses of Central and South Americans, about 90 percent of whom are foreign-born. Borjas points to several reasons why selection should not affect wages, in "Self-Selection and the Earnings of Immigrants," *American Economic Review* 77 (September 1987):531–553.

56. Studies about the impact of social ties in determining wages in the more general population find few associations. See, for example, Peter V. Marsden and Jeanne S. Hurlbert, "Social Resources and Mobility Outcomes: A Replication and Extension," *Social Forces* 66, no. 4 (1988):1038–1059; William P. Bridges and Wayne J. Villemez, "Informal Hiring and Income in the Labor Market," *American Sociological Review* 51, no. 4 (1986):574–582. When more varied measures of social ties are used and studied in specific communities (that is, immigrant communities), the findings show more effects. Few differences have been found in the impact of social ties comparing different immigrant groups. This suggests a systemic quality here present across nationality groups.

57. Barbara F. Reskin, ed., *Sex Segregation in the Workplace: Trends, Explanations, Remedies* (Washington, D.C.: National Academy Press, 1984).

58. Lisa Greenwell, Julie DaVanzo, and R. Burciaga Valdez, "Social Ties, Wages, and Gender among Salvadorean and Filipino Immigrants"; Tienda, "Sex, Ethnicity, and Chicano Status Attainment."

59. Gilbertson and Gurak, "Broadening the Enclave Debate."

60. Zhou and Logan, "Returns on Human Capital in Ethnic Enclaves."

61. Herbert J. Gans, "Second-Generation Decline: Scenarios for the Economic and Ethnic Futures of the Post-1965 American Immigrants," *Ethnic and Racial Studies* 15, no. 2 (1992):173–192.

62. Saskia Sassen-Koob, "Immigrants and Minority Workers in the Organization of the Labor Process," *Journal of Ethnic Studies* 8 (Spring 1980):1–34.

63. Clark, "Toward an Alternative Conception of Job-Search Theory and Policy." See also Roberts, this volume.

64. See Fernández Kelly, this volume.

65. A theoretical question is whether this conception of information alters the logic of the model since the latter can be seen as having factored in all that other information (potentially in various forms: from imperfect information to premarket differences). One could then paraphrase what has been said about firms: even if potential immigrants do not use the neoclassical utility calculus, they may well act as if they did.

66. G. L. Clark, "Fluctuations and Rigidities in Local Labour Markets, Part 1: Theory and Evidence," *Environment and Planning A* 15 (1983):165–185. Doreen Massey, *Spatial Divisions of Labour: Social Structures and the Geography of Production* (London: Macmillan, 1984). Allen J. Scott, "Low-Wage Workers in a High-Technology Manufacturing Complex: The Southern California Electronics Assembly Industry," *Urban Studies* 29, no. 8 (1992):1231–1246.

67. Hanson and Pratt, "Dynamic Dependencies."

68. Michael Storper and Richard Walker, "The Labor Theory of Location," *International Journal of Urban and Regional Research* 7 (1) (1983):1–41; Clark, "Fluctuations and Rigidities in Local Labour Markets"; Clark, "Government Policy and the Form of Local Labour Markets," *Urban Geography* 4 (1983):1–15.

69. But it is also clear that location is not enough to explain labor market outcomes of population groups affected by these changes. Regarding the weight of race as a determinant of labor market outcomes, see N. Fainstein, "The Underclass/Mismatch Hypothesis as an Explanation for Black Economic Deprivation," *Politics and Society* 15, no. 4 (1986):403–451.

70. W. J. Wilson, *The Truly Disadvantaged: The Inner City, the Underclass and Public Policy* (Chicago: University of Chicago Press, 1987).

71. Cf. the evidence showing that women in female-typed jobs work closer to home than other women, and, perhaps even more to the point, the recent evidence that men in female-typed jobs have shorter trips to work than other men (Hanson and Johnston, "Gender Differences in Worktrip Length."

72. Scott, "Low-Wage Workers in a High-Technology Manufacturing Complex."

73. See Fernández Kelly and Sassen, "Hispanic Women in the Garment and Electronics Industries" for a detailed discussion.

74. Roberto M. Fernandez, *Race, Space, and Job Accessibility: Evidence from a Plant Relocation* (Northwestern University, Department of Sociology and Center for Urban Affairs and Policy Research, 1991)

75. Fernández Kelly and Sassen, "Hispanic Women in the Garment and Electronics Industries." See also Bailey and Waldinger, "Primary, Secondary, and Enclave Labor Markets."

76. Hanson and Pratt, "Job Search and the Occupational Segregation of Women." See also Fernández Kelly and Sassen, "Hispanic Women in the Garment and Electronics Industries."

77. Hanson and Pratt, "Spatial Dimensions of the Gender Division of Labor in a Local Labor Market," *Urban Geography* 9, no. 2 (1988):180–202. See also Fernández Kelly and Sassen, "Hispanic Woman in the Garment and Electronics Industries."

78. Mark Granovetter, "Economic Action and Social Structure: The Problem of Embeddedness," in Mark Granovetter and Richard Swedberg, eds., *The Sociology of Economic Life* (Boulder, Colo.: Westview Press, 1992), pp. 53–84.

79. Fernández Kelly and Sassen, "Hispanic Women in the Garment and Electronics Industries."

80. I have explored this elsewhere (Sassen, *The Global City*, Chapter 9) and have begun a new research project on the subject that can be seen as a parallel study to the one here on immigrant workers.

81. Carol Zabin, "Labor Market Interdependence between Mexico and the United States: Wage Convergence or New Gender and Ethnic Hierarchies in California and Baja California Agriculture?" Center for Latin American Studies, Tulane University, New Orleans, La., February 8, 1993.

82. Zabin also found that the migration of very poor Mixtecs from southern Mexico to Baja creates a bridge for male Mixtecs to eventually go to California, a somewhat new pattern. Since Mixtecs are very poor even by Mexican standards, they are more willing to work at lower wages than other Mexican migrants in both Baja and California. They are also mostly undocumented, which will only add to downward pressures on wages in California.

4

The Economic Sociology
of Firms and Entrepreneurs

Mark Granovetter

Development, Modernization, and Social Structure

In this chapter I analyze some of the ways in which social structure determines the scope of economic action, with special attention to the significance for the emergence of entrepreneurial activity of the complex social networks found in many ethnic and immigrant communities.

One of the obvious facts of economic life is that some individuals not only have others with whom they regularly coordinate economic activity, but also assemble relationships with them into organized combinations of activity that we call "firms." Although the question of why firms should exist was asked relatively late in the history of neoclassical economic theory, their prevalence and emergence from a more undifferentiated matrix was nevertheless taken as a signal of "modernization" in much of the literature on economic development that dates from the 1940s through the 1970s.

But this literature, whether in sociology, economics, or political science, typically assumed that any embeddedness of economic action in noneconomic relations, such as those we focus on in this chapter, was a barrier to "true" economic development. In sociology, neoevolutionists such as Parsons[1] made an argument similar—in this respect—to that of Polanyi's *The Great Transformation*,[2] claiming that the more modern the economy, the more the economic functions, like other functions, become differentiated (that is, come to reside separately in distinct social formations and institutions).

Unlike Polanyi, Parsons and most other development theorists of the period saw this shift as fundamentally positive, leading to greater efficiency in an environment that required economic activity to be detached from the noneconomic demands of family and friends and from the necessity in more traditional settings of giving work to people because of their relationship to you rather than because of their ability. In a characteristic formulation of this period, Marion Levy stated that

> industrialization carried with it an emphasis hitherto unequaled in so-cial history on what the sociologists speak of as highly rational, highly universalistic and highly functionally specific relationships. . . . In regard to choosing people for jobs . . . [one] has to place great em-phasis on what a person can do that is germane to the reasons for which he is chosen—on his abilities rather than on who he is. . . . Under highly industrialized conditions relatively small differences in skill may have tremendous implications both in terms of what is ac-complished and in terms of accidents prevented. . . . Finally, in many of the relationships in a highly industrialized situation the obli-gations, etc. involved in a relationship must be precisely defined and delimited regardless of how complex they may be. . . . In this sense an emphasis is placed by modern industry on functionally specific re-lationships rather than on functionally diffuse ones.[3]

Although it was well known from the study of "underdeveloped" economies that existing firms were typically organized along kinship and family lines and that capital was often raised for such firms through informal links among family and friends, this was seen as a fundamentally backward way to organize economic activity, since it did not show the requisite levels of functional differentiation—separation between economic and noneconomic aspects of activity. It followed that such organization prevented these economies from realizing their full potential.

The implication of this position was that existing economic insti-tutions in many settings were poorly adapted to the needs of the economy and needed to be changed or readjusted. This was consis-tent with what Lal has called the "*dirigiste* dogma," that only inter-vention from government could get economies onto the appropriate development track.[4]

Within economics, these views shifted beginning in the 1970s, as they conflicted with the general orientation of the New Institutional Economics, which tended to interpret any existing economic institu-tions as having evolved in some efficient way to solve economic problems. Thus the organization of economic activity around kin and friends underwent a reinterpretation that transformed it from a retrograde vestige of traditional times to a clever solution for difficult problems.

Ben-Porath's important contribution to this reinterpretation moved decisively away from the neoclassical depiction of economic relations as impersonal; he thus points out that investment in resources "specific to a relationship between identified parties can save transaction costs and stimulate trade. . . . The family is the locale of transactions in which identity dominates; however, identity is also important in much of what we consider the 'market.' "[5] Because some transactions are carried out with more focus on identity than others, there must be, by the tenets of the New Institutional Economics, an efficiency reason for these differences; thus, "one can analyze the transactions in which families have an advantage over other institutions, the conditions that make families of various types more or less efficient than the alternatives in any given transaction, the sorting of individuals into families, and the implications of family membership for transactions with others."[6]

Ben-Porath asserts an advantage for families and friends only when "modern" institutions are poorly developed.[7] By contrast, modern developments such as "social enforcement of private contracts, ready access to adjudication, morality, and religious pressure for generalized honesty (in contrast to 'contextual morality') all tend to reduce the importance of identity, to facilitate transactions between strangers, and to reduce the need for specific mutual investment by trading parties, allowing people to trade with a wider circle of others and narrowing the range of goods and services in which any pair or small group deals."[8] This argument is similar to that of Posner and Landa, who posit that personalized transactions arise as a transitional form to fill gaps in market institutions and are thus efficient in their context, but should be increasingly supplanted as markets attain their correct, modern form.[9] I argue instead that the centrality of social structure in entrepreneurship does not depend on the failure or absence of modern institutions.[10] On the contrary, I draw on a series of illuminating cases from the empirical literature to show how the social ties of immigrant, ethnic, and other bounded communities can, under specified conditions, furnish the resources necessary for firms to prosper in a modern setting.

The Emergence of Firms
and the Social Organization of Entrepreneurial Groups

The central issue I want to address is how it is possible for entrepreneurs to assemble the capital and labor required to sustain the cooperative venture we call a "firm." Although firms will find it difficult to survive in an economic environment that affords them no profit, I argue that the possibility of profits—that is, profits above and beyond those available in other uses of resources, or what are sometimes called "excess profits"—is also not a sufficient condition for such emergence; instead, one must study the social structure within which individuals and groups attempt the construction of firms.

Homo Economicus
and the Problem of Trust in Entrepreneurship

The New Institutional Economics leads us to expect that the scale of economic operations in any system will be just the one appropriate to the transaction costs and types found there. But the literature on economic and political development is quite different in this respect, implying that the existing scale is too small in many less-developed settings so that one must find the "obstacles" to the organization of firms and larger-scale activity.

The view of traditional development theory that embeddedness of economic action in noneconomic obligations inhibits economic expansion implies that the problem is a deficiency in the numbers of *homines economici*, individuals whose motivations are unalloyedly economic and thereby not entangled in kinship or other social obligations. But empirical studies of settings with many such individuals make clear that where the undersocialized model of human action [11] actually does approximate reality, the problems of trust that I have argued it implies become paramount and have a profoundly chilling effect on the expansion of economic activity.[12]

I shall catalogue a series of striking examples from Java [13] and from the Philippines [14] and speculate on their theoretical significance. Dewey notes that in the Javanese town (dubbed "Modjokuto") studied by her and also by Geertz, commercial relations typically did not overlap with those of kinship or neighborhood but were almost purely economic in nature.[15] Though most of the urban traders are from rural backgrounds, the population density is so high that few have carried previous relations from the village over to the urban setting. Contracts are correspondingly difficult to enforce given the absence of support from mutual kin, neighbors, or other social groupings.[16] Modjokuto is lacking in persisting ties between buyers and sellers. The same is true for ties among the merchants themselves. There are a few crops, like onions, that lend themselves to large-scale trade, and then Javanese traders do form groups, pooling capital and labor to buy in quantity at lower prices. But the groups are formed to handle a single transaction only, and then dissolve; each trader belongs to more than one group at a time, which spreads the risk.[17] Credit is difficult to find in part because information about credit risks is scarce and costly in this atomized setting.[18] Geertz puts more stress than Dewey on the frequency of alliances between small traders, but affirms also their short-lived character.[19] He argues that what is lacking here among the (typically) Islamic small businessmen "is not capital, for . . . their resources are not inadequate; not drive, for they display the typically 'Protestant' virtues of industry, frugality, independence, and determination in almost excessive abundance; certainly not a sufficient market. . . . What they lack is the power to mobilize their capital and channel their drive in such a way as to exploit the existing market possibilities. They lack the capacity to form efficient economic institutions; they are entrepreneurs without enterprises."[20]

The rugged individualism characteristic of traders in the Modjokuto bazaar economy leads to some attempts at enterprise but "also involves very important limitations on the capacity to grow, by limiting the effective range of collective organization. Modjokuto enterprises seem to grow so large and then no larger, because the next step means widening the social base of the enterprise beyond the immediate family connections to which, given that lack of trust which is the inverse of individualism, they are limited."[21]

In the bazaar economy Geertz studied in Morocco, buyer-seller relations are by comparison quite long-term; cooperation among *sellers*, however, is still minimal. Correspondingly, vertical integration between merchants and artisans is absent; there are no integrated craft-commercial enterprises or permanent connections between the two, and the artisans are concerned to avoid such connections, fearing the dependence this would involve. This is so despite the sharp division of labor between the roles: artisans almost never market their own products, but rather sell them to merchants who then resell them to other merchants or consumers.[22] Even craft workshops where a group of artisans work together are conceived as a cluster of two-person arrangements.[23]

In the Philippines, the city of Estancia shows that a pattern empirically very similar to that found in Modjokuto and Morocco can arise from a very different cultural and social-structural situation.[24] As in

Modjokuto, there are partnerships in buying, where a group pools its resources; these are also short-lived, shifting arrangements. But despite rapid economic growth in Estancia, spearheaded especially by the fishing industry, small family enterprises have not given way to larger corporate institutions. Even in the largest enterprises, everyone is totally dependent on the owner, and the operation rises and falls with that individual. Why? In Estancia, one of the

> most powerful and obvious impediments to corporate economic activities is a pervasive mistrust of others, fortified by innumerable accounts of economic double-dealing in the town. Even within a nuclear family, when it comes to business matters, trust between individuals is often limited. The common assumption is that people are primarily concerned with their own personal welfare or short-term benefit and will take advantage of a situation of trust, whenever possible. . . . The leaders of large organizations—economic or other—are always suspected of using the position, members, or resources for their own personal purposes, and they often do. This of course justifies similar action by lower-echelon members. The expectation that others work only for their own advantage is so powerful that even partnerships between kinsmen or close friends rarely last more than a few weeks or months. . . . Groups larger than a simple partnership are obviously all the more vulnerable. Given this atmosphere of distrust, the most circumstantial and unfounded charges are likely to be accepted.[25]

This sounds very much like the problems of mistrust in Modjokuto. But unlike the highly individualistic Moslem traders of that Javanese city, Estancia residents are predominantly Catholic, live in a small city where there are elaborate networks of noneconomic relations overlaid on the economic ones, and have well-developed personalized ties between clients and customers and among vendors.[26] A sense of "moral economy" operates in Estancia among subsistence vendors, so this is a setting where at least within a well-defined local group people have a feeling of responsibility for one another.[27] But a broader look at the culture and social structure shows that despite this strong sense of the "right to survive," and despite an elaborate network of horizontal linkages, there is also a marked sense of competitiveness among individuals at the *same* hierarchical level. In Modjokuto a similar competitiveness comes from the absence of social connections. In Estancia it seems instead to arise from a social structure that is densely connected, but in a way that stresses vertical, hierarchical, patron-client relations. This lowland Philippine system was originally oriented to landlord-tenant relations, and the pattern has continued with local politicians taking the superior's role. Culturally, interaction in such a system is smooth, Szanton argues, where status differences are clearcut and mutual obligations clearly understood. But then, among the "relatively poor, be they tenants or other traditional workers, horizontal ties to others of similar status are of limited value both because they usually have few resources to spare, and more important, because they are often in competition with one another for support and aid from the same higher status figures. . . . Horizontal solidarity is not characteristic of traditional [Philippine] lowland society."[28] In times of crisis it is vertical ties that will make the difference for you. Basically, economic goods move down the hierarchy and social and political support move up. Thus, the "most significant solidarities, cleavages, and oppositions in the social pyramid tend to be vertical (and factional) rather than horizontal (and ideological) as they are in class-structured societies."[29]

So far we see that social systems with a lack of horizontal solidarity—*which can arise in various ways*—are deficient in the trust required to build enterprises larger than those run by individuals or families. The Philippine example is an important contrast to that of Java because it shows that the lack of trust among individuals need not be the result of an atomized social structure that isolates individuals from one another, but may occur instead because of the particular way even a dense structure is connected.

Does it follow that a high level of horizontal solidarity is the prescription for expansion? This would be the exact reverse of what traditional development theory claimed, and even the most inadequate theories rarely give way to their exact opposites. Consider Geertz's account of economic enterprise in a small (population 12,000) Balinese town.[30] Though Tabanan is, like Modjokuto, administratively part of Indonesia and the two towns are not far apart geographically, they are light-years apart in culture and social structure. Not so long ago, Tabanan was ruled by princes and aristocrats, and though deprived of political power in the new regime, they continue to be involved in a "complex network of specific and explicit ties both with one another and with the great mass of commoners they once ruled."[31] This matters a great deal because it is from this group of displaced rulers that the entrepreneurial class in Tabanan is almost entirely drawn.

The strong vertical solidarities here are similar to those of the lowland Philippines. But Bali is quite different in that there is strong horizontal solidarity as well. Balinese social structure is characterized by social groups called *seka*, formed on the basis of religious, political, economic, or other criteria. "Every Balinese belongs to from three or four up to nearly a dozen of these groups, and the value of *seka* loyalty, putting the needs of one's group above one's own, is, along with caste pride, a central value in Balinese social life. This *seka* pattern of organization gives to Balinese village social structure both a strongly collective and yet a peculiarly complex and flexible pattern. Balinese do almost everything, even the simplest of undertakings, in groups which . . . almost invariably involve personnel clearly far in excess of what is technically necessary."[32] Given the centrality of these groups, "almost the whole of Balinese economic life is realized through one or another of these *seka*, strictly individual activity being rather rare."[33]

From this description, it sounds as if the problems of Modjokuto and of Estancia are nicely overcome in Tabanan. The entrepreneurs are highly prestigious in local eyes. They are aristocrats and thus "have at their disposal a quantity of cultural capital in the form of traditional social loyalties and expectations which Modjokuto's self-made shopkeepers entirely lack."[34] Adding to this the horizontal solidarity of Balinese culture, how can enterprises lose? And in fact, enterprises start fairly readily in Tabanan and even undergo some moderate level of expansion. But there is a fly in the ointment, and it is just what traditional development theory highlighted—that the firm anchored in noneconomic loyalties "has a tendency to behave uneconomically because of the 'social welfare' pressures of its members who, for the most part, are not basically growth-minded. Not only is there great pressure to divide profits rather than reinvest them, but there is also a tendency to employ overly large staffs in an attempt by the directorate to appease the rank and file. . . . 'The trouble with Balinese-owned concerns,' the abdicated king of Tabanan, who runs his hotel by himself, said to me with some shrewdness, 'is that they turn into relief organizations rather than businesses.'"[35] There is, here, a kind of moral economy that militates against the rationalization of firms if this appears to be at the expense of the community. Both commoners and nobles expect and demand that economic decisions "will lead to a higher level of welfare for the organic community as a whole and not just to an enrichment of a self-interested, emergent managerial class."[36] Thus, whereas Modjokuto's firms cannot expand to the most economic level, those in Tabanan tend to expand beyond that point because of their noneconomic commitments.

But this account raises the question of why a system with strong hierarchical but weak horizontal solidarity, as in the Philippines, does not use the vertical ties to build enterprises that can then be rationalized because there is less pressure to operate them as social welfare programs than there is in a Balinese-type system. And in fact there is some evidence from Estancia that this is a real possibility. Szanton reports that the Filipino vertical model of relations has been applied to all economic enterprises. Thus, in commercial fishing outfits, the owner "was cast in the role of the landlord/politician responsible for the maintenance of his crewmen and their families. The crew were structurally equivalent to the tenants, and provided political support to the owners."[37] But given the lack of horizontal solidarity, such a pattern may work better in a firm like a fishing outfit, where the level of horizontal cooperation and complexity required is low, than in one with a more elaborate division of labor, which requires cooperation and trust rather than competition for the patron's favor. This in itself would be a severe limitation.

But it turns out also that even the fishing outfit pattern is more vulnerable than it might seem. Szanton indicates that such operations worked well before World War II, but since then the sense of mutual obligation has declined between owners and workers; the former now feel less responsibility and correspondingly get less political and other kinds of support from their workers. What has led to this has been an increase in the proportion of young, mobile, migrant fishermen without families. The patron-client system, as with other vertically oriented moral economy systems, is highly personalized and localized. It is easier for patrons to decline their traditional responsibilities to young, single newcomers than it would be to known individuals with long-standing local family connections. Although there is no systematic data over time as to what has caused this, it appears from Szanton's account[38] that an unravelling process has taken place: After the war, the owners' costs began to increase, especially the costs of capital investment. This led them to reduce the sharing of profits that they had previously practiced. The worsened situation for the workers led to an outflux of those with local family connections and an influx of young newcomers with little sense of obligation to the owner, with less concern regarding aid from above in a possible crisis and more for maximizing personal incomes. But this change in workers' attitudes, and correspondingly in their practices—for example, surreptitiously selling fish at sea without the owner's knowledge—put more pressure on the owner's practice of moral economy, which in turn led to further shift in the composition of crews, in a process of mutual feedback. What this shows is that the old pattern was stable as long as the set of individuals involved remained localized; but when forces arose that brought in new workers who did not belong to the old set of social arrangements that held the operation together, the system broke down. It could be sustained only in the context of a working ideology approximating that of "moral economy."

Conditions for Entrepreneurial Success: The Case of the Rotating Credit Association

So far we see that individuals and groups attempting to assemble firms may face on the one hand the problem of insufficient solidarity among themselves, which produces a failure of trust, and on the other hand the problem of uncontrolled solidarity, which produces excessive noneconomic claims on an enterprise. Under what conditions can these mirror-image problems be overcome? We can gain further insight into this issue from examination of one of the most successful informal institutions for raising capital in many parts of the world: the rotating credit association.

In developing and developed countries alike, small new firms have always had difficulty raising capital from formal institutions such as banks, which have no good way to assess the risks of these ventures and, given their small scale, would not find it economical to invest in acquiring such information. Thus it is commonplace to observe the raising of capital from family and friends. But the amount of capital that can be so raised is always small, and this creates a comparative advantage for the rotating credit association.

Such associations are spread widely over the world, and have received special attention in Japan, China, Southeast Asia, India, West Africa, and the Caribbean. They occur with many variations, but as Geertz indicates,

> [the] basic principle upon which the rotating credit association is founded is everywhere the same: a lump sum fund composed of fixed contributions from each member of the association is distributed, at fixed intervals and as a whole, to each member of the association in turn. Thus, if there are ten members of the association, if the association meets weekly, and if the weekly contribution from each member is one dollar, then each week over a ten-week period a different member will receive ten dollars. . . . If interest payments are calculated . . . the numerical simplicity is destroyed, but the essential principle of rotating access to a continually reconstituted capital fund remains intact. Whether the fund is in kind or in cash; whether the order the members receive the fund is fixed by lot, by agreement, or by bidding; whether the time period over which the society runs is many years or a few weeks; whether the sums involved are minute or rather large; whether the members are few or many; and whether the association

is composed of urban traders or rural peasants, of men or women, the general structure of the institution is constant.[39]

From the description it is obvious that the rotating credit association is a way to save money and raise capital. Compared to individual savings at home, it has the macroeconomic advantage of always keeping money in circulation, and compared to schemes in which a designated individual acts as a banker and treasurer, holding deposits from others, it has the advantage that at each periodic meeting the fund is distributed to a member and cannot therefore be embezzled.[40] Because each meeting is typically a social occasion, often at the home of a member, and members are usually in some way socially connected to one another, this form of saving has a personal and social element that carries its own rewards, increases social solidarity, and provides additional incentives to participate. Unlike most other situations where one receives a loan and is thereby in the position of supplicant, in a rotating credit association "the recipient of a fund, far from suffering a loss of dignity, is often the member of honour or host at a feast or some other form of entertainment."[41]

Ardener notes that such an arrangement will fail unless all members meet their obligations, but suggests that the

> pressure of public opinion within the membership may be enough to ensure this. It is interesting to note the very great importance placed upon these obligations in some communities. . . . The member who defaults in one association may suffer to such an extent that he may not be accepted as a member of any other. In some communities the rotating credit institution has become so rooted in the economic and social system that exclusion would be a serious deprivation. . . . A member may go to great lengths, such as stealing . . . or selling a daughter into prostitution . . . in order to fulfill his obligations to his association; failure to meet obligations can even lead to suicide.[42]

These pressures nicely illustrate what Portes calls "enforceable trust"—in which transactions among members of a community are "undergirded by certainty that no one will shirk in their eventual repayment."[43]

Ardener also points out that such associations may function as money markets, since members who have not yet received funds can obtain loans from those who have.[44] This and other banking aspects of these associations raise the natural question of where such associations stand with respect to banks in communities that may contain both. Geertz, writing in a period when development theory pointed to impersonal institutions as the most efficient possible mode of economic functioning, described the rotating credit association as a "middle rung" in economic development, since it is

> obviously limited in the scale and complexity of commercial activity which it can support. . . . In the more developed cases, the traditional elements weaken and the stress comes to be placed on . . . bureaucratic organization and the like. . . . In this sense, the form is . . . self-liquidating, being replaced ultimately by banks, cooperatives, and other economically more rational types of credit institutions. But these latter can only function when the differentiation of a specific economic pattern of norms has occurred—when courts will enforce contracts, when managers worry about their business reputations and keep honest books, and when investors feel safe in giving cash resources to debtors to whom they are not related. Cultural change of this sort takes place, however, in steps rather than all at once, and in the intermediary stages the association fulfills a valuable function in organizing traditional and rational economic attitudes in such a way that the process continues rather than stultifies or breaks down into anomie.[45]

But Ardener was critical of this argument, noting that purely economic or rational aspects do not always predominate in the larger or more sophisticated associations of this kind and that even when the rotating credit associations are professionally organized, such aspects as feasting and conviviality may be important. She reports:

> In Vietnam, for instance, where associations are comparatively businesslike (with government registration, the keeping of books, and so forth), feasting is still required and meetings must be "gay" and "elegant". . . . The persistence of the institutions in communities in which banks and co-operatives exist, such as in Great Britain, Japan, and South Africa, and the recent formation of an association by bank employees in the Sudan, suggests that there is still a place for these institutions alongside "other more economically rational" types of institution.[46]

Even in countries such as Cameroon, where rotating credit associations are illegal, they are widely supported by large segments of the community, including those who are actively involved in more formal varieties of banking. This is an example of the persistence of institutions based on personal relations long past the point of demise predicted by the argument that optimally efficient markets must be based on impersonal transactions.

We note also that because rotating credit associations include many individuals who would not normally be considered creditworthy by formal banking institutions, in part because the investigation required to support small loans would be uneconomical, they efficiently serve an important share of the credit market that would otherwise be without funds for entrepreneurship. For this reason, some formal institutions have explicitly copied the techniques of the rotating credit association, creating a new set of institutions often called "peer lending" or "micro-lending," in which loans are collateralized not by goods but by a set of other individuals, assembled by the borrower, who take corporate responsibility for the loan and who cannot themselves receive loans until the books are at least partially cleared on the original loan. The Grameen Bank of Bangladesh has made the largest number of such loans, and this movement appears to be spreading rapidly.[47] In this light the rotating credit association, rather than being a transient middle rung to be replaced by more advanced institutions, turns out to be more advanced in certain respects than the usual impersonal models, in that it makes use of naturally occurring social capital,[48] a low-cost strategy.

The importance of rotating credit associations for entrepreneurship in the advanced industrial societies was highlighted by the work of Ivan Light on the comparative entrepreneurial performance in the United States of Chinese, Japanese, and blacks.[49] Chinese and Japanese (especially before World War II), and to some extent West Indian blacks, successfully developed small businesses by raising capital through rotating credit associations. But blacks who migrated to industrial cities from the southern United States did not make use of rotating credit associations and had great difficulty in raising capital for businesses. What explains this difference?

We know that rotating credit associations require, for their successful operation, a set of members who are sufficiently solidary with one another that they scrupulously avoid defaulting on their obligations to contribute regularly. Those who organize the associations must have enough information about potential members to make accurate judgments of this solidarity. In countries where members of rotating credit associations are natives, local kinship and friendship networks suffice to assure this. Among immigrants, some other form of assurance is required. The key, Light argues, was that Japanese and Chinese who immigrated to the United States before World War II came from just a few areas of their home countries. Eighty-nine percent of Japanese emigrated from eleven southern prefectures, and virtually all Chinese from one of seven districts in Kwangtung province, whose main city is Canton (now Guangdong).[50]

Both groups erected an elaborate structure of organizations based on the exact locale of emigration. These organizations were ascriptive (that is, geographic origins and not preferences determined membership) so there was no possibility of the different organizations competing for members or of the dilution of loyalty through multiple memberships. Moreover, the obligations owed to one another by those from the same home area were matched by the reluctance of those from other areas to help (in finding employment, for example, or giving financial assistance). In addition to performing other functions, such associations became the nuclei of rotating credit associations which thereby flourished and provided the capital needed for opening small businesses and investing in real estate. Light's discussion of West Indian blacks is much briefer, but a similar pattern appears in which home area in the West Indies formed the core for their version of rotating credit associations, which had reached the islands from West Africa with slaves who were transported there.

American blacks, on the other hand, had lost this organizational arrangement from their "cultural repertoire."[51] They had lost touch with their particular African origins and had no opportunity during slavery, as did West Indians, to set up independent businesses which they financed on their own; nor was there much chance to acquire such businesses after emancipation. Moreover, black migrants to northern cities did not especially identify with their home areas in the south and, like white migrants, had virtually no organizations based on these origins. Light explains this difference between the black and the Asian experience by suggesting that "[i]nternational migration is a more drastic form of uprooting than is interstate migration . . . [so] it is not surprising that neither black nor white interstate migrants have felt it necessary to erect organizational monuments to their state of origin."[52] Also, whereas the Chinese and Japanese were nostalgic about their background and often intended (at least in principle) to return someday, southern-born blacks were happy to leave their background behind.

This is not to say that northern blacks had no organizational life. On the contrary, there was a rich variety of voluntary organizations, but to Light this is precisely the problem: these organizations did not have the hold of moral solidarity over their members and had to compete among themselves for membership. Many fraternal organizations had overlapping membership, which diluted any special hold any single one might have. Then any businesses based in one such organization would have to cope with noneconomic claims from co-members of the many overlapping organizations. It was simply too difficult to create moral solidarity "among a voluntary membership which was ascriptively unrelated."[53] Ethical discipline and solidarity would have been facilitated by the social isolation of the membership in the community, so that members would always be in one another's company. Asian groups could do so because they had a putative cultural differentiation: "Cantonese from Toi-shan spontaneously spent their waking hours in one another's company. In part this pattern reflected a preference . . . but it also reflected the unwillingness of non-Toi-shanese to associate with Toi-shanese (and vice-versa) and the subsequent necessity for Toi-shanese to band together."[54]

Thus the black community did not generate the localized solidarities required to sustain such institutions as rotating credit associations, even if these had been in their cultural repertoire. Instead, large and impersonal organizations like the Urban League and the National Negro Business League, staffed by the black elite, tried to recruit poor blacks to the idea of small business; but since the "league chapters were structurally isolated voluntary associations of the wealthy, they were unable to reach lower-class black youth."[55]

And beyond the matter of raising capital, the Japanese and Chinese organizations offered assistance of all sorts to ethnic businesses, including regulation of competition and price supports. This was possible because of the nonoverlapping, clearly organized structure of these groups; no such assistance could arise from the black community. The only exceptions to the general underrepresentation of blacks in business occurred when organizations were formed that could create ascriptive-like solidarities. Since territoriality could not be used in this way, an alternative was the religious sect; Father Divine, a black religious leader who emerged in the Great Depression, mobilized at least a half-million blacks as his followers and by the 1950s had erected a large network of small businesses which they owned and operated. The "secret of Father Divine's miracles was his special ability to induce sect members to cooperate."[56] But this all depended on belief in his divinity, which was necessarily fragile; thus when he died in 1965, his "kingdom" evaporated.

The Balance between Coupling and Decoupling: The Case of the Overseas Chinese

The discussion of rotating credit associations shows that the solidarity required for assembling coherent combinations of economic activity depends on a well-defined collection of people who identify one another as belonging to the same collectivity by ethnic or even more specific markers such as place of origin. This indicates that at least as important as the intensity of interaction is the clearly defined boundary beyond which such intensity and trust falls off sharply. Such a boundary is required in order to sustain trust internally, but also to limit the extent of the group that can make claims on the economic organization that has been constructed.

This is illustrated especially well by the overseas Chinese—the one group that has successfully put together efficient firms in Southeast Asia, an achievement notable for its rarity in the context of the Philippine and Indonesian difficulties I have catalogued. Empirically this success is well documented.[57] The temptation is great to explain it in terms of Chinese culture, and indeed it would be hard to argue that the culture of overseas Chinese is not in fact importantly different in ways that facilitate business success. But cultural understandings and practices do not emerge out of thin air; they are shaped by and in turn shape structures of social interaction.

All accounts agree that Chinese businesses experience dramatically lower operating costs because of the existence of trust within that community. Credit is extended and capital pooled with the expectation that commitments will be met; delegation of authority takes place without fear that agents will pursue their own interests at the expense of the principal's. Rotating credit associations are just one mechanism successfully used for these purposes.

Why is this so among the Chinese? Overseas Chinese constitute small, cohesive minorities with extensive family and organizational connections that shape noneconomic and economic activities alike. In Modjokuto, for example, Dewey reports that Chinese families organize themselves into *bangsa*, groups based on common descent from some specific area of China. "Such a group speaks the same Chinese dialect and for the most part marries endogamously. The relations between the members are formalized in various associations, burial societies, sports groups, commercial associations, and the like."[58] There is a tendency for members of one *bangsa* all to be in the same business and to deal mostly with one another. Within these groupings, and to some extent (not clearly specified by Dewey) across them in the Chinese community as a whole, "ties of kinship and comembership in the various types of associations reinforce and are reinforced by the commercial relationships so that a series of closely knit communities is created, with connections reaching all over Java and often beyond."[59] In building these structures, local Chinese are making use of classical Chinese culture as a "tool kit":[60] "old Chinese models of family, secret society, and association are used as a basis for extending commercial relations beyond the nuclear family and the local group."[61] In this close-knit, cohesive community, norms of proper behavior become clearly crystallized and internalized; deviance cannot be hidden and will be swiftly dealt with if it does occur. Given the enormous advantages of dealing within the closed *bangsa* community of businesspeople, the penalty of having to move outside of it in one's dealings is very stiff.

But the Chinese social structure that facilitates their business relations sounds suspiciously similar to that of the Balinese described by Geertz,[62] who run up against the problem that the diffuse claims of friends and relatives against the economic resources of business organizations prevent those businesses from being run efficiently. Yet Chinese businesses do not seem to suffer from this problem. The abdicated king of Tabanan commented to Geertz that if you go into a Balinese business, "there are a half-dozen directors, a bookkeeper or two, several clerks, some truckdrivers and a hoard *(sic)* of semi-idle workers; if you go into a Chinese concern of the same size there is just the proprietor, his wife, and his ten-year-old boy, but they are getting even more work done."[63] What then shields Chinese businesses from the excessive claims of friends and relatives? Dewey suggests about Java that "one factor which may be important is the minority position of the Chinese. . . . In relation to the Javanese they are a small community. (In Modjokuto they numbered about 1,800 out of a total of approximately 18,000.) The number of people who will call on a given merchant for favored treatment is limited by the size of the community, and further by the split between *Peranakan* [Chinese in Java for several generations] and *Totok* [recent immigrants] and by the division of the latter into *bangsa*. This limitation keeps demands from becoming so burdensome as to nullify the economic advantage. . . . [By contrast] for the Javanese . . . the lack of focused groupings would open a merchant to demands from an unlimited number of other Javanese."[64] The Balinese also have well-defined groupings, the *seka* mentioned above. But unlike Chinese *bangsa* members, each Balinese (like the northern blacks described by Ivan Light) belongs typically to numerous *seka*,[65] and though these groupings do organize economic life, the overlap in membership among these groupings means that if one *seka* is the core of a business, members of that group may still be subject to diffuse claims from fellow members of other *seka*.

A related argument is made by Davis, based on his observations in Baguio City in the Philippines. Trying to explain why Chinese merchants are so much more successful than Filipino ones, he provides evidence *against* the general propositions that Chinese sellers work harder or that they are more clever businessmen. He then notes that Filipino kinship is bilateral so that kin groups are not well defined. Since you inherit some relatives from each parent, your own kin group is different from that of either parent and is exactly the same only for full siblings. In this context, Omohundro, in his study of the Filipino Chinese merchant community, observes that "employees and suppliers operated on the not-unfounded assumption that a man who married a Filipino was either already financially shaky or soon would be, when Filipino relatives made their demands on him," and so would not give him credit any more.[66]

Chinese, by contrast, have corporate kinship groups traced through the male line—a well-defined set of relatives that makes collective action and the mobilization and management of resources easier. The eldest male is in charge, whereas in Filipino kinship groups no one is obviously in charge. "Therefore the Chinese kin group has several important features like those of stock corporations, with perhaps the greatest difference being that kinship limits participation."[67] The better-defined kinship groups of the Chinese, therefore, not only limit the diffuse noneconomic claims that may be made of the business but also provide a stronger base for collective action and a more effective structure of authority. One Chinese informant told Davis that "[m]embers of Filipino families are always fighting among themselves, but we put someone in charge."[68]

What we must look for then, in understanding successful entrepreneurial activity, is some combination of social cohesion sufficient to enforce standards of fair business dealing and an atmosphere of trust, along with circumstances that limit the noneconomic claims on a business that prevent its rationalization. The relatively small size and cohesive social structure of groups that are minorities in their location (and if they are beleaguered and despised minorities, they are that much more likely to pull together socially and culturally) may often provide just the right combination of these factors, thus helping to explain the often-noted economic success of expatriate minority groups.[69] Even in settings where hardly any integrated enterprises exist we may expect that those that do exist have such origins—for example, the very few integrated craft-commercial enterprises reported by Geertz in Sefrou, Morocco, are Jewish in origin.[70]

More generally, immigrants have an advantage over natives in achieving the right balance between what might be called "coupling" and "decoupling." Chinese in China, despite the obvious presence of Chinese culture, can suffer from excessive claims. Thus Wong suggests that it has been typical of entrepreneurs in China to "leave their native homes to conduct business" so that "relatives will not be abundant in the communities in which they work."[71] In moving to regions where they have fewer ties, they gain some of the advantages of immigrants.[72]

Conversely, immigrant minorities rarely suffer from the problem of excessive claims, in part because their solidarity is emergent and constructed and thus likely to have clear boundaries.[73] It may also be the case that immigrant enterprises, especially in the early stages, are sufficiently fragile that claims on their resources are muted; then once they are successful, especially in a multiethnic environment, claims can be warded off by hiring employees from other ethnic groups, to whom no special allegiance is owed.[74]

Intergroup Relations and the Advantages of Minorities

Thus far I have discussed the characteristics of groups that succeed or fail in constructing enterprises. But this level of argument must be supplemented with an analysis of how such groups relate to others. One aspect of this analysis involves cultural differences among groups. For the overseas Chinese, for example, there was no stigma in lending or borrowing money—it merely demonstrated one's high level of ambition.[75] For other groups such as Thais and Malays, however, to be in debt was a source of shame, so indigenous producers preferred to borrow secretly from Chinese traders rather than from local institutions or families, where the debt could become public knowledge.[76] Debtor-creditor relations are stigmatized in these cultures by moral economy norms, or what Gosling refers to as a "distributive ethic" reinforced by Buddhism and Islam: If you have a surplus, you share it. Status results from distributing this surplus to achieve "social capital." You are then owed obligations that could be discharged with labor—creating, in effect, a patron-client system.[77]

There are other practical reasons why locals like to deal with Chinese businessmen. One is the distance it provides from bureaucratic control systems such as tax collection agencies, which would enter the picture in the case of a loan from a bank.[78] Another is that the contact with a member of a different group, who is attuned to a wide outside network, provides valuable information that is not redundant with that available within one's own group and may be useful for understanding the current business environment.[79]

If there are reasons why native-born prefer to deal with merchants and businesses from outside their own group, there are also reasons why this preference is reciprocated by the outsiders. One such important reason is that it is difficult to pursue commercial roles *within* a community that is close-knit and stresses a norm of mutual help and obligation. Foster, writing on Thailand, notes that a trader who was subject to the traditional social obligations and constraints would find it very difficult to run a viable business. If, for example, he were fully part of the village society and subject to the constraints of the society, he would be expected to be generous in the traditional way to those in need. It would be difficult for him to refuse credit, and it would not be possible to collect debts. . . . The inherent conflict of interest in a face-to-face market transaction would make proper etiquette impossible or would at least strain it severely, which is an important factor in Thai social relations. . . . If, however, a person is not a member of the society, his obligations may be different, as may the power of the society over his behavior; this has important implications for the conduct of trade. Members of different ethnic groups are in many ways outside the community. . . . [E]xpectations of generosity decrease markedly for members of other ethnic groups in contrast with one's own.[80]

This theme is echoed in other cultures. Waldinger and his coauthors[81] cite Wong's study of Chinese grocers in the Watts section of Los Angeles as showing that "social distance from their black customers allows . . . competitive practices that black storekeepers, with social ties to the community, cannot follow."[82] Or in Amsterdam, Boissevain and Grotenberg note that more than three-quarters of clients of Chinese and Hindustani Surinamese merchants "come from outside their ethnic group, [thus] it is far easier for them to deny credit and to be more strict and businesslike about collecting debts."[83] Though the trading group may be less wedded to moral economy norms than its customers, their advantage is fundamentally based on social-structural decoupling from customers rather than on a different ideology; it thus appears to retain its force even in situations where the traders and their customers are members of separate ethnic groups that are virtually identical culturally, such as the Mons minority trading with Thai customers.[84]

Indeed, there is no special reason why a local minority must be *ethnically* different at all from the majority in order to experience some of these advantages, and Szanton reports that in Estancia the Protestant minority, divided into four sects, is more successful in business than the Catholic majority. He points out that "whereas a Roman Catholic entrepreneur may have difficulty denying requested favors from the great bulk of the similarly Catholic townspeople, the Protestant businessman with more limited social ties to relatively like-minded persons can more easily say no, and maintain more narrowly contractual relations with others."[85] Migrants to Estancia, also less entangled in local obligations, are disproportionately represented among successful entrepreneurs.[86] Thus, any cultural device that can decouple one group from another may facilitate commerce.

Because of the advantages of separation, groups may retain their ethnic distinction to a degree that they would not otherwise undertake. As against the sociologically naive idea that ethnicity is a primordial characteristic of individuals determined by nature and biology, many recent writers have stressed the "construction of ethnicity" for political and economic purposes.[87] The extreme version of this view is proposed in the New Institutional Economics—that groups "choose" to emphasize ethnic traits as the optimal strategy to maximize income in certain situations. La Croix, for example, suggests that groups solve their economic problems by choosing "a common ('homogeneous') asset—a collection of characteristics—that is less costly for the group to acquire than outsiders, that yields a stream of utility or income generating a normal rate of return to the asset, and that is sufficiently specific and valuable to generate the appropriately large stream of quasi-rents. The choice of ethnic, religious, and genealogical characteristics fulfills these criteria. . . ."[88]

A more prudent analysis would take account of the historical, cultural, and social-structural constraints on such "choices" and of the circumstances that may generate strong ethnic identities for noneconomic reasons. But there is certainly some evidence that ethnic separateness is cultivated in situations where it is of economic value. Foster reports that the minority Mons of Thailand are far more likely to preserve their distinctive ethnic traits when they are engaged in commerce, where the traits pay off, than when in farming, where they do not.[89] Gosling observes that the Chinese in Thailand and Malaysia must retain their Chinese identity because it "permits the antisocial behavior required in commerce and stresses the fact that the game must be played by the dealer-shopkeeper's rules. Once the Chinese acts like a Malay or Thai, he is expected to behave like a Malay or Thai and loses the advantage of ethnic difference."[90] This "chosenness" of cultural difference can be closely attuned to situations. Gosling observed a Chinese shopkeeper in a Malay village who "appeared to be considerably acculturated to Malay culture, and was scrupulously sensitive to Malays in every way, including the normal wearing of sarong, quiet and polite Malay speech, and a humble and affable manner. However, at harvest time when he would go to the field to collect crops on which he had advanced credit, he would put on his Chinese costume of shorts and undershirt, and speak in a much more abrupt fashion, acting, as one Malay farmer put it, 'just like a Chinese.' This behavior was to insure that he would not be treated like a fellow Malay who might be expected to be more generous on price or credit terms."[91]

While it is illuminating to think of the keeping and manipulating of ethnic identity as a matter of rational choice, such analysis usually takes as given the most interesting part of the problem—the factors that make it cost-effective to do so in the first place, for a particular group. Thus, one reason why overseas Chinese pay a stiff penalty for malfeasance within their own group is that in most of Southeast Asia, their opportunities outside of business are limited. In the Philippine city studied by Omohundro, "to cease to be a merchant is to cease to be Chinese."[92] This is partly because native groups disdain commerce, partly because the Chinese do not have the contacts required to enter other fields, and partly because official policy actively prevents their entry. Thus, even if Chinese settlers wanted to enter agriculture, it would have been difficult for them to do so.

Compare the situation of overseas Chinese to that of the Kenyan businessmen studied by Marris and Somerset, who "seldom find a way to assimilate kinship successfully within a hierarchy of managerial authority" which, contrary to the precepts of development theory, puts them at a massive disadvantage in relation to Asian and especially Indian businesses, which are built along kinship lines.[93] This results in part because the Asians, "as a minority excluded from agriculture by colonial policy, could bring much stronger sanctions to bear in their business relationships. A man who cheated his family or caste could be ostracized from commercial employment and had few other sources of livelihood to turn to."[94]

But business is a peripheral activity in African communities, so the sanctions for malfeasance or intransigence that one can mobilize against a relative are weak, since there are usually alternative lines of work available. Indeed, many of the African businessmen interviewed in this study thought that jealousy and insubordination were more likely with relatives than strangers. Marris and Somerset suggest that as business becomes more and land less important, so that a commercial class consolidates, the family may become more significant in African businesses. Note this nicely ironic reversal: rather than family involvement reflecting an early stage of development in the economic process, such involvement is difficult at this early stage and can only be constructed once the process of development has reached a certain plateau.

The discrimination that minority groups face can actually generate an advantage in constructing family businesses, since even if the children of successful business owners become well educated, their opportunities outside the ethnic business sector will be severely limited and the likelihood of their remaining in a family business and putting their talents to work there is much higher. Once this discrimination fades, intergenerational continuity in businesses is harder to sustain, since in most times and places the educated children of entrepreneurial parents seek occupations more associated with their level of education, such as the independent professions.[95] Indeed, Marion Levy has argued that one reason Japan industrialized more successfully than China was that in China the class system was more open, so merchants' and industrialists' sons could rise into the more esteemed social roles of officials and landowners, whereas in Japan the incumbents of these economic roles were assigned ethnic-like traits as a group, in a feudal hierarchy, and prevented from moving into other institutional spheres. Talent was thus confined within the business community and a level of cohesion achieved that was less accessible under Chinese conditions, where both talent and resources were continuously drained from business.[96]

In modern settings we also see numerous instances where discrimination against a group served as a double-edged sword, preventing them from entering most occupations but pushing them into a niche that they were able to dominate, in part by virtue of the enforced ethnic cohesion within that niche. The general point is that conditions "that raise the salience of group boundaries and identity, leading persons to form new social ties and action-sets, increase the likelihood of entrepreneurial attempts by persons within that group and raise the probability of success."[97] This is clear in the case of Japanese domination of truck farming and gardening in California between the two world wars.[98] Thus, the optimal balance between coupling and decoupling may ironically be forced on a group by circumstances beyond its control.

Local decoupling of a group from other groups may actually facilitate a network of weak ties to similar groups in other areas, by freeing time and energy for such relations. Thus successful entrepreneurial groups, compared to other groups, often have a wider network of relationships with individuals—typically of their own group—in other locations. Geertz points out, for example, that both the Moslem entrepreneurs of Modjokuto and the Hinduized aristocratic ones of Tabanan "stand outside the immediate purview of village social structure, as did the traditional groups from which they have emerged. Further, both groups are primarily interlocal in their outlook, some of their most important ties being with groups and individuals in areas other than their own, and this too is a heritage from their progenitors."[99] Extensive connections into other communities are also characteristic of the Chinese in Indonesia and the Philippines,[100] and minority groups such as Parsees and Marwaris who dominate the industrial economy of India.[101] This wider network can be both cause and effect of vertical integration in an economic sector controlled by one group, as for the Japanese hold on truck farming at the levels of production, wholesaling, and retailing in interwar California.[102]

Such interlocal connections can arise in several different ways. The Islamic entrepreneurs of Modjokuto are descended from itinerant market-circuit traders who, hundreds of years ago, maintained commercial ties all over Java, a pattern they have continued. In Bali, "horizontality grew out of the sophisticated court culture. . . . Tabanan's aristocracy not only formed a regional ruling group, but had and still has important and intimate social relationships with similar groups in the other regional capitals of the island."[103] Both groups are "insulated by occupation or by rank from the localized bonds of village society,"[104] which then must be both cause and consequence of their extensive ties to other areas. Chinese minorities are all the more insulated, typically occupying a very low, disdained social status in the local village or town, and so have some of their social energies freed for more long-distance relationships—relationships that may also be facilitated by being able to identify kinsmen and migrants from one's home region of China in other towns and cities.

The ability to call on personalized contacts over a wide geographic area affords considerable advantage in smoothing backward and forward transactions. There are information advantages as well, as Davis tells us of Chinese wholesale grocers in Baguio City, Philippines, whose "commercial relationships with the large Manila supply houses . . . provide them with better price information than is available to Filipino stallholders with whom they deal. . . . [T]hey are able to take advantage of impending price increases by withholding items in order to obtain higher future prices."[105] And not being locally rooted can be a great advantage when economic opportunities shift: "In the early 1960s when the expansion of motorization brought commercial fishing to the more distant islands and the southern coast of Masbate, and Estancia became a major marketing and transshipping point, . . . Chinese quickly reestablished themselves in these newly developing areas, often as the sole merchant buying the local catch in exchange for marine and household goods. . . . Since their most important ties were to other Chinese merchants in the urban areas, they could more easily set aside temporary local relationships to shift operations to more profitable locales. Filipino merchants, with overlapping social, political, and economic ties in their home communities, seem more likely to remain in them even if somewhat larger profits beckon elsewhere."[106]

The Conditions for Ethnic Group Advantage

The discussion thus far suggests that in settings where firms first emerge from more undifferentiated economic activity, certain well-defined social groups have special advantages that resolve the dual and somewhat opposite problems of trust and of diffusion of business success into the provision of community welfare. It has been especially (though not exclusively) immigrant and other minority groups that have appeared in such accounts.

A close look at economic history suggests, however, that although we can pick out many striking cases where such groups have an advantage and dominate economic activity and the construction of firms, there are also settings where economic activity is beginning but no such groups can be identified. There are a number of possible explanations of this.

One is that although conditions exist that would give advantage to a group of the sort I have discussed, no such group is able to construct its distinctive ethnic or other markers in a way that allows it to play this role. Functionalist arguments suggest that good solutions can always be constructed, but this neglects the requirement that solutions be constructed out of existing materials. The Chinese in Southeast Asia and the Indians of East Africa were already present in the locales where they came to dominate certain lines of economic activity, partly because they saw the opportunities and migrated there and partly because colonial powers intentionally used those groups as buffers between themselves and local groups, in order to soften the impact of domination (this was especially clear in the British policy of "indirect rule"). In other words, what Portes has called the "mode of incorporation" of these groups created the potential for economic advantage.[107] But even where minority groups are present in a promising situation, there is no guarantee that they will be able to manage their social structure in a way that optimizes their opportunities.

Another possibility is that although no group is clearly identified by analysts or perhaps even by contemporaries, there nevertheless exists in that setting some group of families whose social structure approximates that which solves the dual problems cited here. Analysis of business success has not been oriented to such social structural considerations so groups like this, if not clearly flagged by ethnic markers, may be missed in attempts to explain the economic situation.

In these first two explanations of the apparent absence of coherent minorities from their frequently strong role in economic activity, I supposed that conditions in fact were favorable for minorities to play such a role, which they may not always be. For example, one favorable—and historically common—condition is cultural: it occurs when the majority group disdains the search for profit. This disdain is evident when those who trade in subsistence goods are seen as not belonging to the moral community if their trade is oriented to profit and carried out at prices arrived at outside the local moral economy. Where such separation is in place, only outsiders who do not partake of the moral economy and suffer relatively little from its sanctions can be effective entrepreneurs. Thus Ortiz notes that among the Paez, only the most marginal in the community sold food for profit at market prices, violating local mores.[108] In Southeast Asia, as I have noted above, the Chinese filled this role.

The economic historian Gerschenkron, opposing the sociological argument of the 1950s and 1960s which posited that values would have to change before development could take place, noted that this is "in obvious conflict with the facts," since there were European instances "where magnificent entrepreneurial activities were conducted in the face of a dominant value system that was violently opposed to such activities and continued regarding the working of the land . . . as the only economic activity that was pleasing in the eyes of the Lord."[109]

Even if such values don't *prevent* entrepreneurial activity, they may still impose serious *costs* on it, and I suggest that it is under just such circumstances that minority ethnic groups have a comparative advantage.

Conversely, in seventeenth century Philadelphia where entrepreneurs were *not* drawn from any particular ethnic background, Doerflinger reports that the setting was distinguished, as few in history have been, by a "spirit of enterprise, a driving compulsion to swiftly develop a powerful dynamic economy,"[110] and that making a fortune was considered quite a respectable ambition. We may thus propose that in settings where the dominant system of values is broadly favorable to profit-making and economic pursuits, immigrant and minority groups will be less likely to find advantage.

We need also to inquire whether the advantages of groups such as those I have discussed obtain equally under all *economic* circumstances. The usual undifferentiated macroeconomic argument would suggest that a "rising tide lifts all boats."[111] Then we would expect minority groups, like others, to have difficulty in hard times but to succeed during an economic boom. I want to argue the opposite:

that minority or other groups whose patterns of coupling and decoupling solve the problems I have described find their main advantage under difficult economic conditions.

This appears to be the case for the Javanese and Philippine examples I have cited, where Chinese dominate commerce. In her account of Estancia, in the Philippines, M. Szanton notes that market conditions worsened considerably after World War II; there was a considerable influx of traders and thus "subsistence vending" provided economic security for those who might otherwise be unemployed. "The marketplace," she suggests, "seems so devised as to be able to continuously absorb more persons and provide them with at least minimal income for survival."[112]

In the Javanese town of Modjokuto, Geertz and Dewey document the advantage of Chinese over local Moslem traders.[113] This was not always the case: before the Depression, there existed large, well-integrated, Moslem-dominated trade organizations that were able to "pool resources, distribute routes and enforce debts within the groups. . . . After the Depression, the combination of a weakened economy and an overcrowding of the market network with an increasing number of marginal traders sapped the dynamic of the merchant class" and now, "the few outstanding efforts by members of the old merchant class to create more efficient productive and distributive institutions in the town are nearly swamped by the hundreds of small-scale petty traders trying to squeeze a marginal living out of traditional commerce."[114]

In Doerflinger's account of Philadelphia wholesale merchants in the eighteenth and nineteenth centuries, it seems clear that no particular ethnic group dominated trade, although there were some real ethnic and quasi-ethnic divisions. What is common to this case and the case of Modjokuto in the 1920s is a highly favorable macroeconomic situation in which entry of firms is relatively easy, capital can be raised without difficulty, and profits have not yet been squeezed. Doerflinger notes, for example, that much of the trade in Philadelphia was in imports and exports and that capital was available from English merchants who extended it freely even without knowing much about the borrowers.[115]

This general argument may help us also to see in what *sectors* of an economy groups will have an advantage. Wong, in his study of Shanghainese textile firms in Hong Kong, argues that it is in industries with especially low entry barriers, like textiles—where there are few economies of scale, proprietary technologies, or product differentiations—that one may expect the use of particularistic criteria to form solidary groups that fend off intruders.[116] In other words, ties of group solidarity can substitute for "natural" factors that create barriers to entry, and so we may expect to see solidary groups in markets that on purely economic grounds would be expected to be competitive, but empirically are not.

Another factor is that the advantage of ethnic businesses seems most robust where the most problematic commodity required is trust. On the other hand, where it is technical knowledge, the ethnic advantage may fade. This is one reason why "middleman" occupations present a special opportunity for the visiting ethnic.[117] Not that there is no technical aspect to these occupations: certainly there are complex bookkeeping and other matters that must be mastered before businesses like these can be run. But such knowledge is relatively static, and once acquired within the group is no longer problematic; trust in one's coworkers is the main problem. Where technical knowledge of a constantly changing variety is required in employees, the advantages of ethnically closed kinship networks may diminish, and Lim thus argues that Chinese firms in Hong Kong that specialize in high-tech areas no longer find an advantage in traditional Chinese management practices; this is confirmed by her empirical study of Chinese export-oriented electronics firms in Singapore and Malaysia, where access to capital, technology, labor, and overseas marketing outlets are determined "by the relationship of Chinese business, not to other Chinese organizations but to foreign firms on the one hand and local governments on the other."[118] But few sectors of any modern economy fit this requirement of constant technical change, so the ethnic advantage may be quite substantial over a large area of economic life.

So it appears that the advantages of immigrant or minority ethnic groups are especially pertinent where profit is disdained, under difficult economic conditions, where credit is tight and the industry barely under way, in industries with low barriers to entry, and where trust rather than technical knowledge is the most valuable commodity. Under such conditions, even temporary setbacks may sink a firm, and there is no margin for error. In more favorable conditions, the ethnic advantage fades. An ethnic group may even become underrepresented in such a case since its ability to monopolize under adverse circumstances is eliminated, and without such a monopoly, its status as a group of second-class citizens may then be highlighted and militate against successful enterprise.

It does not follow that majority groups in good economic times have no problems of trust or of noneconomic claims. These problems appear under all conditions, and can be dealt with only at a cost. Under sufficiently favorable macroeconomic conditions, as in

Java in the 1920s, the difficulties and costs of getting credit, building an organization, and finding ways to either trust subordinates or monitor their behavior without a cohesive social grouping can be borne. But even in that setting I would argue that these still *are* difficulties and costs, and that under more difficult conditions they simply cannot be borne, and will sink altogether any attempt to expand economic activity; then, only groups who can manage these problems at lower cost can sustain commerce.

Conclusion

While my analysis points clearly to the importance of noneconomic and institutional factors as determinants of entrepreneurship, it adds to the study of norms and values the more concrete issue of how social structure and exchange are patterned. I take these factors not as competing with economic variables, but rather as part of an account that must consider both.

I have especially highlighted patterns of group solidarity that give immigrants and other minorities advantage in the construction of enterprise. The argument is that even if external conditions are favorable to their playing this role, such groups must also be characterized by a complex balance of internal coupling with decoupling from outside groups. This balance is determined in large part by historical and economic conjunctures outside of individuals' control, though it is subject to some manipulation at the margins. This manipulation is the subject of rational choice arguments offered by institutional economists, and must not be ignored; it is useful only, however, if supplemented by the type of historical and contextual analysis I have suggested.

I have focused on the small scale of enterprise formation, neglecting some of the larger problems in the study of economic development, such as the way enterprises agglomerate into large-scale business groups and how they interact with other institutional sectors such as labor, government, and consumers. The important topic of agglomeration, though beyond the scope of the present analysis, is an especially natural extension of the discussion of immigrants and minority groups in the economy, since such groups may form large industrial conglomerates or sets of loosely affiliated firms that dominate the most modern industrial sector of an economy, as did the Chinese in Indonesia or the Marwaris in India.[119]

To explain how this occurs requires an argument beyond that advanced here. I have so far outlined as a solution to the problem of enterprise a strategy based on trust and limited liability that seems to be very well-suited to the successful construction of small firms, but would appear thereby to have a built-in barrier to expansion. The number of family members or co-ethnics whom the entrepreneur can know well enough to trust implicitly must necessarily be small. Rather than expanding a business to its most profitable size, many owners whose enterprise is based on family or co-ethnics expand instead by putting some trusted individual in charge of *another* business, sometimes a branch but sometimes unrelated. This is one reason for the frequent observation that entrepreneurs in developing countries have a number of irons in the fire—often in different branches of economic activity.[120]

But it does not follow from this that the road to progress away from small enterprise and toward more familiar large-scale capitalistic units is best traversed by moving to "modern," impersonal economic institutions. Instead, many large industrial empires, including very substantial financial institutions, have been built out of smaller personalized arrangements based on family and friends. Quite elaborate structures of alliance and control have been built by ethnic minorities who have used ties of kin and friendship in artful combination with bureaucratic structures which provide the scaffolding for much larger-scale operations than could be mounted by family alone.[121] It suffices to conclude here by noting that as we progress in our understanding of the sociology of the economy, we will find a surprisingly large role for the supposedly archaic categories of ethnicity and kinship; the idea that these are superseded in the economy of the modern world by efficient and impersonal institutions is a wishful vestige of Enlightenment idealism that careful analysis does not sustain.

This chapter is drawn largely from draft chapters of my book-in-progress, which will be published by Harvard University Press as *Society and Economy: The Social Construction of Economic Institutions.* I am grateful to Alejandro Portes, Patricia Fernández Kelly, Bryan Roberts, and Saskia Sassen for their critical comments on the earlier draft.

Notes

1. Talcott Parsons, *Societies: Comparative and Evolutionary Perspectives* (Englewood Cliffs, N.J.: Prentice-Hall, 1976).

2. Karl Polanyi, *The Great Transformation* (Boston: Beacon Press, 1944).

3. Marion Levy, "Contrasting Factors in the Modernization of China and Japan," *Economic Development and Cultural Change* 2, no. 3 (1953):174–175.

4. Deepak Lal, *The Poverty of "Development Economics"* (Cambridge: Harvard University Press, 1985).

5. Yoram Ben-Porath, "The F-Connection: Families, Friends and Firms in the Organization of Exchange," *Population and Development Review* 6, no. 1 (1980):1.

6. Ibid., p. 2.

7. The functionalist tone of the argument that transactions are carried out via families when and only when this reduces transaction costs is parallel to another literature, not referenced in these discussions, on the "functions of the family" in the structural-functional sociology of the 1950s and 1960s, where, for example, Eugene Litwak and his associates laid out in some detail the circumstances under which families had advantages over other more complex organizations in carrying out specified activities. See, for example, Eugene Litwak and Henry Meyer, "The School and the Family: Linking Organizations and External Primary Groups," in Paul Lazarsfeld, William Sewell, and Harold Wilensky, eds., *The Uses of Sociology* (New York: Basic Books, 1967), pp. 522–543; and Eugene Litwak and Josefina Figueira, "Technological Innovation and Theoretical Functions of Primary Groups and Bureaucratic Structures," *American Journal of Sociology* 73, no. 4 (1968):468–481. But by the 1960s, functionally oriented sociologists had learned to be cautious and to avoid arguing that just because families had advantages in carrying out certain activities, one would always see them specializing in just such activities. This level of caution has yet to be attained by the New Institutional Economics.

8. Ben-Porath, "F-Connection," p. 13.

9. Richard Posner, "A Theory of Primitive Society, with Special Reference to Law," *Journal of Law and Economics* 23 (1980):1–56; Janet Landa, "A Theory of the Ethnically Homogeneous Middleman Group: An Institutional Alternative to Contract Law," *Journal of Legal Studies* 10 (1981):349–362.

10. An historical account of the way entrepreneurship has been conceived in the various social sciences can be found in Chapter 4 of Mark Granovetter's book manuscript, *Society and Economy: The Social Construction of Economic Institutions,* to be published by Harvard University Press.

11. Cf. Mark Granovetter, "Economic Action and Social Structure: The Problem of Embeddedness," *American Journal of Sociology* 91, no. 3 (November 1985):481–510.

12. The concept of trust deserves a more explicit theoretical discussion, which space limitations preclude here. See pp. 38–47 of my "Problems of Explanation in Economic Sociology," in N. Nohria and R. Eccles, eds., *Networks and Organizations: Structure, Form and Action* (Boston: Harvard Business School Press, 1992).

13. Alice Dewey, *Peasant Marketing in Java* (Glencoe, Ill.: Free Press, 1962); Clifford Geertz, *Peddlers and Princes* (Chicago: University of Chicago Press, 1963).

14. William G. Davis, *Social Relations in a Philippine Market: Self-Interest and Subjectivity* (Berkeley: University of California Press, 1973); David L. Szanton, *Estancia in Transition: Economic Growth in a Rural Philippine Community* (Quezon City, Philippines: Ateneo de Manila University Press, 1971).

15. Dewey, *Peasant Marketing*, p. 31.

16. Ibid., p. 42.

17. Ibid., p. 88.

18. Ibid., p. 92.

19. Geertz, *Peddlers*, p. 40.

20. Ibid., p. 28.

21. Ibid., p. 126.

22. Clifford Geertz, "Suq: The Bazaar Economy in Sefrou," in C. Geertz, H. Geertz, and L. Rosen, eds., *Meaning and Order in Moroccan Society* (New York: Cambridge University Press, 1979), pp. 183–185.

23. Ibid., p. 191.

24. D. Szanton, *Estancia.*

25. Ibid., p. 51.

26. See Maria C. B. Szanton, *A Right to Survive: Subsistence Marketing in a Lowland Philippine Town* (University Park, Penn.: Penn State University Press, 1972).

27. The concept of "moral economy" is used in this chapter in the sense introduced by E. P. Thompson's landmark essay on English collective action in the eighteenth century, " The Moral Economy of the English Crowd in the Eighteenth Century," *Past and Present* 50 (February 1971):76–136. It denotes a situation where there is widespread agreement in a population that economic processes must meet certain specified moral standards in order to be legitimate. This is a special case of the postulate of "socially oriented economic action" proposed by Portes (this volume).

28. D. Szanton, *Estancia*, p. 87.

29. Ibid., p. 89n. Such a pattern is widely reported for Mediterranean countries, but also in other widely separated parts of the world, such as Holland and Thailand, where Hanks refers to factions as "entourages." See L. M. Hanks, "The Corporation and the Entourage: A Comparison of Thai and American Social Organization," in S. Schmidt, L. Guasti, C. Lande, and J. Scott, eds., *Friends, Followers and Factions* (Berkeley: University of California Press, 1977), pp. 161–167.

30. Geertz, *Peddlers*.

31. Ibid., p. 83.

32. Ibid., p. 84.

33. Ibid., p. 85.

34. Ibid., p. 106.

35. Ibid., p. 123.

36. Ibid., p. 125.

37. D. Szanton, *Estancia*, p. 89.

38. Ibid., pp. 89–91.

39. Clifford Geertz, "The Rotating Credit Association: A 'Middle-Rung' in Development," *Economic Development and Cultural Change* 10, no. 3 (1962):243.

40. Shirley Ardener, "The Comparative Study of Rotating Credit Associations," *Journal of the Royal Anthropological Institute* 94, Part 2 (1963):217.

41. Ibid., p. 221.

42. Ibid., p. 216.

43. Portes, this volume.

44. Ardener, "Comparative Study," p. 220.

45. Geertz, "Rotating Credit," pp. 262–263.

46. Ardener, "Comparative Study," p. 222.

47. Marguerite Holloway and Paul Wallich, "A Risk Worth Taking," *Scientific American* 267, no. 5: (November 1992):126.

48. See Portes, this volume.

49. Ivan Light, *Ethnic Enterprise in America: Business and Welfare Among Chinese, Japanese and Blacks* (Berkeley: University of California Press, 1972).

50. Ibid., pp. 62, 81.

51. Ibid., p. 36.

52. Ibid., p. 102.

53. Ibid., p. 131.

54. Ibid., p. 133.

55. Ibid., p. 117.

56. Ibid., p. 148.

57. For Indonesia see Dewey, *Peasant Marketing*, pp. 42–50 and Geertz, *Peddlers;* for the Philippines see Davis, *Social Relations*, pp. 198–202 and D. Szanton, *Estancia*, pp. 97–99.

58. Dewey, *Peasant Marketing*, pp. 44–45.

59. Ibid., p. 45.

60. Ann Swidler, "Culture in Action: Symbols and Strategies," *American Sociological Review* 51, no. 2 (1986):273–286.

61. Dewey, *Peasant Marketing*, p. 45.

62. Geertz, *Peddlers*.

63. Ibid., p. 123.

64. Dewey, *Peasant Marketing*, p. 46.

65. Geertz, *Peddlers*, pp. 84–85.

66. John Omohundro, *Chinese Merchant Families in Iloilo: Commerce and Kin in a Central Philippine City* (Athens, Ohio: Ohio University Press, 1981).

67. Davis, *Social Relations*, p. 200.

68. Ibid., p. 200.

69. See, for example, Landa, "Homogeneous Middleman."

70. Geertz, "Suq," p. 252 n. 101.

71. Siu-Lun Wong, "Industrial Entrepreneurship and Ethnicity: A Study of the Shanghainese Cotton Spinners in Hong Kong" (Ph.D. diss., Wolfson College, Oxford, 1979), p. 284.

72. He argues also that it is humiliating in China for a kinsman to make claims on an entrepreneur (Ibid., p. 284).

73. See Portes, this volume.

74. These points were impressed upon me by Alejandro Portes and Bryan Roberts, in discussion at the Russell Sage Foundation meetings on economic sociology of immigration.

75. Peter Gosling, "Chinese Crop Dealers in Malaysia and Thailand: The Myth of the Merciless Monopsonistic Middleman," in Linda Y. C. Lim and L. A. Peter Gosling, eds., *The Chinese in Southeast Asia*, Vol. I, *Ethnicity and Economic Activity* (Singapore: Maruzen Asia, 1983), p. 143, and Maurice Freedman, "The Handling of Money: A Note on the Background to the Economic Sophistication of Overseas Chinese" *Man* 59, item no. 89 (1959):64–65.

76. Linda Lim, "Chinese Economic Activity in Southeast Asia: An Introductory Review," in Lim and Gosling, eds., *The Chinese in Southeast Asia*, Vol. I, *Ethnicity and Economic Activity*, p. 9. One informant observed to Gosling that borrowing from local cooperatives was "better than the radio if you want everyone to know how much money you owe" (Gosling, "Crop Dealers," p. 144). Not only was borrowing from the Chinese merchants a less formal procedure in the sense of not involving paperwork, but the entire transaction could be carried out with exquisite sensitivity to the cultural need to avoid the *appearance* of a loan. Gosling's account is worth citing in detail: "I have watched Malays borrow from a Chinese shopkeeper without ever knowing that a financial transaction was in progress. A cigarette is shared; the shop-

keeper asks if there is anything the client wants. The client makes vague humorous remarks about how his wife pesters him for a sewing machine and his children like sweets and they exchange some common remarks about the jump in prices, the high costs of living and the wasteful ways of their wives and children. The shopkeeper then suggests that he has not yet banked the proceeds from the store and that if the client needs something to tide him over, he is welcome to it. The client usually buys a pack of cigarettes (which is put on his account) and takes the money folded into a small wad with the cigarettes, an invisible transaction unless one is watching closely. After the client has left the shop, the shopkeeper writes the loan and the pack of cigarettes in his ledger" (p. 166).

77. Gosling, "Crop Dealers," p. 143–144.

78. Aram Yengoyan, "The Buying of Futures: Chinese Merchants and the Fishing Industry in Capiz, Philippines," in Lim and Gosling, eds., *The Chinese in Southeast Asia*, Vol. I, *Ethnicity and Economic Activity*, pp. 117–130.

79. Gosling, "Crop Dealers," p. 138; cf. Mark Granovetter, "The Strength of Weak Ties," *American Journal of Sociology* 78, no. 6 (May 1973):1360–1380.

80. Brian Foster, "Ethnicity and Commerce," *American Ethnologist* 1, no. 3 (1974):441.

81. Roger Waldinger, Robin Ward, and Howard Aldrich, "Ethnic Business and Occupational Mobility in Advanced Societies," *Sociology* 19 (1985):586–597.

82. Charles Choy Wong, "Black and Chinese Grocery Stores in Los Angeles' Black Ghetto," *Urban Life* 5 (1977):439–464.

83. Jeremy Boissevain and Hanneke Grotenberg, "Culture, Structure and Ethnic Enterprise: The Surinamese of Amsterdam," *Ethnic and Racial Studies* 9 (January 1986):13.

84. Brian Foster, "Minority Traders in Thai Village Social Networks," *Ethnic Groups* 2 (1980):223.

85. D. Szanton, *Estancia*, p. 97.

86. Ibid., p. 95. Szanton reports that in addition to migrants, Protestants and Chinese, one other group in Estancia provides more than its share of entrepreneurs: women. The local cultural pattern is such that women more easily than men can limit the diffuse claims against their businesses that might prevent them from running efficiently. Men are judged "largely on their adherence to the traditional hierarchical interpersonal role behavior patterns demanding generosity and magnanimity towards others in the larger society," but women are judged mainly on how well they manage their family's internal economic affairs. Thus they are "expected to be thrifty and to haggle in the marketplace which

is, in a culturally real sense, beneath a man's dignity." So if you ask a woman for a loan or for rice, she can more easily say no or request repayment of a loan, on the grounds of her family's needs. Wives, in this setting, are thus often the marketing agents for fishermen or farmers (D. Szanton, *Estancia*, p. 94). Furthermore, women are less likely than men, when provoked, to engage in physical violence. Thus it is "literally safer for a woman to enter 'hard,' narrowly contractual economic relationships with others. Their ability to deny credit or demand payment of debts without fear of violence is essential to commercial enterprises in which goods produced elsewhere . . . are purchased from dealers outside the town, dealers who similarly demand payment in full and on time" (Ibid., p. 95). It is hard to know how widespread such a cultural pattern is, but with the exception of the Middle East, where women's roles are severely limited by Islamic culture, most reports of marketing and commerce in less developed settings show a preponderance of women in the most important roles. Whether they have as distinct entrepreneurial advantages in these other settings as in Estancia seems to me hard to establish on the basis of existing studies.

87. See, for example, the essays in Susan Olzak and Joanne Nagel, eds., *Competitive Ethnic Relations* (Orlando, Fla.: Academic Press, 1986).

88. Sumner La Croix, "Homogeneous Middleman Groups: What Determines the Homogeneity?" *Journal of Law, Economics and Organization* 5, no. 1 (1989):219.

89. Brian Foster, "Minority Traders in Thai Village Social Networks," *Ethnic Groups* 2 (1980):223, 239.

90. Gosling, "Crop Dealers", p. 156.

91. Peter Gosling, "Changing Chinese Identities in Southeast Asia," in Gosling and Lim, eds., *The Chinese in Southeast Asia*, Vol. II, *Identity, Culture and Politics* (Singapore: Maruzen Asia, 1983), p. 4.

92. Omohundro, *Merchant Families*, p. 12.

93. Peter Marris and Anthony Somerset, *The African Businessman: A Study of Entrepreneurship and Development in Kenya* (London: Routledge and Kegan Paul, 1971), p. 135.

94. Ibid., p. 145.

95. Cf. Edna Bonacich and John Modell, *The Economic Basic of Ethnic Solidarity: Small Business in the Japanese American Community* (Berkeley: University of California Press, 1980).

96. Levy, "Contrasting Factors," p. 187.

97. Howard Aldrich and Catherine Zimmer, "Entrepreneurship Through Social Networks," in Raymond Smilor and Donald Sexton, eds., *The Art and Science of Entrepreneurship* (Cambridge, Mass.: Ballinger, 1985), p. 14.

98. Leonard Broom and Ruth Riemer, *Removal and Return: The Socio-Economic Effects of the War on Japanese Americans* (Berkeley: University of California Press, 1949); Bonacich and Modell, *Economic Basis*; and Robert Jiobu, "Ethnic Hegemony and the Japanese of California," *American Sociological Review* 53 (June 1988):353–367.

99. Geertz, *Peddlers*, p. 148.

100. Dewey, *Peasant Marketing*, p. 45; D. Szanton, *Estancia*, p. 99; Davis, *Social Relations*, p. 203.

101. Thomas Timberg, *The Marwaris: From Traders to Industrialists* (New Delhi: Vikas, 1978).

102. Broom and Riemer, *Removal*.

103. Geertz, *Peddlers*, p. 149.

104. Ibid., p. 149.

105. Davis, *Social Relations*, pp. 202–203.

106. D. Szanton, *Estancia*, p. 99.

107. See Portes, this volume.

108. Sutti Ortiz, *Uncertainties in Peasant Farming: A Colombian Case* (New York: Humanities Press, 1973).

109. Alexander Gerschenkron, "The Modernization of Entrepreneurship," in Myron Weiner, ed., *Modernization: The Dynamics of Growth* (New York: Basic Books, 1966), p. 253.

110. Thomas Doerflinger, *A Vigorous Spirit of Enterprise: Merchants and Economic Development in Revolutionary Philadelphia* (Chapel Hill: University of North Carolina Press, 1986), p. 5.

111. Ivan Light and Carolyn Rosenstein Light, "Demand Factors in Entrepreneurship" (Department of Sociology, University of California, Los Angeles, 1989, mimeographed).

112. M. Szanton, *Right to Survive*, p. 138.

113. Geertz, *Peddlers*; Dewey, *Peasant Marketing*.

114. Geertz, *Peddlers*, pp. 13, 17.

115. Doerflinger, *Spirit*, p. 68.

116. Siu-Lun Wong, "Individual Entrepreneurship," p. 254.

117. See Edna Bonacich, "A Theory of Middleman Minorities," *American Sociological Review* 38 (October 1973):583–594.

118. Linda Lim, "Chinese Business, Multinationals and the State: Manufacturing for Export in Malaysia and Singapore," in Lim and Gosling, eds., *The Chinese in Southeast Asia*, Vol. I, *Ethnicity and Economic Activity*, p. 246.

119. Richard Robison, *Indonesia: The Rise of Capital* (Sydney: Allen & Unwin, 1986); Timberg, *Marwaris*.

120. See, for example, Norman Long, "Multiple Enterprise in the Central Highlands of Peru," in S. Greenfield, A. Strockon, and R. Aubey, eds., *Entrepreneurs in Cultural Context* (Albequerque: University of New Mexico Press, 1979).

121. A fuller account of these processes can be found in Mark Granovetter, "Business Groups," in Neil Smelser and Richard Swedberg, eds., *Handbook of Economic Sociology* (New York: Russell Sage Foundation and Princeton University Press, 1994), Chap. 22.

5

Expanding
the Interaction Theory
of Entrepreneurship

IVAN LIGHT AND CAROLYN ROSENSTEIN

$\mathbf{M}$AX WEBER declared that economic sociology must start from the desire for utilities and the provision to furnish them.[1] Adhering to this tradition, textbooks have long claimed that both supply and demand require attention in a complete explanation of entrepreneurship.[2] Smelser writes that "like all markets, the market for entrepreneurial services has a demand and a supply side," underscoring the fact that both sides require attention.[3] Yet, despite the theoretical centrality of these terms, definitions of demand and supply are few.[4] Berg and DiMaggio discuss demand, but neither defines it.[5] Neither Stinchcombe nor Martinelli and Smelser index either demand or supply, though theirs are leading texts in the sociology of economic life.[6]

Only Parsons and Smelser offer analytical definitions.[7] They define supply as "the production of utility or economic value." Entrepreneurs are useful because of the goods and services they produce or cause to be produced.[8] Therefore, the supply side of entrepreneurship includes demographic features of feeder populations that affect their willingness and ability to produce. These features include their mean age, their sex ratio, and their number. But entrepreneurial capability also depends upon sociocultural resources such as socially oriented action patterns, embedded transactions, social networks, and social capital (Portes, this volume). The more abundant these productive resources, the greater the entrepreneurship of a group.

Parsons and Smelser define demand as "the disposition to pay" for goods and services "in a process of market exchange."[9] Following Friedman, the demand curve traces how many entrepreneurs the market will support at various price levels. But demand neither exists prior to and independent of supply nor does it beget supply.[10] First, the meeting of groups creates new demands, as when Germans learn to appreciate Turkish cuisine because Turks work in German cities. Second, consumer demand does not guarantee any supplier response, nor does it guarantee that the entrepreneurial response will exhaust the demand. No matter how strong the demand for gambling halls, serious Baptists will not run them, nor will Quakers manufacture poison gas and nuclear weapons, lucrative though they certainly are.

Market Opportunities

The economist's term "demand" corresponds to "market opportunity," a virtual synonym common in sociology. We somewhat prefer the term demand to market opportunity in this context. Opportunity has a valid and autonomous meaning in status attainment studies where it stands for a vacant prestige niche.[11] Weber meant by market opportunity the privilege of trading where the right is not routinely available to all.[12] However, in the context of entrepreneurship research, "market opportunity" is synonymous with demand.[13] Waldinger, Aldrich, and Ward stress the importance of "opportunity structures" and then define "opportunity structures" as "market conditions."[14] In the last analysis, market conditions offer "opportunity" because of money rewards. If money returns are abundant, opportunity is abundant; if returns are nil, opportunity is nil. Limitless opportunities to perform unpaid services do not create an opportunity structure for housewives. In practice, therefore, market opportunity and opportunity structure boil down to buyers.

Sometimes opportunity is defined ostensively. Ostensive definitions list the conditions under which a phenomenon appears. Waldinger, Aldrich, and Ward have offered an ostensive definition of "the types of economic environments" that offer entrepreneurial opportunity: co-ethnic consumer products, underserved or abandoned markets, markets with low returns to economies of scale, markets with unstable or uncertain demand, and markets for exotic goods.[15] In the same spirit, Waldinger earlier declares demand for small firms a product of "markets whose small size, heterogeneity, or susceptibility to flux and instability limit the potential for mass distribution and mass production."[16]

Ostensive definitions suffer from two limitations. First, since they explain from precursors, they do not isolate causality. Knowing that tooth decay occurs after eating chocolate, candy, doughnuts, and pop tarts, one still does not know that sugar causes tooth decay. Additionally, ostensive definitions are subject to reappraisal whenever someone discovers new categories. Waldinger's early list resembles but is shorter than Waldinger, Aldrich, and Ward's list, so the expansion of the list has already begun.[17] Others have also compiled different but equally good lists.[18] If these lists are added together, the number of precursors becomes embarrassingly large with no guarantee that additional categories will not shortly appear.

Research Design

Although demand and supply always contribute jointly to entrepreneurship, research designs sometimes suppress one in the interest of highlighting the other—a valid application of J. S. Mills's method of difference.[19] Designs that focus on the same group in different locations hold group resources roughly constant while varying demand environments.[20] Such designs exclude supply-side resource effects from the explanation. For example, Patterson compared Chinese migrants in Guyana and Jamaica.[21] He found that only the Jamaica Chinese became entrepreneurs in significant numbers, a result he attributed to uneven economic conditions in the two countries, a demand-side explanation. Within the limits of his evidence, Patterson's design could not disclose any supply influences on Chinese entrepreneurship even if any were present. Patterson treated the Chinese in Jamaica and the Chinese in Guyana as if they were identical in resource endowments but confronted different demand environments. Therefore, Patterson's results do not disprove the existence of supply-side influences that his design rendered invisible, nor of course were they intended to do so.

Studies that focus on different groups in the same location have the opposite kind of blind spot. For example, Kallen and Kelner compared the entrepreneurship of Italians, Jews, and white Protestants in Toronto; Kim, Hurh, and Fernandez compared the entrepreneurship of Chinese, Gujerati Indians, and non-Gujerati Indians in Chicago.[22] Here the "same" location residually stands for a constant demand environment whether that environment be a county, a city, a state, or even the earth. In such cases, location encompasses the demand-side variables. Because a constant cannot explain a change, and location is constant, the only possible explanation of intergroup differences in entrepreneurship then lies on the supply side. Another example is Light's analysis of Japanese, Chinese, and black entrepreneurship.[23] Treating the location as invariant—a handful of northern cities in a half century—this research had to find cultural explanations for intergroup differences. Even if demand-side explanations existed, the research design rendered it impossible to observe them.

Although a valid research tool, Mills's method can support disciplinary myopia if researchers always select that aspect of the problem their discipline explains best and ignore other aspects. In reaction to this problem, recent researchers have recommended balanced explanations that acknowledge the interaction of supply and demand factors, a position compatible with but more advanced than the textbook view. Thus, Waldinger, Ward, and Aldrich observe that a "common objection to cultural analysis" is its lack of attention to "the economic environment in which immigrant entrepreneurs function." They recommend "an interactive approach" which looks at the "congruence between the demands of the economic environment and the informal resources of the ethnic population."[24]

In an enhanced discussion of the interaction theory, Waldinger, Aldrich, and Ward build their "interactive model" around characteristics of groups and opportunity structures.[25] "Ethnic strategies emerge from the interaction" of opportunity structure and group characteristics. On the one side, the opportunity structure pays for products and services. On the other, groups can produce certain commodities more efficiently than others. Entrepreneurship becomes a group strategy to the extent that the demand environment pays group members to perform tasks their resources permit. Since it was formulated, this reaction has achieved the strength of a movement of thought in the entrepreneurship literature, within which it is now virtually axiomatic that entrepreneurs emerge from the interaction of supply and demand.[26]

If the interaction theory meant that supply and demand must be present in a complete explanation of entrepreneurship, the interaction theory would only restate the older textbook view. However, the interaction approach does not just return to the earlier textbook generalization. That earlier view makes no reference to the articulation of supply and demand. It only insists that a complete explanation requires both without specifying how the two connect. Transcending this limitation, the interaction theory describes how supply and demand combine. Specifically, the interaction theory claims that the entrepreneurial performance of groups depends upon the fit between what they have to offer and what the market demands.[27] The better the fit, the more entrepreneurs; and the same group can experience a good fit in some places and a poor fit in others. Thus, Chinese can operate more restaurants in cities whose American consumers like Chinese food than they can in cities whose consumers do not.[28]

Class and Ethnic Resources

When explaining entrepreneurial supply, the key concepts are class and ethnic resources.[29] All groups possess class and ethnic resources, but their balance varies from group to group; sometimes class resources predominate, sometimes ethnic. Additionally, some groups have more resources than others.[30]

Class resources are the cultural and material endowment of bourgeoisies. Money and education are class resources whose role as capital is already well understood. But class resources also include strictly social features of the bourgeoisie, conceived as a real social group, not a stratum. These social features importantly support and enhance the entrepreneurship of the bourgeoisie in ways obscured by a narrow attention to capital endowments.

Class culture is one such social feature of the bourgeoisie. Class cohesion is the other. Class cohesion includes structural and relational embeddedness in the upper-class, multiplex social networks based on school, religious, and marital affiliations, and enforceable trust deriving from social standing. Therefore, class culture includes the "socially oriented" action patterns introjected during socialization (Portes, this volume). These nonvocational values and beliefs stamp the possessor with a personal character that inspires confidence in business deals with other members of the bourgeoisie. But class character also includes the vocational culture of the bourgeoisie as well as its status culture. This vocational culture includes occupationally relevant and supportive values, attitudes, knowledge, and skills transmitted in the course of primary and adult socialization. Bourgeois vocational culture means vocationally relevant values, skills, attitudes, and knowledge which are characteristic of bourgeoisies around the world and which, furthermore, distinguish bourgeois from nonbourgeois co-ethnics while linking members to non-co-ethnic bourgeois elsewhere.[31]

Structural and relational embeddedness in the upper class regulates the economic transactions of individual members of the bourgeoisie. The more class-conscious and socially exclusive the bourgeoisie, possessing in the extreme case the features of high society, the more social regulation the class system imposes upon opportunism. When *A* and *B* make a deal, the opportunism of either affects their social standing as well as their business standing, a consideration that imposes enforceable trust upon both. Similarly, the multiplex social networks of the upper class, emerging from school, church, club, and resort colony, permit individual members of the bourgeoisie to connect with business partners through mutual friends and acquaintances.[32] These others provide references in advance and, in the event of opportunism, social control.

Ethnic resources are sociocultural features of the whole group which co-ethnic entrepreneurs actively utilize in business or from which their business passively benefits.[33] Ethnic resources include an ethnic culture, structural and relational embeddedness, social capital, and multiplex social networks that connect the entire group. Ethnic resources characterize a whole group. For example, writing of Jews in western Pennsylvania before World War II, Morawska found that "a desire for self-employment" was virtually universal. In about one-third of the cases, this motive characterized families that had been self-employed in Europe. But in two-thirds of the cases, the aspiration for self-employment characterized Jews who had not been self-employed in Europe and who were not currently self-employed. In effect, all Jews aspired to self-employment, not just the Jewish bourgeoisie. Therefore, the aspiration for entrepreneurship was an ethnic resource, not just a class resource.[34]

Like the class culture of a bourgeoisie, ethnic culture inculcates introjected action patterns in the course of socialization. Ethnic groups may also provide for their members the same structural and relational embeddedness that beneficially regulate the economic conduct of the upper class. The multiplex social networks of an ethnic group carry the same economic capacity that they do for the upper class. Indeed, ethnic groups and the bourgeoisie are structurally quite similar, and the similarity is most striking among the most entrepreneurial ethnic minorities.[35] A major difference is the broader scope of ethnic groups, which encompass all status levels whereas the bourgeoisie includes only the rich, excluding everyone else. Ethnic cultures lend varying support to entrepreneurship. Middleman minorities deploy ethnic resources that strongly support the entrepreneurship of members, thus engendering high rates of self-employment.[36] Although the evidence of intergroup variation is strong, its explanations are little understood. Since all ethnic groups have cultures, networks, social capital, and embedded transaction, intergroup differences in entrepreneurship presumably reflect intergroup differences in the extent and strength of these resources rather than their presence or absence.[37]

Reframing the interaction theory of entrepreneurship in terms of ethnic and class resources, we hypothesize that the interaction of supply and demand is the process whereby resources connect to the multiple demands that exist in environments. That is, the demand for plumbers is one demand, the demand for statisticians is another demand, the demand for pretzels is another, and so forth. Although demand profiles change from environment to environment, environments always have multiple demands. In order to respond to any demand for entrepreneurs, groups must have appropriate resources. Every group cannot and will not respond to every demand. Resource-rich groups spurn less profitable demands. Resource-poor groups cannot respond to lucrative demands that require more resources than they possess. Groups also differ in the quality of the resources they possess as well as their quantity. Group resources "hook" or fail to hook the demands that float past. Knowing how to do electrical work, group A responds to this demand by supplying electricians, whereas it overlooks demand for florists. Resource-rich and resource-versatile groups hook all or many types of demands, appropriating thereby every entrepreneurial opportunity their environment affords. Resource-poor groups cannot hook demands so frequently and they cannot hook some types of demand at all. If group A cannot hook a demand but B can, then A cannot field an entrepreneurial response to that demand. Since B can, A will field a weaker entrepreneurial performance than B. Therefore, other things being equal, a group's rate of self-employment reflects its resource versatility as well as its resource abundance.

Adequacy of the Evidence

Although intuitively convincing and widely proclaimed, the interaction theory's formal basis in evidence is surprisingly weak. Evidence to support the interactionist view comes in three research designs: cases that simultaneously vary both supply and demand conditions, cases that vary demand or supply but not the other, and cases that vary neither. Of these, the simplest is the case study of one group in one demand environment. Enjoying detailed access to all the local evidence, one group/one locality studies permit intensive investigation of theoretically interesting cases. In the context of a larger, more general literature, this design can turn up detailed explanations of how a case came about.

An example is Light and Bonacich's case study of Koreans in Los Angeles.[38] Attempting to treat both supply-side and demand-side causes, the authors examined the ethnic and class resources of Korean immigrants and the characteristics of their economic niche. With regard to the Koreans' niche, they stressed the absence of competition from big retail chains in the inner city, a product of economic disincentives arising from low-income consumers and high-crime business sites. More broadly, they called attention to the selective effects of the "investor's exemption" provision of United States immigration law, the tax advantages of independent contractors, the timely elimination of fair trade laws in liquor retailing, and lax enforcement of wage and sanitary provisions of the labor code. These external influences created an economic niche in which Korean entrepreneurs could exploit their resources, especially their Protestant religion, patriarchal families, and rotating credit associations.

Strictly speaking, however, the one group/one locality design offers no variation on either the supply or demand side. On the demand side is Los Angeles with what it wants to buy; on the supply side are the Korean immigrants with what they can provide. In case study designs like this, both supply and demand are fixed and static; the problem is to explain the case. This particular one group/one locality case was important because of the high entrepreneurship among Koreans in Los Angeles. Their extraordinary level of entrepreneurship rendered the case of interest in itself as well as for the light it threw upon general theory. But this case study could not explain why non-Koreans in Los Angeles did not take more advantage of the same demand conditions that attracted Koreans to the retail liquor industry, dry cleaning, and garment manufacturing, and to the black community. Nor, on the other hand, could it explain why Koreans ignored entrepreneurial niches that attracted Taiwanese, Armenians, and Iranians. Nor, most importantly, could it formally induct the relative importance of supply and demand variables in Korean entrepreneurship.

Other interaction-seeking case studies have stumbled over this methodological problem. In his study of New York City's garment industry, Waldinger stressed the advantages of a balanced treatment that acknowledges "opportunity structures" as well as cultural influences. Waldinger mentioned the economic advantages that lured immigrant Dominican and Chinese entrepreneurs into this industry.[39] These economic advantages included low returns on economies of scale, instability and uncertainty of product demand, small and differentiated product markets, agglomeration advantages, access to cheap labor, and vacant niches caused by exodus of predecessors. These demand-side attractions did not negate what Waldinger called the "predispositions toward entrepreneurship" of the immigrants, and Waldinger acknowledged the predispositions as well as the economic incentives. Waldinger regarded this conclusion as a balanced one that did justice to supply as well as demand influences.[40]

But Waldinger's research varied groups, not demand environments. His two groups/one industry design formally permitted generalizations about the influence of resources upon entrepreneurship. It did not permit generalizations about the influence of demand environment, a constant. From a formal point of view, therefore, Waldinger's "balanced" conclusions were of unequal value. On the one hand, the comparison of Chinese and Dominicans permitted conclusions about the influence of the two groups' resource profiles on their entrepreneurship. On the other hand, Waldinger's design did not authorize conclusions about demand influences.[41]

Bailey's study of New York City's restaurant industry encountered the same problem. Acknowledging the importance of cultural predisposition and ethnic solidarity in restaurant entrepreneurship, Bailey looked for "important causes" that previous studies had "neglected" in the interest of a balanced explanation.[42] These neglected causes turned out to be "market and technological conditions," privileged access to the cheap labor of co-ethnics, and lack of entrepreneurial interest among native-born workers. Bailey's catalog included supply-side and demand-side factors and represented, in this sense, a balanced explanation of restaurant industry entrepreneurship. This balance was an intellectual achievement insofar as previous studies had neglected demand-side explanations. However, Bailey's multiple groups/one industry research design could not offer generalizations about demand effects that had the same inductive power as did his generalizations about supply differences between immigrants and natives, the groups he compared.

In order to expose supply and demand factors, interaction-seeking research must permit variation in supplier groups and demand environments. One interaction-seeking study has met this design requirement.[43] In their research on Asian entrepreneurs in three British cities, Aldrich, Jones, and McEvoy compared the Asians with a sample of white entrepreneurs in respect to directly measured practices thought to reflect ethnic business style, a supply-side factor. They found few differences between Asians and whites in respect to resources but important differences in business environment among the three cities, with all groups demonstrating higher rates of entrepreneurship in some cities than in others.[44]

Reviewing the evidence, they concluded that "immigrant business activity" was more shaped by internal than by external forces. "The opportunity structure of the receiving society outweighs any cultural predisposition towards entrepreneurship."[45] Absent simultaneous variation in both supply conditions (multiple groups) and demand conditions (multiple localities), this judgment would not have been permissible.[46] Ironically, the judgment does not support the interaction theory which Aldrich later developed. After all, when supply and demand interact to create entrepreneurship, each side explains half the variation. If demand explains more than supply or vice versa, then an interaction model does not fit the evidence.

Although examples could be multiplied, this review shows that the vast current literature on immigrant and ethnic entrepreneurship does not provide formal proof of the interaction theory. The basic reason is the absence of research designs that simultaneously vary supply and demand conditions. Only such designs would permit researchers to find the predicted interactions, and this design infrequently appears in the current literature. A paradoxical exception is the intercity research of Aldrich, Jones, and McEvoy, which did have a design capable of finding interaction effects but which did not, in actuality, find them.[47]

Demand Effects

Turning now to a conceptual analysis, we observe that, following the interactive approach, the entrepreneur population of every group emerges from the interaction of its resources and local demand environments. Although an improvement upon earlier formulations, this proposition cannot accomodate general demand effects. When changes in demand expand or contract the entrepreneurial performance of all ethnoracial groups in approximate parity to one another, then we call this demand effect general. As a rising tide raises or lowers all boats in the harbor, so a general demand effect enhances or contracts the entrepreneurship of all ethnoracial categories in its environment. Conversely, when changes in demand expand or contract the entrepreneurship of one group, leaving others unaffected, then this demand effect is specific, not general.[48] If a tide could interact with boats in this way, then a high tide might raise the ocean liner but leave behind the tugboat or vice versa.

An example of a generally favorable change in demand would be an emerging, postrecessionary, full-employment, high-wage local economy in a cheap money environment. Putting money in everyone's pockets, this environment creates consumer demand for a full spectrum of services and products, thus improving every group's entrepreneurial performance. Immigrant and native-born Asian, black, Hispanic, and white entrepreneurs all benefit from cheap money and full employment. Therefore, in response to improved demand conditions, the number of each group's entrepreneurs increases in equal proportion. For example, if increased demand doubles the aggregate population of entrepreneurs and group *A* had 10 percent of entrepreneurs before the change, then after the change group *A* will continue to have 10 percent of all entrepreneurs, but it will have twice as many entrepreneurs.

Aggregate demand is the sum of the separate demand for all the products and services that entrepreneurs create.[49] Aggregate demand need not create entrepreneurs equally in all population segments. That is, given $1 billion of new consumer spending, the number of white, black, Hispanic, and Asian entrepreneurs such spending will support depends upon how consumers spend their money. Consumers may buy books written by whites, music played by blacks, meals prepared by Asians, or garments sewn by Mexicans. Therefore, an increase in aggregate demand need not produce equal across-the-board increases in the demand for entrepreneurs of all ethnoracial backgrounds.

On the other hand, changes in aggregate demand may produce a general demand effect. We cannot just assume that general demand never exists. Indeed, general demand is many researchers' intuitive model of how demand operates. Advancing this view, Swinton and Handy declare, "In a general sense, all business enterprises compete for the same market demand." Therefore, the "rate of growth of opportunities for business expansion in general" constrains the "rate of expansion of black business ownership."[50] This view assumes that when business in general expands, black-owned firms expand too; and when business in general stagnates, black business stagnates too. Swinton and Handy assume a tight linkage between aggregate demand and industrial demand such that all industries benefit equally from enhanced aggregate demand. If the linkage is this tight, then general demand effect is present, and blacks will obtain a proportional share of the additional entrepreneurs generated by additional aggregate demand.

But linkages need not be tight. When "Yuppies" move into the barrio in the course of gentrification, aggregate demand rises, but the new and abundant Yuppie money flows into wine bars and boutiques, businesses owned chiefly by whites. Mexican owners of pre-existing taco stands and bodegas obtain no Yuppie money. When enhanced aggregate demand results in unequal improvement of the entrepreneurial performance of ethnoracial groups, in this case an improvement of native white rates relative to Mexican, then the demand's effect is specific. Specific demand effects mean that some groups appropriate all, most, or much of the demand, some appropriate little, and some none. Therefore, specific demand affects the share of a metropolitan area's total demand that entrepreneurs of various ethnoracial groups supply. For example, if Koreans in Los Angeles monopolize the janitorial industry, then when industrial demand for janitors grows as a result of new office construction, Korean entrepreneurs appropriate the whole increase, while none of the other ethnic groups obtain any share. This appropriation increases the absolute and relative number of Korean entrepreneurs in Los Angeles, thus raising the Koreans' self-employment rate relative to non-Koreans.[51]

Supply Effects

How are specific demand effects possible? That question requires examination of features of the supply environment that govern responsiveness to demand. Supply effects are the effects of supply characteristics of provider groups upon entrepreneurial performance net of demand. According to the interaction theory, supply characteristics affect entrepreneurship in interaction with features of the demand environment, as when Chinese restauranteurs benefit from local demand for Chinese food. But the interaction theory has the same limitations on the supply side that it has with respect to general demand. That is, just as the interaction of supply and demand need not exhaust the ways in which demand affects entrepreneurship, so interaction does not exhaust the manner in which supply affects entrepreneurship. This shortfall arises because ethnoracial groups differ in respect to the levels, types, and versatility of entrepreneurial resources they control. Groups with scant resources cannot respond to entrepreneurial demands that require vast resources. Groups with one type of resource cannot respond to demands that require another. Groups with specific resources can respond only to a narrow spectrum of demands.

Additionally, and independent of the level of class resources, some ethnic resources are of specific rather than general utility in entrepreneurship. *Specific utility* refers to provider characteristics that provide a special advantage in a particular demand context but are not of general use. *General utility* refers to resources that permit versatile response to any and all types of demand. For example, in the restaurant industry, wine connoisseurship confers an advantage in French restaurants but it does not confer the same advantage in Persian restaurants because Muslims do not serve alcohol. Therefore, wine connoisseurship is a less versatile resource than the willingness to work long hours, a useful characteristic in any business. When a universalistic demand collides with the provider populations from which entrepreneurs are recruited, specific resource endowments can produce specific demand effects. This alteration does not arise only because groups have different levels of class resources, some rich and others poor, but also because some resources are specific and some general.

Although the interaction theory illuminates the restaurant industry and others like it, it does not illuminate cases in which ethnoracial or ethnonational groups enjoy general resources. Two examples illustrate general resources. The first is a generalized capacity to do any business, which we call business acumen. If a group enjoys unusual business acumen, then it exploits every demand environment. People who have superior business acumen prosper in the flower business, where that is in demand, and they prosper in construction, where that is in demand. The interaction theory cannot explain this generalized entrepreneurial capacity because the interaction theory requires specific resources, not general.

Again, money to invest and human capital are general resources that encourage entrepreneurship in any demand environment. Rich people can invest in hotels when that industry is profitable, and later redirect their money to hospitals when they become profitable. When groups enjoy generalized resources, aggregate demand matters because entrepreneurs can switch into any industry in which demand expands. The superior educational level of Korean entrepreneurs offers an empirical illustration. Korean entrepreneurs have on average more years of education than do non-Korean entrepreneurs. Therefore, in whatever city they reside, Korean immigrant entrepreneurs have a human capital advantage that supports their entrepreneurial success. Possibly as a result, Koreans in New York City enjoyed their biggest commercial success in the greengrocer business where they introduced ready-to-eat fruits and vegetables in bite-size pieces. Koreans in Los Angeles never specialized in the greengrocer business, nor did Koreans have, as far as anyone can tell, any specific resource affinity for greengroceries. Korean immigrants in Los Angeles operated gasoline service stations, dry cleaning, and liquor stores, not greengroceries. Yet none of these Los Angeles specialties reflects any unique aptitude either. Rather, the Koreans adapted to whatever demand environment they inhabited, New York or Los Angeles, switching resources from industry to industry as necessary.

Interlocal Entrepreneurial Performance

Intermetropolitan comparisons of entrepreneurial performance offer a novel opportunity to examine the interaction theory with evidence.

We distinguish two aspects of entrepreneurial performance: rate and rank. A group's *rate of entrepreneurship* is the number of its members self-employed per 1,000 able-bodied adults in the labor force.[52] A group's *entrepreneurial rank* is its self-employment rate relative to other groups in its locality. That is, in every metropolitan area the group with the highest self-employment rate ranks first, the group with the second-highest rate ranks second, and so on. Entrepreneurial rank and self-employment rate are independent between, but not within, metropolitan areas in that a group can rank first in a low-entrepreneurship locality while manifesting a rate below the lowest-ranking group in a high-entrepreneurship locality. In principal, a low-resource group can even display higher mean rates than a high-resource group provided the low-resource group occupies more favorable demand environments than does the high-resource group.[53]

When supply interacts with demand (as, according to the interaction theory, it always does), new constellations have the potential to revise rank orders. For example, Chinese restauranteurs would be immensely successful in New York, where consumers love their cuisine, but unsuccessful in Little Rock, where consumers avoid novelty. The Chinese would rank higher in New York than in Little Rock as a consequence. If, however, all ethnic and class resources were general and none specific, then even extreme interlocal variations in aggregate demand would be compatible with continuity of rank order within localities. That is, lacking a market for restaurants, the Chinese in Little Rock would enter some other industry. These irregularities do exist. Thus, when blacks ranked first in entrepreneurship in Richland, Washington, as they did in 1980, they ranked higher there than they usually did. Upward and downward shifts may occur because entrepreneurial demand increases some group's rate more than others. In fact, should a group with low resources appropriate a big demand, possibly through set-aside laws, that appropriated demand alone might add enough entrepreneurs to improve the group's rank as well as its rate. If the rate alone increased, the group's rank would not change unless the group also appropriated more than its usual share of demand.

Ethnoracial Composition of Metropolitan Areas

In order to further examine demand and supply effects, we investigate the effects of both upon entrepreneurial rank and rate. However, entrepreneurial rank is only meaningful in those metropolitan areas that contained all five major ethnoracial categories. Unequal ranks would give an unfair advantage to larger groups more commonly present since, in the absence of other groups, they would rank higher than when the other groups are present. For example, even if group *D* always ranks last, it would rank third when three groups were present, fourth when four groups were present, and fifth when all five groups were present. This inequality would elevate its mean rank.[54] Therefore, we examined the actual structure of ethnoracial pluralism in 1980, using the 5 percent public-use sample (PUMS) of the national census. We categorized all 272 metropolitan areas of the United States according to the number of ethnoracial categories they contained.

All five ethnoracial categories enjoyed effective representation in only 167 of the 272 metropolitan areas.[55] We designate these 167 as the matched metropolitan areas. In the other 105 metropolitan areas, one or more of the minority groups were missing.[56] *Minority group* refers to all ethnoracial categories except native white. In fifty metropolitan areas, four of the five categories were represented; thirty areas contained three groups, twenty-two contained two groups, and three areas held only one ethnoracial category above the threshold of effective representation. In these three monoethnic metropolitan areas, native whites were the only ethnoracial group represented above threshold levels. For the record, these three were Altoona, Pennsylvania; St. Cloud, Minnesota; and Wausau, Wisconsin.

Self-employment *rates* are the percentage of each category's labor force receiving income from self-employment. This income-derived definition is broader than the class-of-worker definition normally employed to measure self-employment because it includes part-time self-employment as well as full-time. Self-employment *rank* is a category's ordinal position relative to the other four categories within each metropolitan area. For example, in Abilene, foreign whites ranked first in self-employment rate, Asians ranked second, native whites ranked third, blacks ranked fourth, and Hispanics ranked fifth.

Utilizing only the 167 matched metropolitan areas, we now ascertain how much consistency of rank orders existed among the 167 metropolitan areas. Rank consistency implies recurrently unequal levels of generalizable resources which groups allocate to whatever entrepreneurial opportunities are most accessible in each demand environment. Complete intermetropolitan consistency would exclude interaction effects altogether because interaction effects imply radical inconsistencies of entrepreneurial performance in the presence of unique demand environments. Table 5.1 shows that foreign-born whites ranked first in 59.3 percent of metropolitan areas, second in 29.3 percent, third in 5.4 percent, and so forth. Their mean

Table 5.1   Rank[1] of the Mean Self-Employment Rates[2] of FB Whites,
NB Whites, Asians, Hispanics, and Blacks,
Within each of the 167 Metropolitan Areas[3] (percentages)

Rank	FB Whites (%)	NB Whites (%)	Asians (%)	Hispanics (%)	Blacks (%)	Total[4] (%)
(High) 1	59.3	12.6	25.1	2.4	.6	100.0
2	29.3	48.5	19.8	2.4	0.0	100.0
3	5.4	34.7	37.1	18.0	4.8	100.0
4	4.8	4.2	11.4	58.7	20.4	99.5
4.5[5]	0.0	0.0	.6	.6	0.0	1.2
(Low) 5	1.2	0.0	6.0	18.0	74.3	99.5
Total[6]	100.0	100.0	100.0	100.1[7]	100.1[7]	
Mean SE Rank:	1.6	2.3	2.5	3.9	4.7	

[1] The Mean Self-Employment Rates of FB Whites, NB Whites, Asians, Hispanics, and Blacks were ranked *within* each metropolitan area: 1 = high . . . 5 = low.
[2] The Self-Employment Rates are the percentage of each category's labor force who had income gains or losses from self-employment (census variable INCOME2).
[3] All five categories were present in the civilian labor force in numbers meeting the threshold criteria of 20 persons in the original 5 percent public-use microsample data (or 400 persons in the weighted 100 percent sample).
[4] The Total column equals the summation of the five categories across each rank (row).
[5] In one metropolitan area, Asians and Hispanics were each reassigned a rank of 4.5, because both categories had mean self-employment rates of zero income.
[6] The Total row equals the summation of the distribution of the ranks for each of the five categories (down each column).
[7] Error due to rounding.

rank in the 167 metropolitan areas was 1.6, the highest of any of the five ethnoracial groups. At the opposite extreme, blacks ranked fifth in 74.3 percent of metropolitan areas, fourth in 20.4 percent, and first in only 0.6 percent of areas. The table shows that native whites and Asians traded off second and third rank in approximate parity. But Hispanics and blacks reliably held fourth and fifth rank respectively. The impressive intermetropolitan consistency of rank implies that the five ethnoracial groups had reliably unequal resource endowments which they could shift around to suit whatever demand environment they faced. Therefore, some consistently outranked others.

Table 5.1 also exposes irregularities. Normally high-ranking foreign whites ranked last in 1.2 percent of metropolitan areas, Asians ranked last in 6 percent of areas, and normally low-ranking blacks ranked first in 0.6 percent of metropolitan areas. Irregularities imply that on occasion groups performed appreciably above or below their normal rank. Such inconsistent results could come about in two ways. Groups could perform better in metropolitan areas in which their general resource basis was unusually strong. We call this the variant resources explanation. Alternatively, groups could perform better in metropolitan areas whose demand environments offered unique connections to specific group resources of no moment in most environments. We call this the specific resources explanation. A variant resources explanation assumes that a group had higher or lower general resources than it usually had; therefore, it performed better or worse than it usually did. A specific resources explanation assumes that a group's unique resources fit a particular demand environment better than other environments. Therefore, it performed better than usual.

To pursue this issue, we computed the intragroup ranks of each metropolitan area, ranking in first place the metropolitan area in which each had the highest self-employment rate, and ranking in 167th place the area in which it had the lowest. Other metropolitan areas ranked between these extremes. If general resources predominated, permitting great versatility in demand-responsiveness, then we expect agreement among the groups because all would prosper in the same high-demand environments and languish in the same low-demand environments. In other words, ranking each ethnoracial category across all 167 metropolitan areas, we would find that all five ranked highest in the same entrepreneur-supporting metropolitan area. To illustrate this point, Table 5.2 lists the metropolitan area that ranked first in respect to self-employment rate and mean self-employment income for each of the five ethnoracial categories. In each case, we also show the ranks of each of the other four ethnoracial categories for comparison. For example, Chico, California, ranked first in self-employment rate for Asians and native whites, third for Hispanics, thirteenth for blacks, and thirty-fifth for foreign-born whites. Similarly, Cedar Rapids, Iowa, ranked first in mean self-employment income for blacks, forty-second for foreign whites, 141st for Asians, 125th for native whites, and 94th for Hispanics.

To the extent that general resources predominated in all groups, we expect agreement of the intermetropolitan rank orders[57] among the five ethnoracial categories. In an extreme case, only one metropolitan area should be listed in Table 5.2, as all five ethnoracial categories would share that area's top opportunities. Conversely if intragroup, intermetropolitan ranks are idiosyncratic, with group *A*

Table 5.2   Metropolitan Areas in which One of the Five Ethnoracial
Categories Ranks[1] Number One (Highest) for Mean
Self-Employment Rates and Mean Self-Employment Income,
and the Ranks of the Other Categories in the
same Metropolitan Areas for the 167 Matched Areas, 1980

	NB White	FB White	Black	Asian	Hispanic
SMSAs[2] for Mean Self-Employment Rate					
Chico, CA	1	35	13	1	3
Daytona, FL	7	1	8	9	5
Knoxville, TN	118	4	149	53	1
Santa Cruz, CA	2	12	1.5	24	35
Northeast PA	84	16	1.5	100	11
SMSAs[2] for Mean Self-Employment Income					
Cedar Rapids, IA	125	42	1	141	94
Columbus, OH	91	75	107	87	1
Lansing-E. Lansing, MI	151	143	132	1	124
Norwalk, CN	1	58	23	148	144
Wichita Falls, TX	20	1	138	94.5	104

[1]Intermetropolitan ranks for each category, i.e., 1 = the highest Mean Self-Employment Rate or Income and 167 = the lowest.
[2]Metropolitan areas are listed in alphabetical order.

doing very well where B does poorly and vice-versa, then specific resources may explain unusual success and failure. Table 5.2 shows the results of this exercise. Although perfect agreement is missing, Table 5.2 nonetheless shows some agreement. Chico, California, was in fact the top-ranking city for two ethnoracial categories, and that central California city also ranked high for the other three. This coincidence suggests a favorable general demand environment in Chico that permitted all groups to exploit their general resources. Daytona, Florida, also provided a favorable entrepreneurial environment for all five ethnoracial categories in terms of mean self-employment rates. But Table 5.2 also displays some rank disagreements incompatible with a high resources/general demand explanation. For example, Knoxville, Tennessee, provided the first-ranked economic environment for Hispanics, and foreign whites clearly benefitted from the same economic environment. Knoxville provided the fourth most favorable environment for foreign whites. However, for blacks the Knoxville metropolitan area ranked only 149th, for Asians 53rd, and for native whites, 118th. If the Knoxville demand environment were generally positive, why did blacks, Asians, and native whites not benefit more from it?

Mean self-employment income offers another measure of a positive demand environment. Other things being equal, demand environments are favorable where self-employment incomes are high.[58] Therefore, to the extent that demand effects were general, the rank order of groups ought to coincide in respect to mean self-employment income as well as in respect to mean self-employment rate. The bottom half of Table 5.2 shows the rank orders of ethnoracial categories in respect to mean self-employment income. In this bottom panel the tendency toward disagreement is more pronounced than in the top. Thus Cedar Rapids, Iowa, ranked number one in self-employment income among blacks. That result signifies that the mean black self-employment income was higher in Cedar Rapids than in any other of the 167 matched metropolitan areas. If Cedar Rapids generally rewarded entrepreneurs well, all groups should have basked in its economic sunshine. In fact, only blacks found Cedar Rapids the most rewarding economic environment of any in the United States. For some reason, Cedar Rapids was relatively better for blacks than for nonblacks.

Spearman correlation coefficients measure the extent to which category rank orders agreed so that higher-ranking metropolitan areas for one group tended to be higher-ranking areas for another.[59] Therefore, we computed the simple rank order correlation for each pair of ethnoracial categories in respect to both self-employment rate and self-employment income. The Spearman rank correlations are displayed above the diagonal in Table 5.3. This evidence summarizes the general demand effects. The rank order coefficients are significant in seven of the ten paired comparisons with respect to self-employment rate, and in five of ten paired comparisons with respect to self-employment income. The mean rank order correlation of the four minorities with native whites is .34 for self-employment rate and .21 for self-employment income. In general, Asians correlated least successfully with other groups, suggesting that the demand-side determinants of Asian self-employment rates and incomes were, of all the categories, the most independent. The two underdog categories, blacks and Hispanics, correlated less well with one another than with native-born whites in respect to self-employment rates. We repeated this analysis using Pearson correlation coefficients. Displayed below the diagonal in Table 5.3, results are similar to those obtained with rank order correlation.

Table 5.3   Spearman Rank Correlations[1] and Pearson Correlations[2] of the Ranks[3] of the Mean Self-Employment Rates and Mean Self-Employment Income for Five Ethnoracial Categories in 167 Matched Metropolitan Areas

	NB White	FB White	Black	Asian	Hispanic
For Ranks of Self-Employment Rates:					
NB White	1.00	.41**	.52**	.13	.27**
FB White	.38**	1.00	.25**	.27**	.30*
Black	.43**	.28*	1.00	.06	.17*
Asian	.17*	.22**	.04	1.00	.14
Hispanic	.37**	.33**	.19*	.17*	1.00
For Ranks of Mean Self-Employment Income:					
NB White	1.00	.33**	.33**	.14	.03
FB White	.33**	1.00	.20*	.11	.08
Black	.33**	.20**	1.00	.13	.23**
Asian	.14	.11	.13	1.00	.25**
Hispanic	.03	.08	.23**	.25**	1.00

$*p<.05; **p<.01.$
[1] Spearman Rank Correlations are above the diagonal.
[2] Pearson Correlations are below the diagonal.
[3] See discussion in text.

Regression Analysis

The rest of this chapter uses OLS regression to evaluate the joint effects of supply and demand upon self-employment rates. The names and operational definitions of variables appear in Table 5.4. We examine the effects of supply and demand on self-employment rates for 272 metropolitan areas for pooled samples of five ethnoracial categories.[60] We distinguish between variant and invariant supply. *Invariant supply* denotes respondent characteristics that do not vary within each ethnoracial category across different metropolitan areas. Here ethnic identification is the invariant feature. Census takers asked respondents to identify an ethnoracial category to which they belonged and, regardless of locality, the people classified within each category all selected that ethnoracial identity. Naturally, ethnic identification connects with ethnic resources such as social networks, values, attitudes toward self-employment and thrift, religion, cultural institutions and family structure, and what Coleman

Table 5.4 Variables Used in the Analyses[1]

Variables	Name and Operational Description of Variables
Dependent Variable	
CATMSER	Income-Based Definition of Mean Self-Employment Rate[2]
Supply Independent Variables	
Invariant Supply (Intercept Variables):[3]	
FBW	Dummy variable (Foreign-Born Whites = 1; Else = 0)
BLACK	Dummy variable (Blacks = 1; Else = 0)
ASIAN	Dummy variable (Asians = 1; Else = 0)
HISPANIC	Dummy variable (Hispanics = 1; Else = 0)
Variant Supply:[4]	
CCATSIZE	(Category mean labor force size/10,000) − .30552
CCATPCTM	Category mean percentage male − .54
CCATED	Category mean years of education − 12.56
CCATAGE	Category mean years of age − 36.67
Supply Interaction Variables:[5]	
4 Supply Intercept Variables ×	
4 Variant Supply Variables	

Demand Independent Variables[4]
General Demand:
Metropolitan Demand:
Aggregate Consumer Demand:
    CSMSAI1   (Mean Wage & Salary Income/10,000) − 1.22563

Area Industrial Structure:[6]
    CCONIND   Mean % in Construction industry − .07
    CMANUIND   Mean % in Manufacturing industry − .23
    CRETIND   Mean % in Retail industry − .18
    CFININD   Mean % in Finance industry − .06
    CBUSIND   Mean % in Business Services industry − .04
    CPERSIND   Mean % in Personal Services industry − .03
    CPROFIND   Mean % in Professional industry − .21
    CPUBIND   Mean % in Public Administration industry − .06

Regional Economic Differences:[7]
    NYNJPA   Dummy variable (SMSA in NY, NJ, or PA = 1; Else = 0)
    ECENTRAL   Dummy variable (SMSA in East Central = 1; Else = 0)
    WCENTRAL   Dummy variable (SMSA in West Central = 1; Else = 0)
    SATLANTC   Dummy variable (SMSA in South Atlantic = 1; Else = 0)
    TNKYMSAL   Dummy variable (SMSA in TN, KY, MS, or AL = 1; Else = 0)
    CENTRLSO   Dummy variable (SMSA in Central South = 1; Else = 0)
    WESTMTNS   Dummy variable (SMSA in Western Mountains = 1; Else = 0)
    PACIFIC   Dummy variable (SMSA in Pacific = 1; Else = 0)

Demand Interaction Variables:[8]
    17 General Demand ×
        4 Supply Intercept Variables

Table 5.4 (continued)

[1] Based on 1980 PUMS Census data, U.S. Department of Commerce, Bureau of the Census. *Census of the Population and Housing, 1980: Public-Use Microdata Sample A; Technical Documentation* (Washington, D.C.: U.S. Government Printing Office, 1983).

[2] Respondents were defined as self-employed (=1) if they had reported any income gains or losses from self-employment (INCOME2). We calculated the self-employment rate by dividing the number of persons who reported self-employment income (NINCOME2) by the total number of persons in the civilian labor force for each category.

[3] Native-Born White is the omitted reference category. Aiken and West advise that dummy coded variables *not* be centered. Leona S. Aiken and Stephen G. West, *Multiple Regression: Testing and Interpreting Interactions* (Newbury Park, Calif.: Sage, 1991), pp. 116, 130.

[4] These continuous variables were centered, as recommended by Aiken and West, because the range of values for none of these variables encompassed a meaningful zero (where the linear regression line or plane transects the axis of the dependent variable for "raw" or metric coefficients). Centered variables were created by subtracting the mean for the total pooled sample from the "raw" data for each respective variable. These means are indicated in each of the operationalizations described in Table 5.4. Ibid., pp. 37, 119–138, and footnote 3.

[5] There are no native-born white interaction variables, because native-born white is the omitted reference group. The variant supply variables were first centered, but not the dummy variables.

[6] The reference group deleted was the percentage in the following industries: Mining, Transportation, Wholesale, and Entertainment and Recreation Services.

[7] Each region is a dummy variable. New England is the omitted region.

[8] There are no native-born white interaction variables, because native-born white is the omitted reference group. The SMSA industrial structure variables were first centered, but not the dummy variables.

has labelled "social capital."[61] It would be preferable to measure these variables directly. Since census data do not treat these topics, we resort to residual measurement, treating ethnic identity as a dummy variable (0,1) for each of four categories—foreign whites (FBW), blacks, Asians, and Hispanics—and omitting native whites as the reference group.[62] Ethnic identity stands in for direct measures of ethnic resources.

Variant supply means resource-related group characteristics that vary among metropolitan areas. Two types are demographic advantage and human capital. We test two measures of demographic advantage: the absolute size of each category (CCATSIZE) and the percentage of each category's labor force that was male in 1980 (CCATPCTM). Lieberson has proposed that group size and self-employment rate vary inversely because of compositional effects.[63] The absolute size of each category (CCATSIZE) tests the effects of group size upon entrepreneurial performance. Since men were more frequently self-employed than women in 1980, we supposed that in metropolitan areas where ethnoracial categories had a higher proportion of men in the labor force, their self-employment rate might be higher.[64]

Two human capital measures are also tested: a group's mean years of education in the metropolitan area (CCATED) and the mean age of the category's labor force (CCATAGE). Since those more educated are normally more likely to be self-employed, we expect a positive relationship between the mean years of education of a category and the category's self-employment rate. Similarly, since the self-employed are older than wage workers, we supposed that in metropolitan areas where a category's labor force was older, the category's self-employment rate should be higher as well.

We examined the possibility that demographic and human capital characteristics had different consequences for different groups. When variant and invariant supply variables are interacted, the result highlights any unique processes on the supply side. We multiplied each of the four invariant dummy categorical variables by each of the four general variant supply variables described above, creating sixteen interaction variables. The four general variant supply variables we first centered, but the dummy categorical variables we did not center.[65]

Demand Variables

Following Boyd and Razin, Rekers, Dijest, and Van Kempen, we measure local demand for entrepreneurs in terms of local influences upon self-employment rates.[66] The 272 metropolitan areas in our data encompass all the nation's metropolitan regions in 1980. More than 200 million people resided in these metropolitan areas. Each metropolitan area offers a semi-unique demand environment, and together the 272 metropolitan regions span the entire demand spectrum. Seventeen demand variables measure the economic characteristics thought to govern the local economy's need for self-employment. We distinguished three components of demand. The first is the aggregate consumer demand of each metropolitan area. We assigned this component one measure:[67] the metropolitan area's mean wage and salary income (CSMSAI1) in ten thousands. Arguably, this measure promotes self-employment in that higher-income localities permit entrepreneurs to tap a wealthy constituency, thus buoying self-employment rates. Alternatively, if the effect of mean wage and salary income is negative, this measure might indicate that disgruntled workers undertake self-employment to offset low wages.

The second component is industrial structure. We measured industrial structure in terms of the percentage of the locality's labor force that was employed in eight industries.[68] Five of these eight industries contain heavy proportions of self-employed workers (retail trade, business and repair services, personal services, finance, insurance, and real estate, professional, and related services) so metropolitan areas heavy on these industries ought to have heavy demand for entrepreneurs too.

The third component is the regional economy. We used eight dummy variables to measure it. The omitted region is New England, which has the lowest mean self-employment rate of any region. Regional economy permits us to establish the effects of supply upon self-employment rates net of category differences in regional settlement.

The interaction theory predicts that demand and supply jointly determine entrepreneurship. To mirror this assumption, we interact the invariant supply and demand. This procedure creates sixty-eight interaction variables. Guided by Aiken and West, we analyze a succession of regression models, testing first a model of only the four measures of ethnoracial identity. Model 1 tests whether the mean self-employment rates of any of the four ethnoracial groups differ significantly from those of the reference group, native whites. In the second and third models, we test whether the relative effects of supply variables are the same for every ethnoracial group. First we add the variant supply variables to the second model and then, in the third model, add the supply interaction variables. We retained individually significant variables in the model and deleted nonsignificant interactions to create the third, modified model.[69] We then again tested whether the remaining supply interactions added to the variance explained. If none of the specific supply interaction variables were significant, but some or all of the variant supply variables were significant, then we would have shown that the effects of supply are the same for all five groups.

Model 4 adds demand variables to Model 3. Finally, in Model 5, we add the demand/ethnic identity interactions to Model 4 and, as we did for the supply variables, check whether demand effects vary by ethnoracial group. We then modified the model to retain only those interaction variables that were significant and deleted any of the demand interaction variables that were nonsignificant.

In summary, utilizing the PUMS data, we organized a maximum of 109 independent variables into lower-order and higher-order measures of supply and demand. We then regressed the broad income-based measure of mean self-employment rate on these independent variables in successively more complex equations. Only the five most parsimonious versions are presented in Table 5.5. In the first, only measures of invariant supply appear as independent variables. In the second, we combine invariant and variant supply variables. In the third, we combine all three supply variables (invariant, general, and supply interaction). Model 3 affords a measure of what supply explains without demand. We examined whether the interacted effects of supply on self-employment were the same for all five groups or whether the effects of these supply variables for any or all of the four groups differed from native whites.

Next we added demand variables to the model and then, in equation five, we added invariant supply/demand interactions. We checked these last two models to see whether demand effects were general or specific. The models were modified to retain only those interaction variables that significantly explained variation. Table 5.5 presents the five models and their respective adjusted R^2 for the sequential models. Table 5.5 presents only the standardized coefficients for these models.

Empirical Results

In the first model, the constant, b_0, represents the predicted mean of native whites (7.5 percent). The ethnoracial identity variables indicate each group's difference from the native white self-employment rate, b_0. Three of the minority groups have net predicted means which differ significantly from native whites. The predicted mean self-employment rate of foreign whites is 9.6 percent, of blacks 2.5

Table 5.5 Regression of Mean Self-Employment Rates[1] on Supply and Demand in 272 Metropolitan Areas, N = 1,172 (standardized coefficients)

	Models				
	1	2	3[2]	4[2]	5[2]
Supply					
Invariant[3]					
FB White	.217****	.093**	.113**	.087*	.066
Black	−.502****	−.388****	−.317****	−.300****	−.242****
Asian	.014	−.014	.097*	.069	.187****
Hispanic	−.334****	−.165****	−.126***	−.100**	−.085*
Variant[4]					
CCATSIZE[5]		−.035	−.063**	−.035	−.029
CCATPCTM		.051*	.077**	.104****	.123****
CCATED		.229****	.706****	.609****	.476***
CCATAGE		.253****	.283****	.354****	.369****
Supply Interactions[6]					
CCATED × Foreign White			−.185***	−.164**	−.111
CCATED × Black			−.112*	−.097*	−.027
CCATED × Asian			−.381****	−.256**	−.187*
CCATED × Hispanic			−.244***	−.191**	−.114
Demand[4]					
Aggregate Consumer Demand					
CSMSAII[5]				−.054	−.049

Industrial Structure[7]		
% Construction	.000	.009
% Manufacturing	−.069	−.064
% Retail	.096**	.127*
% Finance	.017	.022
% Business Services	−.036	−.034
% Personal Services	−.013	−.008
% Professional	−.037	−.024
% Public Administration	−.071*	−.068*
Regional Economic Difference[8]		
NY, NJ, and PA	−.009	−.011
East Central	.015	.012
West Central	−.019	.049
South Atlantic	.067	.067
TN, KY, MS, and AL	.056	.057
Central South	.105*	.159**
Western Mountains	.043	.100*
Pacific	.187****	.252****
Demand Interactions[6]		
% Retail × Foreign White		−.054
% Retail × Black		−.048
% Retail × Asian		.091**
% Retail × Hispanic		−.046
West Central × Foreign White		−.059*
West Central × Black		−.014
West Central × Asian		−.061*
West Central × Hispanic		−.026

Table 5.5 (*continued*)

			Models		
	1	2	3²	4²	5²
Central South × Foreign White					.004
Central South × Black					−.043
Central South × Asian					−.088**
Central South × Hispanic					−.009
Western Mountains × Foreign White					.006
Western Mountains × Black					−.050
Western Mountains × Asian					−.075**
Western Mountains × Hispanic					−.023
Pacific × Foreign White					.026
Pacific × Black					−.071*
Pacific × Asian					−.107**
Pacific × Hispanic					−.034
Adj R²	.42	.47	.48	.54	.56

****LE .0001 ***LE .001 **LE .01 *LE .05

[1] See footnote 2 in Table 5.4.

[2] Modified version in which interaction variables with one or more significant coefficients were included in the model.

[3] See footnote 3 in Table 5.4.

[4] All continuous independent variables have been centered. See footnote 4, Table 5.4.

[5] In tens of thousands.

[6] All possible supply and demand interactions were tested, but only those variables with significant effects were retained in the model as reported in this table. These interaction variables are interpreted in terms of how each differs from the same effects for native whites (the reference category).

[7] See footnote 6, Table 5.4.

[8] See footnote 7, Table 5.4.

percent, and of Hispanics 4.1 percent. Only Asians are almost identical to native whites at 7.7 percent.[70] The ethnoracial categories explain 42 percent of the variance in the mean self-employment rates of these five groups.

When we add the four variant supply variables,[71] adjusted R^2 increases to 47 percent, a significant improvement.[72] Three of the four variant supply variables significantly increase self-employment rates. A category's percentage male, its mean years of education, and its mean age all increased its self-employment. If the percentage of males in all of the categories increased by 1 percent, their mean self-employment rate would increase by 2.9 percent; if their mean years of education increased by one year, their mean self-employment rate would increase by 0.7 percent; and, finally, if their mean years of age increased by one year, their mean self-employment rate would increase by 0.3 percent. However, an increase in the category's absolute size would have no effect upon the category's self-employment rate.[73]

In the second model, the constant, b_0, represents the predicted mean self-employment rate of native whites (7.3 percent), at the mean value of each of the four general supply variables.[74] Three of the minority groups retain net predicted means which differ significantly from native whites: 8.2 percent for foreign whites, but only 3.5 percent for blacks and 5.6 percent for Hispanics. At 7.1 percent self-employed, Asian rates remain almost identical to those of native whites.

Next, in original Model 3,[75] we first add the sixteen interaction variables to the four ethnoracial dummy variables and the four variant supply variables. This offers a test of the interaction theory, which can explain interactions but not main effects. Adjusted R^2 increases slightly to 48 percent, short of statistical significance. We then deleted twelve nonsignificant supply interaction variables, retaining only the interaction of mean years of education and ethnoracial category.[76]

All four minority groups differed from native whites in the effect of their mean years of education on self-employment rates. For each additional year of mean education, the mean self-employment rates of native whites increased by about 2.1 percent, but only by 0.8 percent for foreign whites, 1 percent for blacks, 0.2 percent for Asians, and 0.7 percent for Hispanics.[77] This result indicates that education produced a weaker self-employment effect for minorities than it did for native whites. Moreover, education has a significant interaction effect upon the minorities, rather than an identical main effect for all five groups.

Even with the education interactions added, the other three variant supply variables remain significant, indicating three main effects of variant supply. We now find a significant inverse relationship between the absolute size of the category's labor force and the mean self-employment rate for the categories, as Lieberson proposed, but since this relationship disappears in models 4 and 5 we do not discuss it here. These data yield no support for Lieberson's compositional hypothesis.[78] As expected, higher percentages of males and older workers increase the self-employment rates of all five ethnoracial categories. In terms of the invariant supply variables, the predicted net mean self-employment rates of all four minority categories become significantly different from native whites, whose predicted mean self-employment rate is 6.9 percent. The predicted mean self-employment rates of foreign whites and Asians is 8 percent, exceeding the rate of native whites by 16 percent. In contrast, the self-employment rates of blacks and Hispanics fall below that of native whites (3.8 percent and 5.6 percent).

Adding Demand Variables

The fourth model adds seventeen measures of demand. We begin by adding demand variables to modified Model 3:[79] one for aggregate consumer demand in each metropolitan area, eight for the industrial structure of the metropolitan area, and eight for the regional economy.[80] These demand variables increased the explained variance in the mean self-employment rates of the pooled sample by 6 percent, bringing adjusted R^2 to 54 percent.

Four demand variables are significant in this model. First, the percentage of a metropolitan area's labor force engaged in retail trade is the only one of eight measures of industrial structure that significantly *increases* categories' mean self-employment rates. A 1 percent increase in a metropolitan area's retail trade increases self-employment rate by almost 17 percent. As expected, metropolitan areas with larger sectors of their labor force in retail trade also have significantly higher self-employment rates for all ethnoracial categories. Second, self-employment declines in metropolitan areas with higher percentages of the labor force employed by government. A 1 percent increase in percentage employed in public administration decreases self-employment by 8.5 percent. Finally, all groups have higher mean self-employment rates in the metropolitan areas of two regions that have higher self-employment rates. That is, working in a metropolitan area in the Central Southern states increases self-employment rates by 1.3 percent relative to New England; working in the Pacific states increases self-employment by 2.2 percent.

Net of demand, three of four minority ethnoracial categories still explain variation in mean self-employment rates. As in the preceding models, the one supply interaction variable, mean years of education, remains significant for all four of the minority groups. Of the variant supply measures, absolute mean size of the categories loses significance, but percentage male and mean age remain significant. A 1 percent increase in percentage male increases the predicted mean self-employment rate of all groups by 6.0 percent. A one year increase in local mean category age raises self-employment of all groups by 0.4 percent.

Our final model is modified Model 5. To create this model, we initially tested the effects of sixty-eight supply/demand interactions that we added to modified Model 4. These sixty-eight increased the adjusted R^2 by 2 percent. We next reduced the number of demand/ invariant supply variables to twenty by deleting nonsignificant variables.[81] Five supply/demand interactions have one or more significant coefficients: percentage working in the retail trade industry plus four of the regional areas. A 1 percent increase in the percentage in retail trade in a metropolitan area produced a 64.5 percent net increase in mean self-employment rate for Asians, but only a 22.4 percent increase for native whites. The other three minorities do not differ significantly from the effects of retail trade upon native whites. The five ethnoracial groups do not respond identically to each of the four economic regions with the highest mean self-employment rates. In each high-entrepreneurship region, one or more of the ethnoracial groups has significantly lower self-employment rates than native whites: foreign whites in the Western Central states; blacks in the Pacific region; and Asians in all four regions. Hispanics, however, do not differ from native whites in any of the regions.

Percentage employed in public administration universally reduces the percentages who might otherwise seek self-employment. A 1 percent increase in public administration employment in a metropolitan region corresponds to an 8.1 percent decrease in self-employment. Mean wage and salary income of metropolitan areas continues to have no impact on the variation in self-employment rates of the five ethnoracial groups; higher wages do not provide the capital for investment or consumption, nor do low wages push groups into self-employment.

The addition of supply/demand interactions reduces the supply interaction of mean years of education, theretofore significant, such that only Asians still differ significantly from native whites. A one-year increase in mean years of education is associated with a 1.4 percent increase in mean self-employment rates for native whites, but only a 0.5 percent increase for Asians. Age and percentage male remain significant. A 1 percent increase in males is associated with a 7.1 percent increase in mean self-employment rates for all of the groups. A one-year increase in category mean years of age produces a 0.4 percent increase in self-employment.

Finally, the addition of demand measures and of supply/demand interactions reduced but did not eliminate the significance of ethno-racial identification. Native white ethnic identification yields a base-line net mean self-employment rate of 6.0 percent. Foreign whites do not significantly differ: their rate is 6.7 percent. Asians have a rate of 8.1 percent, higher than either white rate, but blacks and Hispanics lag behind whites with 3.6 percent and 5.1 percent.

Discussion

Reviewing the regression results, especially Model 5, one observes interactions and main effects. The main effects are bigger than the interaction effects, which explain only small additional variation. These results resemble those reported elsewhere.[82] On the face of it, these results do not support the interaction theory, which proposes that supply and demand *interact* to generate entrepreneurship. If that theory were valid, the interaction terms ought to explain every-thing and the main effects nothing.

However, when reinterpreted in the light of our theoretical discussion above, these results are compatible with the interaction theory. After all, dominant main effects need not mean that supply/demand interactions did not occur. Indeed, that paradoxical conclusion is hard to accept because supply's unmediated effect upon entrepreneurship is like the sound of one hand clapping. Rather, the dominance of main effects just as plausibly indicates that real interactions are *statistically invisible*. That surprising possibility hinges on our new distinction between general and specific resources. On the supply side, general resources translate into entrepreneurial versatility, the ability to re-spond to a wide variety of demands, and in the limiting case to any and all demands. Thus construed, the dominant main effects of in-variant and variant supply betoken versatility that straddles demand environments. For example, the positive main effects of age and education imply that better-educated and more experienced groups produced more entrepreneurs *everywhere* because education assists entrepreneurship *everywhere*.

On the demand side, similar explanations pertain to main effects apparently unmediated by interaction with supply. Positive main effects of demand betoken economic conditions that generate entrepreneurship everywhere because all ethnoracial groups *have the resources* to respond.[83] Precisely because all the groups can respond, the interaction of supply and demand becomes statistically invisible. Thus, the main effect of percentage retail suggests that this structural condition is one to which all ethnoracial groups responded with expanded entrepreneurship because all groups possessed the necessary resources. The census data cannot identify these general resources, but they are probably baseline endowments of ethnic and class resources so basic that all groups possess them. Literacy is a baseline resource like this. Tasks that require only the ability to read will not distinguish among literate groups, but that failure will not prove that groups do not require literacy to accomplish such tasks.

Summary of Findings

Although popular and intuitively satisfactory, the interaction theory of entrepreneurship does not rest on a body of evidence broad enough to raise the issues our research design has posed. As one result, the interaction theory has not had to confront the problem of general and specific resources. The interaction theory claims that the interaction of supply and demand links specific competencies and specific demands. That relationship does exist, but our theoretical analysis shows that general demand effects and general supply effects exist too, especially the latter. General demand and general supply effects are inexplicable so long as the interaction theory defines the interaction of supply and demand narrowly as the linkage between specific competencies and specific industrial demands.

Statistically interpreted, this theoretical dilemma turns into the problem of how to deal with main effects of demand and supply. Strictly speaking, the interaction theory predicts that no main effects of demand or supply can occur. If main effects of supply and demand were nil, interactions would explain everything, thus completely vindicating the interaction theory. Conversely, if we find only main effects and no interactions, then the interaction theory would be flatly wrong. Our data fall between these extremes. However, in our data the main effects are more powerful than the interaction effects. Since these main effects overpower interactions, a major part of our explanation does not display the requisite interaction, challenging the interaction theory. This situation tempts us to ask whether supply or demand "explains more" of the variation in self-employment. But according to the interaction theory, supply and demand must each explain half the variation, so such an imbalance is theoretically uninterpretable. If the entrepreneur population arises from interaction of supply and demand, supply cannot explain more than demand, nor vice-versa.

The interaction theory can be salvaged if we add a distinction between specific and general resources to the existing distinction between ethnic and class resources.[84] General and specific resources may be class resources, ethnic resources, or both. The examples that best illustrate the interaction theory stress specific resources (for example, the ability to cook Chinese food), but many overlooked resources are general. Versatile resources enable groups to thrive everywhere, entering whatever industries offer the best local opportunity. As a result, the interaction of resources and environment remains statistically invisible. Similarly, some demand environments require such a low level of resources that all ethnoracial groups always possess them. When this situation obtains, general demand effects appear in the regression equations, leaving the puzzling impression that this time, at least, demand did not interact with supply. In actuality, however, the requisite interaction did occur but was statistically invisible because all groups possessed the resources necessary to hook this demand.

This distinction between general and specific resources is a new one. In our data education and work experience, both class resources, are general resources too. This result is surprising since lawyers cannot be physicians or vice versa, yet both are highly educated. However, since our measures are aggregated, these results need not mean that education's effects are invariably general. Similarly, the results need not imply that work experience in a specific trade prepares one for entrepreneurship in general rather than entrepreneurship in the trade in which one obtained one's experience. Rather, one concludes that a group's high level of education and of work experience are generalized resources which confer upon the group a versatile competence in entrepreneurship. Individual-level research will be necessary to ascertain the extent to which individual education and experience fit a person for entrepreneurship in a narrow range of trades rather than generally.

The main effects of ethnic identity are particularly interesting. They indicate a generalized resource of the whole group independent of age, gender composition, or education. Although based on residual measurement, the main effects of ethnic identity support the claims so often encountered in the literature that ethnoracial groups have different endowments of social capital, network multiplexity, action orientations, and the like. The principal argument against this position has held that apparent intergroup differences in entrepreneurship are spurious products of unequal human capital endowment. Portes and Zhou already showed that human capital did not explain away the superior entrepreneurship of four national origin groups (Chinese, Japanese, Koreans, Cubans), and our analysis extends their demonstration for much larger ethnoracial categories among 200 million Americans.[85] True, four of these broad categories are purely nominative. Asians, Hispanics, whites, and foreign-born whites are agglomerations of internally heterogeneous ethnic stocks. If the internal proportions of each category were changed (more high-entrepreneurship and fewer low-entrepreneurship subgroups, or vice-versa) the aggregate's performance would change too. Therefore, the concrete meaning of the ethnic identity coefficient is fuzzy even if its general meaning is clear.

But the same objection does not apply to blacks. Because the number of foreign-born blacks was so modest in 1980, our intermetropolitan data really measure the entrepreneurship of black Americans, a homogeneous and historic ethnic group. Blacks are not a nominal category like the others. The negative main effect of black ethnic identity upon entrepreneurship implies a generalized shortfall of entrepreneurial resources in any and all economic environments. This negative effect is reduced by controls for human capital and percentage male but it is not eliminated. Net of human capital, age, and percentage male, black entrepreneurship is still lower than it should be relative to native whites. That is, the ethnic resources of blacks do not support entrepreneurship. All blacks have is a slender basis of class resources which is not backed up by ethnic resources.

Conclusion

Entrepreneurship is an obvious and significant juncture at which society affects economic development and growth. A society's or a group's entrepreneurship is suboptimal when economies do not fully exploit all the opportunities an environment affords. In such cases, opportunities are missed altogether, delayed, or lost to external competitors.

If markets generated the entrepreneurs they needed by price signals, then shortages of entrepreneurs would rarely or never occur, and real economic growth would rarely or never fall short of the potential immanent in demand. Such a healthy situation could plausibly exist if the supply of entrepreneurs depended only upon the prior supply of investment capital. In that case, markets would unerringly allocate society's limited human and financial capital to entrepreneurship in exactly the right proportion to maximize growth.

However, that orthodoxy has collapsed, with all its comforting intellectual consistency, leaving a theoretical puzzle. We now know that human and financial capital do not guarantee optimal entrepreneurship. This is the point at which the sociology of immigration makes a theoretical as well as practical contribution to our understanding of economic development. Were it not for immigration, societies would consist of labor forces whose members were culturally homogeneous. Homogeneity would inhibit attention to internal characteristics of groups that support entrepreneurship. However, immigration eventuates in a pluralistic society whose labor force consists of initially diverse groups still unequally assimilated and acculturated. In economic terms, cultural diversity means a mosaic of groups that differ in respect to socially oriented action patterns, embeddedness, social networks, social capital, ethnic resources, and so forth (Portes, this volume). A now-quite-impressive array of case studies has documented the contributions that these ethnocultural differences make to entrepreneurship. Studies find that ethnic resources (families, rotating credit associations, enforceable trust, multiplex social networks, ideologies, religion, etc.) encourage and support the founding of new business firms especially by people short of money and education.

Additionally, quantitative analyses of census data, like ours, now find that money and human capital do not explain away intergroup differences in entrepreneurial responsiveness. Therefore one turns to the internal characteristics of groups for an explanation of persistent intergroup differences in entrepreneurial responsiveness. Some of these differences are cultural; others are not. Similarly, some intergroup differences arise because ethnic leadership has selected one policy priority rather than another. Ever since the Niagara Conference of 1909, at which the followers of W. E. B. DuBois routed the followers of Booker T. Washington, African American leadership in the mainstream has stressed education and job opportunity over entrepreneurship. That was a policy choice, not a cultural heritage.

Intergroup differences in entrepreneurship that arise from policy choices are more amenable to change than differences that arise from basic cultural features of the groups. Broadly speaking, enduring features of group structure that affect entrepreneurship have cultural origins. That said, we do not wish to reify cultural differences. Culture implies change-resistance, not changelessness. We agree with Max Weber's expectation that markets encourage cultural changes that improve the fit between market and culture. In the historic short-run, however, markets operate in social contexts that often resist them. Karl Polanyi called this resistance the embeddedness of the economy in society. One form of resistance is total noncompliance of society to market. Noncompliance arises where societies or social groups cannot or will not produce what the market wants. For example, when adults conscientiously refuse to work for wages, markets experience total noncompliance. Another resistance is a slow-down. Here, society's resistance reduces the speed at which markets produce economic change because too-rapid economic change threatens to smash the cultural underpinnings that hold society together.

Taking society seriously means accepting the reality of society, the priority of society to market, and acting accordingly. The reality of society means the reality of group structures, norms, values, institutions, and the like. These exist. Liked closed doors, one ignores them at one's peril. The priority of society to market means the dependence of every economy upon a functioning society which constrains it but also makes it possible. Societies cannot change as fast as markets, and societies recurrently slow down the rate of economic change that markets would otherwise impose.

Getting back to entrepreneurship, we conclude that markets will not make entrepreneurs out of disadvantaged Americans who lack the resources entrepreneurship requires. Racketeers and petty thieves are the only kinds of entrepreneurs poor and disadvantaged people have the resources to become. True, poverty and disadvantage create a motive for entrepreneurship, but these conditions do not provide the necessary resources. Ambition without resources turns into frustration, and frustration often into aggression. Social policies that endow groups with resources also endow them with the capacity to respond by entrepreneurship to economic opportunities. Enhanced economic growth then pays back the earlier investment in resources. Our data show that education is such a resource. Strengthening education will not eliminate the antientrepreneurial baggage that the disadvantaged carry into the modern era from the past. However, strengthened education provides a compensatory resource that reduces the negative impact of historical disadvantage, bringing a disadvantaged group's cultural repertoire slowly into closer conformity with the needs of a market economy.

Notes

1. Richard Swedberg, "Economic Sociology: Past and Present," *Contemporary Sociology* 35 (1987):29.

2. Peter Kilby, "Hunting the Heffalump," in P. Kilby, ed., *Entrepreneurship and Economic Development* (New York: Free Press, 1971), pp. 1–40.

3. Neil J. Smelser, *The Sociology of Economic Life*, 2nd ed. (Englewood Cliffs, N.J.: Prentice-Hall, 1976), p. 126. This point would need no restatement but for disciplinary traditions that equip researchers with conceptual tools that better fit one side or the other. Economists, geographers, human ecologists, and Marxists have emphasized demand-side explanations of entrepreneurship. Demand-derived explanations fit their disciplinary paradigms. On the other hand, anthropologists, psychologists, and sociologists have stressed supply-side explanations, which better fit their paradigms. See James Wilken, *Entrepreneurship: A Comparative and Historical Study* (Norwood, N.J.: Ablex, 1979), p. 7; Alex P. Alexander, "The Supply of Industrial Entrepreneurship," *Explorations in Entrepreneurial History* 4 (1967):136–149; and Ivan Light and Stavros Karageorgis, "The Ethnic Economy," in N. Smelser and R. Swedberg, eds., *Handbook of Economic Sociology* (New York: Russell Sage Foundation, 1994), pp. 646–671.

4. Granovetter mentions the reluctance of sociologists and economists to utilize one another's concepts. The reluctance probably applies particularly well to this case since, as Bearse has observed, the concept of market "demand for entrepreneurs" is cloudy because "the conventional concept of market demand may not apply to more than a minor part of the phenomenon." See Mark Granovetter, "Toward a Sociological Theory of Income Differences," in Ivar Berg, ed., *Sociological Perspectives on Labor Markets* (New York: Academic Press, 1981), p. 32; Peter J. Bearse, "A Study of Entrepreneurship by Region and SMSA Size," *Frontiers of Entrepreneurship Research* (Wellesley, Mass.: Babson College, 1981).

5. Ivar Berg, "Introduction," in I. Berg, ed., *Sociological Perspectives on Labor Markets* (New York: Academic Press, 1981), p. 3–6; Paul DiMaggio, "Cultural Aspects of Economic Action and Organization," in R. Friedland and A. F. Robertson, eds., *Beyond the Marketplace* (New York: Aldine de Gruyter, 1990), pp. 123–128.

6. Arthur Stinchcombe, *Economic Sociology* (New York: Academic Press, 1983). Alberto Martinelli and Neil J. Smelser, eds., *Economy and Society* (Newbury Park, Calif.: Sage, 1990).

7. Talcott Parsons and Neil J. Smelser, *Economy and Society* (Glencoe, Ill.: Free Press, 1956), pp. 9–10.

8. Consumers do not buy entrepreneurs; they buy their products and services. Therefore, entrepreneurs are a producer good. For this reason, many economists treat entrepreneurs as a fourth factor of production along with land, labor, and capital. Alternatively, Light and Bonacich treat entrepreneurship as a special form of labor service, subsumable under the general category of labor as a factor of production. Either

way, entrepreneurs are a factor of production. Ivan Light and Edna Bonacich, *Immigrant Entrepreneurs: Koreans in Los Angeles, 1965–1982* (Berkeley: University of California Press, 1988), Pt. 4.

9. Parsons and Smelser, *Economy and Society*, p. 9.

10. Milton Friedman, *Price Theory* (Chicago: Aldine de Gruyter, 1976), p. 13; Ivan Light, "The Ethnic Vice District," *American Sociological Review* 43 (1977):475.

11. David L. Featherman and Robert M. Hauser, *Opportunity and Change* (New York: Academic Press, 1978).

12. Max Weber, "The Economic Relationships of Organized Groups," in *Economy and Society*, Vol. 1 (New York: Bedminster, 1968), Chap. 2.

13. Opportunity is the right concept when one is discussing opportunities for minorities to achieve social equality, upward mobility, or prestige. These are frequent and valid uses of the concept because the existence of opportunities depends upon social conditions broader than the capacity to obtain custom.

14. Roger Waldinger, Howard Aldrich, and Robin Ward, "Opportunities, Group Characteristics, and Strategies," in R. Waldinger, H. Aldrich, and R. Ward, eds., *Ethnic Entrepreneurs: Immigrant and Ethnic Business in Western Industrial Societies* (Newbury Park, Calif.: Sage, 1990), p. 21.

15. Waldinger, Aldrich, and Ward, "Opportunities," p. 25.

16. Roger Waldinger, *Through the Eye of the Needle: Immigrants and Enterprise in New York's Garment Trades* (New York: New York University Press, 1986), p. 278.

17. Roger Waldinger, "Immigrant Enterprise in the New York Garment Industry," *Social Problems* 32 (1984):60–71; Waldinger, Aldrich, and Ward, "Opportunities."

18. L. J. White, "The Determinants of the Relative Importance of Small Business," *The Review of Economics and Statistics* 64 (1982):42–49; Peter J. Bearse, "The Ecology of Enterprise" (paper prepared for the Northeast Meetings of the Regional Science Association, Binghamton, N.Y., May 29, 1987).

19. "The demand for small business activities and the supply of existing or potential business owners interact to generate immigrant entrepreneurship." Roger Waldinger, Robin Ward, and Howard Aldrich, "Trend Report: Ethnic Business and Occupational Mobility in Advanced Societies," *Sociology* 19 (1985):591. See also Charles C. Ragin, *The Comparative Method* (Berkeley and Los Angeles: University of California Press, 1987), pp. 36–42.

20. See for example, Swinton and Handy's examination of black entrepreneurship in 155 metropolitan areas. This research disclosed "conditions

in the local economy" that were "major determinants of the overall level of demand" for black business. This is a worthy goal. The study did not and was not intended to examine variation in the ability of blacks to take advantage of market demand. David H. Swinton and John Handy, *The Determinants of the Growth of Black Owned Businesses: A Preliminary Analysis* (Atlanta: Southern Center for Studies in Public Policy of Clark College, 1983). Prepared under contract with U.S. Department of Commerce, Minority Business Development Agency.

21.   Orlando Patterson, "Context and Choice in Ethnic Allegiance: A Theoretical Framework and a Caribbean Case Study," in N. Glazer and D. P. Moynihan, eds., *Ethnicity* (Cambridge: Harvard University Press, 1975), p. 347.

22.   Evelyn Kallen and Merrijoy Kelner, *Ethnicity, Opportunity and Successful Entrepreneurship in Canada* (Toronto: Institute for Behavioral Research of York University, 1983); Kwang Chung Kim, Won Moo Hurh, and Marilyn Fernandez, "Intra-Group Differences in Business Participation: A Comparative Analysis of Three Asian Immigrant Groups," *International Migration Review* 23 (1989):73–95.

23.   Ivan Light, *Ethnic Enterprise in America* (Berkeley and Los Angeles: University of California Press, 1972).

24.   Waldinger, Ward, and Aldrich, "Trend Report," p. 589.

25.   Waldinger, Aldrich, and Ward, "Opportunities," p. 21.

26.   See Roger Waldinger, Mirjana Morokvasic, and Annie Phizacklea, "Business on the Ragged Edge: Immigrant and Minority Business in the Garment Industries in Paris, London, and New York," in Waldinger, Aldrich, and Ward, eds., *Ethnic Entrepreneurs*, Chap. 6; and James Curran and Roger Burrows, "The Social Analysis of Small Business: Some Emerging Themes," in R. Goffee and R. Scase, eds., *Entrepreneurship in Europe* (London: Croom Helm, 1987), Chap. 10.

27.   "We emphasize the fit between immigrant firms and the environments in which they function, including not only economic and social conditions but also the unique historical conditions encountered at the time of immigration." Waldinger, Aldrich, and Ward, "Opportunities," p. 32.

28.   Wilbur Zelinsky, "The Roving Palate: North America's Ethnic Restaurant Cuisines," *Geoforum* 16 (1985):62; Gaye Tuchman and Harry Levine, "New York Jews and Chinese Food," *Journal of Contemporary Ethnography* 22 (1993):396–397.

29.   Light and Karageorgis, "The Ethnic Economy."

30.   Ivan Light, "Immigrant and Ethnic Enterprise in North America," *Ethnic and Racial Studies* 7 (1984):195–216.

31.   Knowing how to read and interpret a balance sheet is such a skill.

32. Michael Useem, "Corporations and the Corporate Elite," *Annual Review of Sociology* 6 (1980):41–77; Davita S. Glasberg and Michael Schwartz, "Ownership and Control of Corporations," *Annual Review of Sociology* 9 (1983):314–317.

33. Kim, Hurh, and Fernandez properly observe that to explain intergroup differences in self-employment in terms of resources, one must specify the resources alleged to cause high self-employment. Yoon operationalized ethnic resources as follows: An entrepreneur received loans from family and/or friends; participated in a rotating credit association; was in partnership with a co-ethnic; participated in a business network of family and kin; had co-ethnic suppliers; worked long hours of unpaid labor. Yoon defined class resources with the following variables: An entrepreneur used personal savings to finance his or her own business; brought money with her or him from homeland; obtained bank or government loans for his or her business. Kim, Hurh, and Fernandez, "Intra-Group Differences," p. 91. See also In-Jin Yoon, "The Changing Significance of Ethnic and Class Resources in Immigrant Business: The Case of Korean Immigrant Businesses in Chicago," *International Migration Review* 25 (1991):303–331; and Light and Karageorgis, "The Ethnic Economy."

34. Ewa Morawska, "Small Town, Slow Pace: Transformations of the Religious Life in the Jewish Community of Johnstown, Pennsylvania (1920–1940)," *Comparative Social Research* 13 (1991):136–137. Similarly, of Taiwanese wage earners, Stites writes that they view their jobs as "a temporary part in a career and a means to eventual entrepreneurship." Richard W. Stites, "Industrial Work as an Entrepreneurial Strategy," *Modern China* 11 (1985):242.

35. Abner Cohen, *Custom and Politics in Urban Africa* (Berkeley and Los Angeles: University of California Press, 1969), pp. 201–214; Abner Cohen, *Two Dimensional Man* (Berkeley, Calif.: University of California Press, 1974), pp. xvi–xvii.

36. Walter Zenner, *Minorities in the Middle* (Albany: State University of New York Press, 1991), pp. 17–25.

37. Light, *Ethnic Enterprise*, Chaps. 3, 4, and 6.

38. Light and Bonacich, *Immigrant Entrepreneurs*.

39. Waldinger, *Through the Eye of the Needle*, p. 10 and Chaps. 1, 4.

40. Ibid., p. 31.

41. Given his design, Waldinger could not explain why, on the supply side, immigrant groups other than Dominicans and Chinese were not drawn into the garment industry, nor, on the demand side, whether other New York City industries did not offer more or equally favorable demand opportunities to Dominicans and Chinese.

42. Thomas R. Bailey, *Immigrant and Native Workers* (Boulder and London: Westview Press, 1987), pp. 22, 53–55.

43. See Paul Ong, "An Ethnic Trade: Chinese Laundries in Early California," *Journal of Ethnic Studies* 8 (1981):95–113; Bearse, "The Ecology of Enterprise"; Eran Razin, "Entrepreneurship among Foreign Immigrants in the Los Angeles and San Francisco Metropolitan Area," *Urban Geography* 9 (1988):283–301; Paul D. Reynolds, "New Firms and Economic Change: Recent Findings and Policy Implications" (paper presented at the Annual Meeting of the American Sociological Association, San Francisco Hilton Hotel, August 13, 1989); Eran Razin, "Immigrant Entrepreneurs in Israel, Canada, and California," in Ivan Light and Parminder Bhachu, eds., *Immigration and Entrepreneurship* (New Brunswick, N.J.: Transaction, 1993).

44. Howard Aldrich, Trevor P. Jones, and David McEvoy, "Ethnic Advantage and Minority Business Development," in R. Ward and R. Jenkins, eds., *Ethnic Communities in Business* (New York: Cambridge University Press, 1984), Chap. 11.

45. Ibid., p. 205.

46. Of course, one might dispute the sweeping conclusion on other grounds. The researchers did not examine demographic or class resources on the supply side, nor did they look into intermetropolitan continuities of rank, a condition discussed in this chapter. These supply issues might have required a modification of their lopsided conclusion that only demand-side influences affected entrepreneurship in the British cities. However, within the realistic limits of their research, their design permitted no conclusion other than the one these researchers drew.

47. Aldrich, Jones, and McEvoy, "Ethnic Advantage."

48. Specific demand arises in at least six ways: public discrimination, law, self-exclusion, unique resources, ethnic channelling, and economic closure. Of these, old-fashioned ethnoracial discrimination is the simplest. If prejudiced purchasers discriminate, they demand suppliers of a particular ethnoracial type, not just qualified suppliers. This case is not just hypothetical. Borjas and Bronars (pp. 581, 592) argue precisely that consumer discrimination against them reduces the self-employment of blacks. Racial discrimination qualifies a purchaser's job description, thus limiting the entrepreneurial chances of qualified black applicants. This is a discriminatory intent whose effect is to enhance or depress the entrepreneurial performance of nonwhite entrepreneurs relative to white ones. Since the effect of discriminatory demand is unequal, the demand effect is specific, not general. George J. Borjas and Stephen G. Bronars, "Consumer Discrimination and Self-Employment," *Journal of Political Economy* 97 (1989):581–605.

49. Lawrence R. Klein, *The Economics of Supply and Demand* (Baltimore: Johns Hopkins University Press, 1983), p. 2.

50. Swinton and Handy, *The Determinants*, pp. 32–33.

51. If the number of janitorial service firms triples among the Koreans, and nothing else changes in the local economy, then the Koreans will have increased their share of the total entrepreneur population.

52. In fact, we use percentage instead; that is, the number of self-employed per 100 persons in the civilian labor force in that category.

53. Antonio Furino and Timothy Bates, *New Perspectives on Minority Business Development: A Study of Minority Business Potential Using the MBDA Financial Research Data Base* (Washington, D.C.: Development through Applied Science for U.S. Department of Commerce, Minority Business Development Agency, 1983), p. 81.

54. For the same reason, we can only study the rank of the five major ethnoracial categories. If we expanded the rank study to all thirteen national-origin groups in our dataset, we would find only a handful of metropolitan areas that contained all thirteen groups. In that case, our N would be too small to permit statistical evaluation of the results.

55. We compared the 167 metropolitan areas with the larger list of 272 from which they were culled in order to ascertain whether the smaller list showed appreciably different self-employment rates than the larger. Mean self-employment rates for each group were virtually identical on the large list of 272 metropolitan areas and the culled list of 167. This result suggests that the smaller list of 167 metropolitan areas was virtually identical to the larger list in respect to the demand environment of entrepreneurship.

56. Native-born whites were present above the threshold level in all 272 metropolitan areas.

57. Intermetropolitan ranks for each category, i.e., 1 = the highest mean self-employment rate or mean self-employment income to 167 = the lowest (among the metropolitan areas in which native whites, foreign whites, blacks, Asians, and Hispanics are present).

58. Robert W. Fairlie and Bruce D. Meyer, "The Ethnic and Racial Character of Self-Employment" (paper presented at the Department of Economics, University of California, Los Angeles, March 19, 1993).

59. Hubert M. Blalock, *Social Statistics* (New York: McGraw Hill, 1960), pp. 317–319.

60. For the maximum number of metropolitan areas that have threshold numbers of each category, i.e., NBW = 272 areas, FBW = 245, Blacks = 245, Asians = 180, and Hispanics = 230, for a total of 1,172 cases.

61. James S. Coleman, "Social Capital in the Creation of Human Capital," *The American Journal of Sociology* 94 (1988):S103.

62. See Leona S. Aiken and Stephen G. West, *Multiple Regression: Testing and Interpreting Interactions* (Newbury Park, Calif.: Sage, 1991), pp. 116–117, 129–130.

63. Stanley Lieberson, *A Piece of the Pie: Blacks and White Immigrants Since 1880* (Berkeley: University of California Press, 1980), pp. 380–382.

64. Victor R. Fuchs, "Self-Employment and Labor Force Participation of Older Males," *The Journal of Human Resources* 17 (1982):339–357.

65. All of the general supply, as well as the general demand variables, are continuous measurements. However, the ranges of these variables do not include a substantively meaningful zero. For example, no ethnoracial group has a mean years of education that is zero. Instead, the range is from 6.3 to 18.5, with a mean of 12.6 years. Aiken and West recommend that such continuous variables be "centered"; that is, that the mean for the total (in this case, pooled) sample be subtracted from each raw data score, so that the y axis is moved from zero (which would be meaningless) to the mean for each of the centered independent variables. Table 5.4 indicates the pooled sample mean that was subtracted from each respective variable in order to create the centered variables. A prefix "C" has been added to the name of each variable to indicate that it has been centered. Aiken and West, *Multiple Regression*, pp. 37, 116, 119–138, Chap. 7 n. 3.

66. Razin, "Entrepreneurship among Foreign Immigrants"; Razin, "Immigrant Entrepreneurs"; A. M. Rekers, M. J. Dijest, and R. Van Kempen, "The Influence of Urban Contexts on Ethnic Enterprises in the Netherlands" (paper presented at the Annual Meeting of the Association of American Geographers, Toronto, Canada, April 19–22, 1990); Robert L. Boyd, "Black Entrepreneurship in 52 Metropolitan Areas," *Sociology and Social Research* 75, no. 3 (1991):158–163.

67. A second measure, the absolute size of the metropolitan area's labor force, was considered but was deleted from the model, because it was highly correlated with the supply variable CCATSIZE, the absolute size of each category in a metropolitan area. For the pooled sample, the r = .56, but it was as high as .98 for native whites.

68. The reference category deleted from the model was composed of four industries: Mining, Transportation, Wholesale, and Entertainment and Recreation Services.

69. Aiken and West, *Multiple Regression*, Chaps. 7, 6.

70. Predicted mean self-employment rates were calculated for each of the four minority racial-ethnic groups. For example, the intercept, which represents the self-employment rate of native whites, was 7.5 percent. To obtain the rate for foreign whites, we add their metric coefficient to the intercept, i.e., 7.5 + 1.1 = 9.6 percent.

71. Model 2, the regression of mean self-employment rates on four invariant supply category dummy variables and four general supply continuous variables, is:

$$Y = \text{eq. 1} + b_5\text{CCATSIZE} + b_6\text{CCATPCTM} + b_7\text{CCATED} + b_8\text{CCATAGE} + b_0 \qquad \text{(Eq. 2)}$$

72. We used Aiken and West's equation 6.5 to test the significance of R^2 change (*Multiple Regression*, pp. 107):

$$F = \frac{(R^2_{in} - R^2_{out}) \, / \, m}{(1 - R^2_{in}) \, / \, (n - k - 1)}; \, df = m, \, (n - k - 1)$$

73. Changes in the dependent variables predicted by independent variables, presented here in the text in metric coefficients, are not reported in Table 5.5.

74. See Aiken and West for the advantages of interpreting the constant and dummy variables, when the continuous variables have been centered. Aiken and West, *Multiple Regression*, pp. 119–123, 138 n. 3.

75. Original Model 3, the regression of mean self-employment rate on four invariant supply category dummy variables, four general supply continuous variables, and sixteen specific variant supply interaction variables is:

Y = eq 2. + b_9(FBW × CCATSIZE) + b_{10}(FBW × CCATPCTM)
+ b_{11}(FBW × CCATED) + b_{12}(FBW × CCATAGE)
+ b_{13}(Black × CCATSIZE) + b_{14}(Black × CCATPCTM)
+ b_{15}(Black × CCATED) + b_{16}(Black × CCATAGE)
+ b_{17}(Asian × CCATSIZE) + b_{18}(Asian × CCATPCTM)
+ b_{19}(Asian × CCATED) + b_{20}(Asian × CCATAGE)
+ b_{21}(Hispanic × CCATSIZE)
+ b_{22}(Hispanic × CCATPCTM)
+ b_{23}(Hispanic × CCATED)
+ b_{24}(Hispanic × CCATAGE) + b_0 (Original eq. 3)

76. Modified Model 3, the regression of mean self-employment rate on four invariant supply category dummy variables, four general supply continuous variables, and four specific variant supply interaction variables is:

Y = eq. 2 + b_{11}(FBW × CCATED) + b_{15}(Black × CCATED)
+ b_{19}(Asian × CCATED) + b_{23}(Hispanic × CCATED)
+ b_0 (Modified eq. 3)

The adjusted R^2 remained at .48 and these four supply interaction variables added a significant increment of explained variance (p. ≤ .01).

77. Metric coefficients calculated from CCATED minus each interaction education variable (for example, for foreign whites: .021 − .013 = .008).

78. Lieberson, *A Piece of the Pie*, p. 366.

79. We also tested the addition of the demand variables to the original Model 3, but the modified Model 3 was still valid, that is, only the same supply interaction variables for education were significant.

80. Original Model 4, the regression of mean self-employment rate on four invariant supply category dummy variables, four general supply continuous variables, sixteen specific variant supply interaction variables, and seventeen general demand variables is:

Y = Modified eq 3. + b_{25}(CSMSAI1) + b_{26}(CCONIND)
   + b_{27}(CMANUIND) + b_{28}(CRETIND) + b_{29}(CFININD)
   + b_{30}(CBUSRIND) + b_{31}(CPERSIND) + b_{32}(CPROFIND)
   + b_{33}(CPUBIND) + b_{34}(NYNJPA) + b_{35}(ECENTRAL)
   + b_{36}(WCENTRAL) + b_{37}(SATLANTC) + b_{38}(TNKYMSAL)
   + b_{39}(CENTRLSO) + b_{40}(WESTMTNS) + b_{41}(PACIFIC) + b_0
                                                    (Original eq. 4)

81. Modified Model 5, the regression of mean self-employment rate on four invariant supply category dummy variables, four general supply continuous variables, four specific variant supply interaction variables, seventeen general demand variables, and twenty specific demand interaction variables is:

Y = Modified eq. 4 + b_{45}(FBW × CRETIND) + b_{53}(FBW × WCENTRAL)
   + b_{56}(FBW × CENTRLSO) + b_{57}(FBW × WESTMTNS)
   + b_{58}(FBW × PACIFIC) + b_{62}(Black × CRETIND)
   + b_{70}(Black × WCENTRAL) + b_{73}(Black × CENTRLSO)
   + b_{74}(Black × WESTMTNS) + b_{75}(Black × PACIFIC)
   + b_{79}(Asian × CRETIND) + b_{87}(Asian × WCENTRAL)
   + b_{90}(Asian × CENTRLSO) + b_{91}(Asian × WESTMTNS)
   + b_{92}(Asian × PACIFIC) + b_{96}(Hispanic × CRETIND)
   + b_{104}(Hispanic × WCENTRAL) + b_{107}(Hispanic × CENTRLSO)
   + b_{108}(Hispanic × WESTMTNS) + b_{109}(Hispanic × PACIFIC)
   + b_0 (Modified eq. 5)

These added twenty demand interaction variables together were significant at the .05 level.

82. Fairlie and Meyer, "The Ethnic and Racial Character."

83. All groups may also react negatively, e.g., avoiding self-employment when opportunities for government employment exist.

84. Light, "Immigrant and Ethnic Enterprise."

85. Alejandro Portes and Min Zhou, "Divergent Destinies: Immigration, Poverty and Entrepreneurship in the United States" (prepared for the Joint Center for Political and Economic Studies, Washington, D.C., 1992).

6

Social and Cultural Capital in the Urban Ghetto: Implications for the Economic Sociology of Immigration

M. Patricia Fernández Kelly

THE PURPOSE of this chapter is to examine the relationship between social and cultural capital. To achieve that end, I focus on early motherhood among impoverished ghetto women. The subject is of interest given differing perspectives that assign causal priority either to anomalous cultural norms and values or to situational factors. I resort to four sets of ideas derived from the field of economic sociology: (a) the effect of membership in social networks characterized by low levels of what Jeremy Boissevain calls *multiplexity*, that is, internal differentiation in terms of role, status, and field of activity; (b) the ensuing truncation of social networks that shape the experience of the poor in ways that differ substantially from how they affect more affluent groups; (c) the distinction between social capital and the quality of resources that may be tapped through relationships of mutuality; and (d) the formation of cultural capital as a repertory of symbols and meanings interactively created and dependent on the conditions that generate social capital.

Although the protagonists of my account are African Americans living in West Baltimore, the details of their experience have implications for the understanding of other populations threatened by poverty and insularity, including some recent immigrants and their children. Several authors have emphasized the immigrant antecedents of American blacks, their commonalities in profile and expectations with other immigrant groups as well as the divergences that eventuated in arrested social, economic, and political mobility. There is an ongoing relationship between ethnicity and migration. Today's ethnic minorities are the immigrants of yesterday and vice versa. With signal exceptions, current research on African Americans focuses not primarily on their immigrant past but on the distressing behavioral complex subsumed under the rubric of the *urban underclass*. Yet one way to envision the experience of impoverished African Americans is as an outcome of migration under particular circumstances.

In *The Truly Disadvantaged: The Inner City, The Underclass, and Public Policy*, William Julius Wilson provides an analysis of the structural and cultural factors explaining the peculiarities of contemporary ghetto experience.[1] This analysis, which has proven to have a lasting impact on research and debate, gives priority to changes in the domestic economy that led to a constriction of the manufacturing sector, the ensuing eviction of vulnerable sectors of the black working class from formal employment, and their concentration in inner-city areas. While acknowledging the structural causes of ghetto poverty, Wilson also gives attention to aberrant behaviors that he attributes in large part to the departure of middle-class blacks to the suburbs. Left without ostensible ties to the labor market and viable role models, impoverished African Americans fell into a social abyss characterized by high rates of persistent unemployment, crime, welfare dependence, family atomization, and adolescent pregnancy.

That interpretation, which combines economic and cultural dimensions, is paralleled by a conservative account which emphasizes deviant values and norms as well as the unintended consequences of welfare programs like Aid for Families with Dependent Children. Although designed to provide temporary relief, public assistance is said to have created incentives for permanent reliance on government support, idleness, and loose sexual behavior. Authors like Charles Murray and Lawrence Mead, among others, attribute ghetto pathologies to the excesses of liberal ideology and recommend stricter eligibility requirements as well as participation in training and employment programs as conditions for welfare grants.[2]

Both liberal and conservative readings of the malaise surrounding impoverished African Americans contain elements of truth. Wilson's insight about the relationship between changing economic conditions, class recomposition, and *underclass* behavior is substantiated by recent empirical research.[3] The situational connection between welfare dependence, persistent unemployment, and adolescent pregnancies is also borne out by the facts. What neither of the two views explains is the sequence of events that leads to specific behavioral outcomes among the poor, or the meaning that those events and resulting behaviors have for the actors engaged in them.

I argue that the form and effects of cultural and social capital are defined by physical vectors, such as the characteristics of urban space, and by collective constructions, such as social class, race, and gender. The fragmentation of experience along those lines leads to multiple, often confounding, behavioral outcomes whose meaning is not evident to the casual observer. The task to be accomplished, then, is to examine the ways in which people in impoverished neighborhoods both talk about values and connect their talk with action or inaction.

Because people derive their knowledge from the physical spaces where they live, they also anticipate that which is probable in their nearby environment, and they recognize as reality that which is defined as such by members of their interpersonal network occupying proximate spheres of intimacy. For that reason, social and cultural capital are *toponomical*, that is, dependent on physical and social location. This is as true for affluent children as for impoverished children, many of whom become parents at an early age.

A proposition derived from this argument is that lived reality organizes the meaning of behavior to a larger extent than a disembodied notion of morality. Many impoverished people, living in racially segregated neighborhoods, express adherence to *mainstream* American mores; hard work, family loyalties, and individual achievement are part of their cultural repertory. Nevertheless, the translation of values into action is shaped by the tangible milieu that encircles them. So, incidentally, is the ability of affluent families to actualize values into behavior.

Clustered in neighborhoods characterized by uniformity in terms of race and socioeconomic status and by minimal investment or opportunity, the experience of impoverished blacks is molded by relative isolation and the absence of *multiplexity*.[4] Social network truncation translates, not into the lack of social capital based on relations of trust and reciprocity, but into a diminished capacity to gain access to resources controlled by larger social groupings. Paradoxically, insularity also leads to the creation of a rich symbolic repertory aimed at transforming vulnerability into precarious displays of individual affirmation, self-individuation, and status. This complex process is illustrated by the trajectory of girls who opt to become mothers while still in adolescence.

The chapter is divided into four parts. First, I provide a theoretical framework. The second section reexamines the debate on the underclass with particular attention to adolescent pregnancies. Then I provide an ethnographic account based on in-depth interviews with a sample of adolescent mothers from West Baltimore. The concluding section summarizes findings and implications.

Social and Cultural Capital in the New Economic Sociology

Rooted in classic texts by Durkheim, Marx, Weber, and Simmel,[5] the concept of social capital was reclaimed for contemporary analysis by Bourdieu in the 1970s and by James Coleman in the 1980s. According to the latter, the term encompasses benefits derived from relations of mutual trust and collaboration; it thus resides in the relations between the members of a group, not in the individuals who compose it. Mutuality can be realized in two complementary ways: first as an effect of assumptions about common interests that can be advanced through social exchanges—"I will cooperate with you now hoping that you will do the same for me later"—and then as an expectation which must be fulfilled within certain time limits in order for the relationship to continue—"I collaborated with you before, thus I anticipate your aid at this time." According to Robert D. Putnam, this kind of reciprocity is what novelist Tom Wolfe calls the "favor bank" in *Bonfire of the Vanities*.[6] Putnam also notes, echoing Albert O. Hirschman, that social capital is a *moral resource*, that is, a benefit whose supply increases through use and which, unlike physical capital, becomes depleted if not used.

The last statement highlights central features in the formation of social capital. Nevertheless, it is not altogether precise to say that social capital is always augmented through use or that it cannot suffer depletion. The reason is that social capital is internally heterogeneous. Temporal parameters, norms of inclusion and exclusion, and physical and social locations are among the factors explaining internal variations in the flow of social capital. I discuss these three vectors below.

The formation of social capital depends on shared understandings about *temporal demarcations* that vary across groups. In some instances, the actualization of benefits obtained through social means is expected to occur within brief intervals; in others it involves long periods of time. Norms of behavior, ranging from civility to ritual, connect moments in the flow of social capital. While it is true that it can expand through use, social capital can also be reduced if the time elapsed between action and anticipated response goes beyond certain temporal limits. For example, the obtention of a job through the recommendation of a friend or acquaintance often creates obligations for the recipient the neglect of which can be costly. In some cases, social capital occurs as a finite number of exchanges at the end of which the account is peaceably closed by the parties involved. Conceptions about time thus circumscribe the limits and potential advantages derived from social capital, and breaches of etiquette can drain an account in the favor bank despite otherwise strong bonds. On the other hand, obligations cannot be created among individuals who are unable, by virtue of circumstance or ability, to secure opportunities for one another. Such is the case of many impoverished populations.

Social capital also depends on processes of identity formation through *norms of exclusion and inclusion*.[7] More often than not, membership in a social network is based on ascriptive criteria such as ethnicity, race, gender, national background, and social class. As a result, the development of social capital entails particularistic rather than universalistic transactions. Women as well as men can partake of benefits through membership in particular communities, but because women tend to occupy subordinate positions, the resources available to them through the deployment of social capital differ from those available to men in the same group.

Finally, social capital surges and subsides in concert with *social and physical locations* including (a) the shifting center defining membership in a group, (b) the effect of social distance, and (c) the tangible space in which networks conduct their exchanges. There are significant differences in the benefits that individuals can claim through membership in various, sometimes overlapping, groups. For example, children can generally rely on large allocations of good will from their immediate families. Nevertheless, the social capital they muster on the basis of kinship can yield meager benefits unless their kin are part of larger networks that control desirable resources. Conversely, individuals may derive substantial advantages from their association with strangers who, despite relative detachment, recognize them as members of their ethnic, religious, or national community. Those dynamics are captured by Mark Granovetter's discussion of *strong* and *weak* social ties.[8]

One way to understand conditions in the urban ghetto is by noting that children living in it often lack meaningful connections beyond their immediate kinship and neighborhood environments. This has two related consequences. First, the social capital generated by their families can only be parlayed into access to resources existing in their physical surroundings, including those made available by public assistance programs. Because those resources tend to be of poor quality, the advantages derived from social capital are few. That, in turn, has an effect upon adults' credibility when trying to control the behavior of children. Second, the truncation of social networks makes it unlikely that most impoverished children can maintain the kind of sustained contact with members of external social networks that would enable them to envision alternative paths out of the ghetto. Examples of this are found in an exhaustive review of the ethnographic literature on impoverished populations conducted by Robin Jarrett, who distinguishes between community-specific and community-bridging behavioral outcomes.[9] The first, she notes, are consistent with *underclass* characterizations and found among children with few ties to external networks. By contrast, community-bridging behaviors, including high aspirations and an interest in formal education, are evident among youngsters whose families have been able to establish sustained contact with an internally diversified social network extending beyond their own neighborhoods.

The unevenness of social capital also depends on the position of individuals within hierarchies of domination. In the relationship between superior and inferior, social distance differs dramatically depending on whether an individual is one or the other.[10] Minimal distance separates those in positions of power from their subordinates. The reverse is not true: a gulf divides subordinates from their benefactors. Social capital may flow in both directions but its content and texture vary. The fluctuating center defining membership in a group, the effect of social distance, and the actual space in which interaction takes place highlight the *toponomical* features of social capital, that is, its dependence on physical and social locations.

With the concept of social capital, sociologists have attempted to refine crude economic characterizations. But the reification of the term can lead to distortions. One of these is the conceit that what distinguishes social networks is the "amount of social capital" they accumulate, and therefore a solution to poverty lies in boosting social capital among the poor. The assumption is that affluent groups are in a better position to generate reciprocal relationships and therefore to muster "more" social capital. That is not the case; research on impoverished populations shows that their survival largely depends on relations of mutuality. The distinction lies in the types and quality of resources that can be tapped through exchanges based on trust and cooperation. For that reason, social capital is best understood as a process that facilitates access to benefits, not as a concrete object appropriated by individuals or networks. This calls for a shift of attention away from the notion of social capital as a quantifiable feature and toward the characteristics of resources available to various social groups. An example will suffice to illustrate the point.

In West Baltimore, male unemployment reaches levels above 30 percent. Most unemployed men do not hold high school diplomas, but more than one-third do. Yet their ability to secure jobs—even those requiring few skills and paying a minimum wage—is not better than that of high school dropouts. Part of the explanation is that, although high school credentials have lost value in the labor market for all populations, a diploma from a high school in an impoverished neighborhood has even less value. An impoverished high school graduate is likely to lack the basic skills required to complete a job application in an effective way. These deficiencies are not solely the result of weaknesses in the public education system but also derive from limited contact and exposure to individuals who "know the ropes." In other words, impoverished men lack the knowledge derived from sustained contact with groups familiar with the informal rules of the labor market.[11]

Unable to trade low levels of human capital for desirable jobs, many men rely on survival strategies made possible by their membership in peer groups. Despite high crime rates and the publicity surrounding them, the fact is that most unemployed men do not engage in criminal acts. They depend instead on maneuvers that combine intermittent work in the informal sector with attempts at lowering the cost of personal reproduction by alternating residence between kin members and the mothers of their children and by exchanging favors with other men. Social capital constitutes the basis of those interactions, but few and inferior are the advantages tapped through the deployment of social capital.

As the example above makes clear, social networks are critical for the understanding of behavioral outcomes. The functions and attributes of interpersonal networks have to be considered in any attempt to elucidate the social underpinnings of economic action. Social networks are assortments of individuals who maintain recurrent contact with one another through occupational, familial, cultural, or affective ties. In addition, they are intricate formations that channel, filter, and interpret information, articulate meanings, allocate resources, and control behavior. Individual choices depend not only on the availability of material and intangible assets in the society at large but also on the way in which interpersonal contacts shape information and relate to structures of opportunity. As noted in the introduction to this volume, characteristics such as size and composition, density, degree of spacial concentration, and the frequency and nature of transactions among their members give social networks particular profiles. Identities forged within networks intersect with others conferred by external groups.[12]

Perhaps the most important characteristic of a network is its *multiplexity*, the degree to which it may be composed of persons with differing social status, linked in a variety of ways, who play multiple roles in several fields of activity. A diversity of linkages and roles facilitates institutional overlap. The integration of groups of various sizes into the whole which we call society takes place through personal connections. Higher degrees of multiplexity increase the probability that information about resources (such as jobs) and knowledge (such as entrepreneurial know-how) will reach individuals on the basis of their ascriptive characteristics. Mark Granovetter's classic study of the ways in which individuals secure jobs underscores the importance of personal contacts and challenges the neoclassical proposition that employment is the simple effect of supply and demand functions.

Social networks do not exist separate from physical location. The attributes of the space occupied by social networks provide concrete, tangible referents that buttress the meaning of experience and shape the character of reciprocity. Boissevain observes that a person's network can be divided into zones formed by individuals who know each other with varying degrees of familiarity. In order for messages diffused throughout the larger society—including messages about values and norms—to acquire concrete meanings for individuals, they must be personalized through iterative transactions in proximate spheres of intimacy. True learning originates in circumscribed spaces. In the same vein, social capital assumes the existence and exchange of intangible forms of knowledge derived from a shared background. That includes conceptions about the body—its movements, appearance, and speech—and notions about time. Finally, social capital depends upon the deployment of symbolic repertoires. It is at this juncture that cultural capital comes into play.

Cultural capital is of interest to economic sociology in three related ways: first, to the extent that it constitutes a repertory of symbols interactively developed, placed into circulation, and tapped by individuals to "make sense" of their experience; second, to the extent that those symbols recreate centers of power within larger structures of domination; and third, to the extent that those symbols affect the relationship between individuals, social networks, and economic structures, including labor markets. This narrow but distinct definition makes for a better understanding of the ways in which cultural practices relate to social and economic phenomena than broader interpretations found elsewhere.

The anthropological literature offers no fewer than two hundred definitions of "culture." That alone should sound a cautionary note in this intellectual battlefield. But despite all ambiguities, cultural interpretations continue to be wielded with abandon by debaters of social policy. Especially noxious is the tendency to use "culture" as a residual category in which such disparate phenomena as beliefs, norms, and collective performance are indiscriminately heaped. Consider, for example, Christopher Jencks's point:

> There is also fairly strong evidence that mainstream American norms of behavior exert less influence on blacks than on whites with the same amount of schooling. Blacks are more likely than whites with the same amount of schooling to have their babies out of wedlock. . . . Such differences can, of course, be seen as part of racism's appalling historical legacy. But if all whites were suddenly struck colorblind, we would not expect these differences to disappear overnight— indeed, they would probably persist for several generations. That is what it means to invoke "culture" as an explanation of such differences.[13]

Three suppositions underpin this set of statements. The first relates to the way in which norms and values are translated into behavior: Jencks assumes that values explain behavior. The second, derived assumption is that disparate outcomes in a similar behavioral plane must indicate corresponding cultural differences and, therefore, diverging values. Finally, the statement is grounded on the belief that culture metastasizes in a relatively autonomous field impervious, for the most part, to economic and social forces. In that respect, Jencks's view is in agreement with earlier perspectives on the *culture of poverty*.[14]

It is possible to articulate a reading, other than the one offered by Jencks, of the varying incidence of out-of-wedlock births among African Americans and whites with analogous levels of schooling. In this reading, values alone do not explain behavior. Given sharp levels of residential segregation and high rates of poverty, African Americans and whites have at their disposal dissimilar types of resources to realize *mainstream* norms and values. A seventeen-year-old white woman about to graduate from high school, living in a middle-class neighborhood, and contemplating college, even with ambivalence, is likely to defer motherhood in order not to jeopardize her other opportunities. In this case, the young woman perceives giving birth to a child out of wedlock not only as a breach of norms but also as an impediment to realistically perceived and desirable options.

A seventeen-year-old black woman about to graduate from high school in an urban ghetto faces a different set of choices. It is less likely, for instance, that her social network will include a significant number of individuals who have pursued educations in "good" colleges and gone on to secure "good" jobs. As a result, many adults and adolescents in her circle may see graduating from high school as the culmination of a life stage that should bring about mature responsibilities. Moreover, the young woman may share with men in her peer group the impression, fostered by *mainstream* values, that parenting qualifies individuals for membership in the adult community. In this case motherhood has a distinct meaning: it is not a deviation from but a path to approximate dominant norms.

As with Jencks's interpretation, this reading is based on assumptions that have to be made explicit. One assumption is that disparate behavioral outcomes can spring from attempted adherence to shared cultural understandings. A second is that the translation of values into behavior is mediated by specific resources and *embodied* experiences (a term to which I will return below), and a third holds that seemingly identical features like "same level of education" may conceal markedly different social contents. Finally, this interpretation is based on the claim that *cultural capital is a byproduct of social capital*; it does not reproduce autonomously but only to the extent that the conditions surrounding the generation of specific forms of social capital are maintained. In other words, symbolic repertories are recreated when the structural conditions that give rise to certain types of social capital are replicated.

Consider, again, the profiles sketched above. Whether the young Caucasian woman is celibate, using contraceptives, or pondering an abortion, she is also likely to favor certain kinds of music, attire, and gestures. Those tastes were fashioned interactively with her peers, the mass media, and the responses of adults. Because she belongs in a network with a high degree of *multiplexity*, she is liable to engage in behaviors considered inappropriate by certain sectors of her group. In considering her options, however, she is unlikely to interview for a job in anything other than acceptable garb, no matter how repugnant she may find it when associating with her friends. In dressing for the interview, unless she has a self-destructive instinct, she is certain not to expose a small tattoo on her breast that recently drove her parents to distraction.

Her counterpart in the ghetto has tastes too. She is likely to be preoccupied by her hair, which members of her inner circle describe as "bad" and "nappy." Her friends have similar problems. They therefore go to great lengths in reshaping their tresses into acceptable, even flamboyant displays of craftsmanship. Vulnerability is recast into power. A bodily part is transformed into a sign of affirmation and individuation. Up to this point, the sparkling mounds of braided hair do not differ much from the tattoo inscribed on the breast of the white woman. But because the African American belongs in a network with a low degree of *multiplexity*, she may not know that her coiffure can severely curtail the probability of success in job interviews. What is wrought as an empowering symbol in an insular milieu becomes a signal that bars access to resources and employment in the larger society.

Whether the young woman in question would modify her appearance or not, on the basis of knowledge obtained through an expanded social network, is a different matter that is best explored in relation to issues of resistance and compliance. The point, in this case, is that intangible forms of knowledge at the disposal of the first woman are not available to the second and vice versa. This is what I mean by *embodied* knowledge.[15]

A series of insights derive from this interpretation. One is that networks generate symbolic repertories to impose meaning upon circumstances; it is therefore impossible to understand the symbols without giving attention to the conditions in which they are deployed. Another is that in subtle ways, knowledge differs from setting to setting and that those differences may be accentuated by social network truncation. Finally, divergent behavioral outcomes may not ensue from disparate values and norms but from the characteristics of resources available to realize them.

With these conceptual tools in mind, I now return to the meaning of adolescent pregnancies in the Baltimore ghetto.

The Debate on Adolescent Pregnancies and Poverty

The relationship between poverty and adolescent pregnancies is germane to the field of economic sociology in two related ways. First, to the extent that teen pregnancy and motherhood create barriers for participation in the labor market, they also define a particular position of individuals and groups vis-à-vis economic structures. Second and similarly, the contest between cultural and situational explanations allows for an examination of the relationship between economy and society. In a narrow sense, appropriate to this discussion, adolescent pregnancies among impoverished African Americans can be viewed as a *strategic research site*.[16] Because these pregnancies occur as an effect of a relatively bounded chain of events, they present an opportunity to ground issues that appear diffuse and unwieldy in larger populations. In this section, I give attention to divergent perspectives on the causes and consequences of adolescent pregnancies in the context of poverty.

The widespread birth of children to adolescents has become the fulcrum of a controversy about the causes and perpetuation of poverty which has theoretical and practical implications. Conservatives see the rise of teen pregnancies as a symptom of moral decline, permissiveness, and the failure of the "welfare state."[17] Early motherhood, they argue, causes poverty. Stricter requirements, increased accountability, and limited access to government support are warranted. Over the last decade this perception has translated into legislative measures. In some states—Maryland included—women receiving Aid for Families with Dependent Children are no longer entitled to additional stipends if they become pregnant while receiving assistance. Critics also believe that welfare programs unwittingly reward idleness, promiscuity, and dependency.[18] Behind closed doors, some proponents of the conservative view reveal their suspicion that adolescent pregnancies among African Americans are caused by cultural and biological features. Images of lustfulness at the expense of the taxpayer simmer below more reasoned appeals for personal responsibility.[19]

Considering the nature of the debate, it is sometimes difficult to remember that—as works by Constance Nathanson and Kristin Luker observe—the vast majority of babies throughout history have been born to adolescents, largely because life spans used to be shorter and because the inception of puberty coincided with the expectation of motherhood within or, in some cases, before marriage.[20] June is still the Month of Brides in the United States, a vestige of an earlier period (extending well into the 1950s) when marriage and babies followed graduation from high school. The stigma attached to adolescent pregnancies is a recent phenomenon centering as much on "illegitimacy" as on the youth of mothers.

Moreover, despite extensive publicity about an "epidemic" of teen pregnancies, pregnancy rates among adolescents declined sharply, falling by about one-third, from the mid-1960s until the late 1980s. Births to adolescents dropped rapidly as oral contraceptives became widespread, then dropped again after abortion became more widely available during the mid-1970s. The rates continued to decline slowly, with black teenage pregnancy rates remaining higher than that of whites but declining faster. To put it succinctly, in 1966 a random sample of one hundred black teenage girls could be expected to produce eighty babies by the time they all turned twenty. For one hundred white girls, the equivalent number would have been forty. By 1986, the count had dropped to fifty-one for blacks and twenty-one for whites.[21] When socioeconomic status and level of education are taken into account, the rates of pregnancy among black and white teenagers have converged more noticeably, although the former remain higher. Thus to some extent the panic over adolescent pregnancies disregards trends at the aggregate level. If there is such a thing as an epidemic, it is concentrated among the members of a comparatively small population formed by the rural and urban poor. The latter have captured the most attention.

The relationship between public aid and poverty has received notice from scholars in various disciplines. Tienda and Steir[22] observe that Aid for Families with Dependent Children originated as a form of insurance to protect minors against extreme deprivation. Nevertheless, since the 1960s, Congress has been concerned that government largesse fosters dependence by discouraging work effort, stimulating out-of-wedlock parenting, and disrupting families. Charles Murray blames public assistance programs for rising male unemployment rates, high adolescent birth rates, and the proliferation of female-headed households among African Americans.[23] Richard P. Taub explains that the growth in the number of unwed teenage mothers is central to the study of poverty, since female-headed households comprise a large percentage of all impoverished people.[24] In addition, the burden of poverty makes it difficult for single mothers to supervise their children who, as they mature, seem more likely to drop out of school and face other troubles, perpetuating a cycle of destitution through the generations. The conclusion is that a family needs at least two adults who both earn adequate incomes to provide proper child care. Daniel Patrick Moynihan has been arguing in this direction since the 1960s.[25] Policy recommendations stemming from this literature tend to focus on the reconstruction of the husband-wife unit in poor areas and on measures to reduce adolescent pregnancy rates.

The original debate over the intergenerational transmission of welfare dependence took two forms. A cultural version emphasized the transmission of values and attitudes through socialization. Oscar Lewis, for example, noted structural constraints but emphasized beliefs and behaviors that once established perpetuated the transmission of poverty.[26] Consistent with this view is the idea that daughters reared in homes receiving public assistance adopt values that denigrate work and make dependency on government aid an acceptable means of support. Economic dependence is thus perpetuated by acquired "tastes" for public aid and the development of a *welfare culture*.

An alternative perspective emphasizes social and economic factors that limit options available to children who grow up in impoverished neighborhoods.[27] Daughters reared in poverty are more likely to be poor than daughters brought up in affluence, not because of deviant values and attitudes, but because of limited opportunities. Tienda and Steir concur with Hannerz that diverse behavioral patterns are situational and that statistically normative patterns do not necessarily imply a deviation from social and cultural norms. In an analysis that created widespread interest, William J. Wilson emphasizes *concentration effects*, which he defines as systematic "differences in the experiences of low-income families who live in inner-city areas [by comparison to] the experiences of those who live in other areas of the central city."[28] He argues that spatial and social isolation from mainstream behavioral norms was partly produced by the exodus of working- and middle-class families from inner-city neighborhoods. In agreement with Hannerz, he maintains that behavioral forms are situationally shaped.

On the surface, situational and cultural explanations of the relationship between poverty, government aid, and adolescent pregnancies hinge on opposite chains of causation. In one case culture explains economic outcomes; in the other, economic factors account for norms and values. In the first instance, adolescent pregnancies and their byproduct, poverty, are said to be induced by *welfare culture*; in the second, resource maldistribution, isolation, and residential segregation are said to explain poverty and, indirectly, teen pregnancies.

A closer examination reveals that neither of the two interpretations is really about culture but about economic processes. So-called "cultural" explanations conceal an agreement with neoclassical outlooks: adolescent women choose motherhood as a mechanism to maximize benefits derived from public assistance and reduce energy expenditure in the form of work effort. They argue that rational calculation is made possible by incentives derived from government aid. *Welfare culture* is, thus, not primarily about values but about the weighing of costs and benefits—a strictly economic exercise. Upon scrutiny, cultural accounts of poverty reveal their true colors: they are the ruminations of *homo economicus* masquerading as Hegel and telling us more about economic transactions than about values, norms, or beliefs.

While cultural versions focus on economic behavior and choice at the individual level, situational renditions give priority to large-scale economic phenomena such as the structure of opportunity and the uneven distribution of resources. Those views are consistent with a radical critique of the neoclassical model by contrast to cultural accounts. To reiterate, the main difference between the two perspectives does not reside in the counterposition of culture and economy but in their varying conceptualization of economic factors and their attention to different levels of analysis. Neither of the two views explains the sequences that lead to behavioral outcomes, in this case adolescent pregnancies, nor do they clarify the role of cultural repertories, either in the transmission of poverty or in the interplay between individual economic decisions and larger economic institutions.

Understanding the chain of events and meanings leading to motherhood among impoverished adolescents is precisely the purpose of the next section.

The Ethnographic Account

On a map, West Baltimore resembles the profile of a reclining hourglass comprising approximately fifteen square miles. To the southeast is Upton; to the northwest, Lower Park Heights. The two sections join at Druid Hill Park, a receding expanse of green where, incongruously, the Baltimore Conservatory and Zoo are located.

Upton is one of the poorest neighborhoods in the city of Baltimore. In that location, poverty means something different and something more than material deprivation. For several generations, the limits of collective life have been shaped by residential segregation and a paucity of productive investment. Ninety-eight percent of Upton residents are of African descent. The majority are renters, not property owners. Mortgages and other loans are virtually unavailable. In 1990, the average price of a home in the neighborhood was $7,442—a bad investment by any measure. Arson and abandonment are frequent (owners find it more profitable to burn down their properties than to repair them), as evidenced by the abundance of charred and boarded-up buildings which often become safe houses for drug dealers. Partly as a result, vacancy rates are high; 30 percent of housing units in Upton are not occupied. Also high are the levels of unemployment and underemployment. Business activity is puny, with the exception of a myriad grocery stores and liquor shops inherited by Korean immigrants from an earlier cohort of Jewish entrepreneurs.

West Baltimore attracts attention for another reason: its incidence of adolescent pregnancies surpasses even that of Baltimore, a city whose rates triple the national average and are among the highest in the country.[29] In 1990, nearly one-quarter of the city's 13,000 births were to teenagers. The same year, almost one-third of girls between the ages of fourteen and nineteen living in West Baltimore had already become mothers to at least one child. Many of those girls had grown up in female-headed households receiving government aid. In Baltimore, as in the nation at large, adolescent mothers are likely to have been born to women who became mothers themselves at an early age and for whom dependence on public assistance often is a permanent source of livelihood. The odds are staggering in that respect: one out of two girls born to adolescents receiving public assistance become mothers before completing their teenage years.[30]

To understand the meaning of adolescent pregnancies in West Baltimore, as well as the interrelated sequences of events that lead to those outcomes, I conducted an ethnographic research project that was partly sponsored by the Department of Health and Human Resources. Between 1989 and 1992 I interviewed the members of fifty families, a total of over 250 individuals. A sample of twenty families was first drawn from a pool of applicants to a new social service delivery program created under the 1988 federal Comprehensive Child Development Act. That core sample was augmented through snow-balling procedures and, in a few cases, through random encounters. Ten families from the larger sample have been especially important to this project. Interviews varied in length; some were concluded at the end of an hour, others continued over several days. In this section, I give attention to a small subsample formed by adolescent mothers from my original pool of informants.

Towanda Forrest was twelve years old when I met her in 1988, a gorgeous woman-child with a grainy inflection and eyes full of dare. During one of our first conversations, she told me:

Only fools get pregnant. They be thinking they so smart but they is fools 'cause you don't gain nothing by having a baby, only worries. I tell the other girls, Towanda's smart, she will never get pregnant; never! Just wait and see.

In December 1991, two months shy of her fifteenth birthday, Towanda was delivered of her first child, a boy named Reggie Shantell Brown. Towanda had pondered over the baby's name for several months but, sadly, she couldn't spell it. Despite almost seven years of instruction, Towanda was then—and is now—almost illiterate. By the time Reggie Shantell was born she had abandoned school. When I chided her about her earlier resolve not to become pregnant she retorted, "Some things are just meant to be." In the spring of 1993, Towanda was expecting her second child. She was seventeen by then.

How did Towanda arrive at her present situation? Is she, together with a growing number of impoverished girls in the nation's ghettos, flouting the values of the larger society? Does she illustrate the contention that welfare programs encourage dependence and sexual misbehavior? Or is she, on the other hand, the pliant victim of conditions over which she has no control?

As part of exploratory research about the conditions surrounding fifty impoverished families in West Baltimore, I asked twenty-seven women between the ages of fourteen and nineteen a series of questions about the circumstances that led them to become mothers. At seventeen, Latanya Williams was expecting her second child when I met her in 1990. She was an outspoken girl who lived with her mother and five siblings in one of several skyscrapers that form the George Murphy Homes, Upton's best-known publicly subsidized housing project. Her mother, a quiet and religious woman, has depended on public assistance for almost twenty years. One hot summer day, while nibbling pumpkin seeds in the yard of a neighboring house, Latanya put forth a typical view:

> I waited for a long time before I had my baby. Anyone can tell you, all my girlfriends had babies before me and I was jealous 'cause when you don't have a child to call your own, you's nothing; you got nothing to be proud of. I couldn't wait. What's there to wait for?

When I asked whether she had considered finishing high school as a way to improve her chances for a better life, she looked at me with skepticism and said:

> It's not like I don't want to get an education but it's not so easy. . . . And besides, I don't know no one, I tell you no one, who has a good job by finishing high school. That's a lie, just a fucking lie! So why waste time to end up at the 7-Eleven? It ain't worth it. What I want is to have my own apartment, my own place . . .

As the conversation continued, I ventured further: was Latanya hoping to marry the father of her children?

> I don't know about that. . . . I like my independence and you can't trust men, they go crazy on you. First, I have to see that he really wants to take care of my babies, test him, you know . . . cause no crazy boy's gonna boss me around, no way!

By the time we got around to the delicate subject of contraceptives, Latanya had achieved momentum:

> What's yo talking about? Man, just because I'm seventeen, it don't mean I don't know nothing. Look, the pill's bad for your health, swells you all up and everything. Rubbers? They's gross; my old man don't like 'em, and abortion, that's a sin, to kill a poor baby. I love my baby. I'm gonna raise him good.

Although characteristic, the views expressed by Latanya were not shared by all the young women with whom I discussed motherhood. Latishia Marvin, a heavy-set girl, was facing the arrival of her first baby with trepidation in 1990. She was eighteen years old:

> I didn't know I could get pregnant, you know, 'cause the doctor said I had a lopsided uterus. But I did and I'm scared but I can't do nothing now.

Her fears were tempered with hope. She told me the arrival of the baby would give her a "new chance." According to her mother, she had held a steady job at the local food store since she was fourteen and was struggling to graduate from a school where teachers spent more time trying to quiet down riotous students than teaching. Latishia had lukewarm expectations about going to college but was having difficulty getting a passing grade in "her English subject." Shortly before the arrival of Byron, her first son, she was able to graduate from high school. Unfortunately, a doctor recommended that she quit her job because the pregnancy had caused her feet to distend. In one stroke, she had completed the requirements to apply for college and moved from membership among the working poor to full dependency on public assistance.

Although Latishia's mother had mixed feelings about her daughter's pregnancy, she didn't see anything extraordinary about the event. She too had become a mother at an early age. "God sends the babies," she told me, "they are our greatest joy."

And then there was Towanda Forrest, whose comments were recorded earlier. Melinda Jordan, her ten-year-old cousin, yearns to have her own baby. "That way," she says, "I can move in with Towanda when she gets her apartment, and we can have our own home."

These testimonies appear to voice calculations about public aid as a means of increasing economic benefits and reducing energy expenditure, thus confirming the indictment of welfare critics. Such calculations, however, entail assessing information and weighing the advantages of competing alternatives. Is any ten-year-old child really "choosing" government subsidy over productive employment when yearning for pregnancy and motherhood? What do children dream about when they long for babies of their own?

Before considering an answer to those questions, I pause to examine the quoted statements in more detail. First, they manifest skepticism about the rewards of education. The girls I interviewed distinguished between educational achievement as an ideal and the reality of the schools they attended. No one regarded schooling with indifference. They agreed that educated—"smart"—people got all the advantages but they did not believe that their academic records or the schools they were attending would unlock opportunities. Their classrooms were crowded and noisy. Instructional materials were unavailable or antiquated and, typically, all of them had started school with major deficits that had only grown over time.[31] Ten-year-old Melinda Jordan had suffered meningitis when she was a toddler. Shuffled between relatives and foster parents, she had ended up living with an affable but alcoholic aunt. Her standardized test scores placed her at the bottom of the national norm group. Eighteen-year-old Latishia Marvin had displayed excellent behavior while growing up but she had struggled with grades all along. Towanda Forrest was almost illiterate at twelve, and a high school dropout by the age of fourteen.

The young women I interviewed had no reason to see education as a path to success. As a result, they perceived schools as social, not educational, arenas where they participated in the small dramas that children of all types are wont to enact. They gossiped, picked friends and adversaries, defied instructors, competed for each other's attention and, especially, they struggled for self-affirmation. When Towanda was Melinda's age, she started receiving suspensions for fighting in school—just like Melinda does at present. Both offer the same justification: "You can't let people walk all over you; you got to get some respect."[32]

The quest for respect is commonplace among adolescents of all class, race, and ethnic backgrounds. However, varying outcomes hinge on the attributes of social networks.[33] Among affluent youngsters, the search for respect depends on an ample pool of resources and potential benefits made available by adults who maintain a distinct position with respect to the young. In impoverished environments, where grown-ups often compete for the same kinds of jobs available to adolescents, the search for respect traverses other avenues; it tends to focus mainly on physical force, the defense of turfs, and corporal adornment. Images of power are thus constructed where other alternatives are not easily accessible.[34]

Second, the young women I interviewed expressed mistrust about the qualifications of men as mates and parents. Other researchers have noticed the clashing interpretations of impoverished African American men and women about each other.[35] Those views, in turn, are widespread in settings characterized by high levels of male unemployment and underemployment, regardless of race or ethnicity. In environments where men have difficulties in securing jobs, the prospects of marriage and family take a distinctive form. Moreover, men and women alike see important differences between available jobs and jobs they deem desirable. Since male identity, according to mainstream norms, strongly depends on the characteristics of employment, men are starkly aware of their inability to fulfill their prescribed role as "providers." Their perceptions about work and jobs influence their orientations toward marriage. Men as well as women may say they do not get married because they wish to protect their independence. It is also the case that they feel they cannot afford marriage.

Furthermore, the relative incomes of prospective spouses have clearly perceived consequences for the balance of power in their relationships. Those who have jobs fear exploitation. Those who are jobless fear domination. Conflicting perceptions emerge from this predicament. The women see the men as untrustworthy, exploitative, flighty, and undeserving of respect. The men, in turn, speak of the women as materialistic hags who have forgotten how to be respectful and whose only interest is in long-term financial security. The debasement of women by reducing them to "bitches" and "hos" conceals a correlative attempt to redefine the locus of power in gender relations. The skepticism of women and their determination to preserve personal autonomy by shunning marriage represent the flip side of the same process. In Taub's words:

> In lieu of a material base where to hang the cloak of honor, impoverished blacks must find honor where possible and hold on to it. Since occupational achievement for men is limited, they have sought alternative sources of status, including the capacity to drink heavily, to be able to fight well, and to have sexual prowess. Terms in ghetto language, such as "pussy" to communicate lack of toughness, and "dissing," both point in the honor direction.[36]

The paradox is that behaviors which appear anomalous to those who are not poor could well be attempts at dealing with normative values in environments where the material basis for implementing those values is insufficient and therefore fragile.

Third, the quotes present motherhood as a desirable condition, not as a calamity. In the light of expert judgments to the contrary, this is perplexing. To unfurl the meaning of motherhood among impoverished adolescents, we must move away for a moment from the women—who, after all, might only be seeking an ex post facto justification—to note the fascination with which even younger children view babies. Tercell Jones, an eight-year-old boy atop wiry limbs when I interviewed him in 1991, condensed a familiar perception:

> Babies, they so cute; when Lisa [his sixteen-year-old sister] had Shatiareia you could tell it made everybody happy—'cause you could see she was so pretty and smart. She makes you feel like you something special and you don't have to worry about other things when she's around. She pays attention; you just have to teach her. . . . she's a good baby.

There is abuse and neglect in the ghetto—as in other, less dispiriting environs populated by wealthier families—but also a striking appreciation for infants. The arrival of a new baby attracts utmost interest among youngsters and adults alike because, to put it bluntly, there are few milestones in poor neighborhoods that people can call upon to separate stages in their life-cycles. Hardly any of the events that mark the passage from childhood to adulthood in richer areas exist in the ghetto. Savings accounts, extracurricular activities, hopes of getting a driver's license, prospects of well-paying jobs— those middle-class perquisites of the journey toward maturity—are rare in poor neighborhoods. Infants galvanize attention and offer possibilities for self-distinction. Having babies, then, is about the articulation of meaning, not solely the consequence of careless behavior.

A related matter concerns adolescents' perceptions about their future prospects. This, in turn, calls into question their notions about time. The extent to which social time differs from chronological or astronomical time is a venerable theme in the social sciences but one that has been undertheorized with respect to impoverished populations. Bearing directly on this point is Robert K. Merton's concept of socially expected durations (SEDs): socially prescribed or collectively patterned expectations about temporal intervals embedded in social structures of various kinds.[37] He distinguishes between structural or institutionalized durations, collectively expected durations, and patterned temporal expectations found in various kinds of interpersonal and social relations. He also observes that SEDs "constitute a fundamental class of patterned expectations linking social structures and individual action."[38] Equally important is the point that socially expected durations affect *anticipatory* social behavior.

In accordance with those sociological ideas, my analysis implies that impoverishment combined with spatial segregation shapes particular conceptions of time and socially expected durations. Poverty and exclusion flatten and compress temporal rhythms. Alex Kotlowitz recounts the experience of African American boys in a Chicago housing project whose responses to the question, "What do you want to be as an adult?" are prefaced by the conditional clause, "If I grow up. . . ." If, not when.[39] Familiarity with violence and death influences their perception about the probable duration of life and produces behavior appropriate to foreshortened phases.

Ethnographic research among ethnic and racial minorities further details the extent to which accelerated development characterizes the experience of impoverished youth.[40] Older children shoulder parental responsibilities for their siblings when adults are unable or unwilling to do so. More frequently than among wealthier groups, impoverished adolescents maintain lateral relationships with parents and older relatives not only because age differences tend to be smaller but because poor adults occupy with their children a similar position vis-à-vis labor market alternatives. In this context, motherhood represents the extension of responsibilities assumed at an early age and expresses a specific relationship with the labor market. That partly explains why, at seventeen, Latanya Williams can state with conviction, "I waited for a long time before I had my baby." That's why she can ask, "What's there to wait for?"

This may be contrasted with the experience of more prosperous groups where parenthood is also associated with the fulfillment of manhood and womanhood but where a larger stockpile of resources is available to achieve the same purpose. The irony is that, in impoverished environments, the absence of resources deemed desirable leads to the perception of newborns as unqualified assets rather than handicaps. Partly for the same reason, there is a link throughout the world between poverty and early pregnancy. In most of those settings, public assistance and welfare programs are unavailable and therefore cannot be held responsible for providing the "wrong" incentives.[41] Even when removed from the insular confines of our own national policy debate, the situational connection between adolescent pregnancies and poverty persists. Pressures exerted by predatory men seeking their own affirmation further complicate matters.

Bereft of actual power, young men and women seek stature through the use of their bodies.

Therefore, when ten-year-old Melinda Jordan speaks about her desire to have a baby, a family of her own, an apartment, she is identifying the attributes of personal autonomy and hoping for circumstances different from those that have surrounded her agitated life in the past. Her perceptions and goals are shaped by previous experience as a member of a social network distinguished by impoverishment and relative isolation, not by reference to the dictates of an abstract morality. Her attempts are likely to fail, of course, but they do not necessarily represent a calculated effort to burden the taxpayer.

All this makes understandable another feature of the statements quoted earlier: although the speakers reveal various areas of ignorance, a lack of familiarity with contraceptives is not one of them. None of the twenty-seven women I interviewed was unaware—or unable to avail herself—of the means for birth control. They attended schools where attention was given to reproductive behavior and where counselors habitually distributed informational booklets and made referrals. Furthermore, in those cases where pregnancy had been involuntary, girls still chose to keep their babies. This calls into question the liberal insight that births to adolescents can be prevented through education alone. My interpretation points to a configuration of events, embodied experiences, and situations that make motherhood a desirable option when other alternatives to define adulthood are unavailable. It may not be pregnancy that causes poverty but the circumstances of poverty that lead to accelerated development and, therefore, to motherhood at an early age.

In neighborhoods like Upton, the vacuums created by the absence of productive investment have been occupied by public assistance programs. This has had at least two major consequences. One is that the experience of many children, their knowledge and expectations, differs markedly from the experience of children whose families relate directly to the market economy. Another, derivative effect is that while the identity and sense of personal efficacy of affluent children is formed through actual or symbolic relations with the market, the identity of impoverished children is shaped instead by frequent iterations with government agencies. In both cases, children strive for adulthood by deploying knowledge rooted in their environments. In both cases, the passage from childhood to maturity is marked by milestones. But the milestones differ, as do the benefits derived from the deployment of social capital in the two contexts.

Moreover, children do not just aspire to become grown-ups; they hope to become men and women. Advancing from childhood to maturity intersects with the process of gender formation. The symbols and behaviors surrounding manhood and womanhood vary in consonance with a finite number of options. And gender plays a part in the transition to maturity in yet another way. The presence of the state in impoverished neighborhoods, a key component in the experience of children, is not neutral; it too bifurcates along gender lines. Public assistance touches the majority of single women and their children. The corrections and criminal justice systems deal primarily with boys and men. That split has repercussions in the lives of children growing into adulthood in the Baltimore ghetto.

Reconsider now Towanda's case. Her grandmother, Missie, migrated with her husband and children from North Carolina to Washington, D.C., in 1956. Towanda's mother, Lydia Johnston, had had a difficult time growing up but at the age of twenty, already with a baby of her own, she married an itinerant mechanic with whom she is still living. Missie moved to Baltimore in 1973 and almost a decade later Lydia, who at the time worked as a maid in Washington, joined her. Towanda grew up in Baltimore, first in a home shared with her grandmother and later in a rat-infested row house where I met her in 1988. By then, Lydia had resorted to public assistance to support four of her five children. The eldest, Lawrence, had been confined to prison since the age of seventeen when he was convicted as an accessory to the murder of a cab driver.

Having faced other pains, Lydia was now worried about Towanda's well-being. The girl had begun to associate with a crowd of older kids. She was skipping school and could not read at the second grade level. She complained that other youngsters were ganging up on her and calling her names. She told me her greatest wish was to go somewhere far away where she did not have to share her bed with other people. She did not trust grown-ups, especially men. When I asked her about her new friends in the neighborhood, she told me:

> They's nice kids no matter what mama says. They like me and I like 'em. They's cool not like the other people. . . . They don't like me in school, always calling me names. . . . I'm no slut. I don't have to take their shit 'cause I can take care of myself and my friends take care of me.

Lydia struggled to keep her daughter out of trouble but her authority had fragile foundations. For one thing, she could not keep Towanda at home. Crowded and damp, the house offered no refuge from the dangers outside, especially during the summer months when temperatures reached suffocating heights. Furthermore, Towanda felt no pride in her mother, who had to clean other people's homes to supplement her welfare stipend. Lydia suffered from a credibility gap: in the eyes of her daughter she could not back up sensible advice with benefits more attractive than those made available by Towanda's new friends.

Lydia blames her children's problems on Calvin, her husband, who never earned enough, drinks heavily, and is an indifferent parent. When she applied for Aid for Families with Dependent Children, she intimated that he had left her. In the eyes of the state, hers is a female-headed household. In actuality, Calvin has always been part of the family. When Lydia was able to move to the projects, he followed along, an obscure presence treated with scorn and resignation but always there. With her four children and invisible husband, she occupies a small house with one lavatory and three bedrooms. Between seven and fourteen children and adults—relatives, friends, and friends of friends—intermittently share that abode.

In discussing the dangers of adolescent pregnancy, I asked Lydia whether she regretted having had children at an early age. Was that not the reason why she had fallen prey to "the welfare"? She replied with uncharacteristic ardor:

Oh no, ma'am, oh no. I never had no problem with them babies. I fed them and I raised them and I always had a job; always earned my keep; it ain't my babies that got me on welfare; it was that I couldn't earn enough to support them by having a job!

With little success, Lydia continues trying to get a high school equivalency degree in the hope of achieving gainful employment. She would like to work with computers or as a nurse's aide. Although the probability of that ever happening is slim, she sees dependence on public assistance as a temporary event. Most women in her situation share the same expectation.

After the move to the Murphy Homes, Towanda's behavior deteriorated further. As a newcomer, she received a far-from-hospitable reception from other youngsters in the area. She formed alliances, developed a style and a presence; someone not to be trifled with. Throughout that period, Lydia received several warnings of eviction stemming from Towanda's transgressions. In 1991, Towanda was caught shoplifting and subsequently was expelled from school for threatening the principal. I asked her whether she realized how difficult she was making life for her family.

I don't mean to be [rotten]. But a girl has to take care of herself; in a 'hood like this you can die if you don't fight for your rights. I want to make something of myself, you know, to have a family, my own home. I want to be with people who think I'm something.

It was around that time that she met Reggie Brown. At twenty-one, Reggie was already a figure to be reckoned with, an entrepreneur of sorts and, by the standards of young people in the neighborhood, "a cool guy." He was the local kingpin, always with cash in his pockets. "It's all drug money," Lydia told me. But for Towanda, tough and streetsmart, he was a logical choice:

A boy like Reggie, he look a bomb! He knows the ins and outs; he knows everything. . . . He aks'd me to be his woman. Well, you can't trust the men but to be his woman, yeah, he alright . . . but I wouldn't marry him because men, they wants to be on top and no one's on top of Towanda, not even mama.

Born in West Baltimore, only a few blocks away from the projects, Reggie Brown represents the trajectory of many ghetto men. When he was only nine and out with a few friends, he took some cookies from the local store. The owner reported the incident to the police and, for two weeks, Reggie was taken to a juvenile detention center where he underwent observation and then was returned to his mother. That experience made an indelible impression partly because it was not an isolated event.

Boys growing up in Upton are fascinated by the police, whom they admire and fear. Many want to become cops to "help people," but if you ask a kid in the 'hood what the verb "to search" means, his first response will be to describe an officer engaging in a bodily probe. The boy is likely to recall the times he has seen men thrust against a wall or a car and asked to put their arms up while the officer inspects their pockets. By the age of sixteen, a boy may have had more than a dozen detentions. Even pranks that would be dismissed in other environments can be taken as evidence of criminal leanings when the poor are involved.

Leroy Forrest, Towanda's younger brother, started his career at age thirteen after he was caught running crack for an older friend. When I discussed the incident with three of his young cousins, aged seven through eleven, they agreed that it was unfair for Leroy to be punished; "after all," one told me, "he was just doin' it to help his family." Now sixteen, Leroy spends most of his time in a correctional center, although he is allowed to visit the family during holidays. In addition to a muscular frame he boasts a gold tooth. Towanda boasts one too. Both are glittering displays of importance gained in the struggle for respect in the neighborhood.

Shortly after Reggie Shantell was born I found myself engaged in a conversation with Lydia Johnston in her small but tidy living room. She was inflamed with Towanda's behavior:

> Them children coming up have no sense; they's always thinking they know better. Towanda, she got an attitude, always got an attitude, I don't know how she came by that attitude!

I was preparing for a continued outburst of moral righteousness when Lydia's expression changed. She asked me whether I wanted to see the baby. I was taken aback; of course I wanted to see him. Like a commander deploying a platoon, she raised her voice to call Reggie. "Ma'am," was the courteous response from the second floor. "Bring the baby down!" Obediently, down the stairs came the young man with his son in his arms, eyes gleaming with pride. Moments later I asked Reggie Senior how he felt about the birth of his son:

> It's good, it's good ma'am. And I was there when he was born, right there in the hospital. I 'bout fainted with all the blood and that, but I was there. . . . I sure was there. Now, I have someone to really live for, someone who needs me and who'll look up to me.

I could not help but wonder whether Lydia's husband had felt the same way when his first child was born or whether Reggie would replicate Calvin's defeats in the years to come. Those thoughts were interrupted by the chatter of family members and friends who joined in admiring expressions. What ensued was a collective demonstration of delight that dissipated any doubt about the extent to which Reggie Shantell was welcome. Sitting in a corner, fourteen-year-old Towanda chewed gum in contentment. Hers was the moment of triumph.

Up to this point, I have focused on behavioral outcomes found among impoverished African Americans. Recent accounts, however, note a surge of adolescent pregnancies since 1987 in areas characterized by the presence of large immigrant clusters. California, for example, is identified in journalistic reports as a state leading the trend toward increased out-of-wedlock pregnancies among teenagers. A closer look at the evidence suggests that the phenomenon is indeed on the rise in places like South Central Los Angeles, which received attention as a result of the most recent riots but which is also conspicuous for the devastation endured as an effect of plant closings and the consequent exacerbation of unemployment, insularity, and concentrated poverty.

In a series of in-depth interviews I conducted among Nicaraguan families in Miami, as part of a larger study of second-generation immigrants, I was impressed by the number of adolescent mothers. Nicaraguans arrived in this country escaping political turmoil but, contrary to the experience of other political refugees, their status has remained uncertain since the mid-1980s. Stuck in legal limbo, many have experienced rapid downward mobility, with older children unable to secure jobs or realize educational aspirations. With some variations, these Nicaraguans represent an instance of thwarted opportunity and arrested incorporation into the labor market. More research is needed among the new waves of immigrants and their children, but the first evidence suggests that Towanda and her peers may not be alone. Their experience could be replicated by recent aliens whose adaptation to this society diverges from earlier patterns of assimilation.[42]

I stated at the beginning of this essay that the immigrant experience was known to earlier generations of African Americans. Works by Philippe Bourgois and others suggest that in assessing the trajectories of their parents and grandparents, younger blacks find little evidence to bolster the expectation that "starting at the bottom" will translate into better prospects for the future. While recently arrived immigrants can imagine entry-level jobs as a necessary transition to enhanced opportunities, African Americans can state, with conviction, that similar hopes among their forebears did not materialize. To the extent that immigrants encounter long-term barriers to occupational and social mobility, they are also likely to experience behavioral syndromes similar to those found among impoverished African Americans. Adolescent pregnancies are a symptom—not a cause—that proliferates in circumstances where the paths toward opportunity and resources are blocked.

Conclusions

In clarifying the meaning of adolescent pregnancies in West Baltimore, this chapter focused on a small number of individuals related by kinship and friendship. However, the plot unraveled is not idiosyncratic. I have attempted to pinpoint the locations of cultural and social capital as they affect economic outcomes and argued that cultural capital is best understood, narrowly, as a reserve of symbols interactively formed and placed into circulation to *make sense* of circumstances. Cultural capital does not reproduce autonomously but only to the extent that the conditions surrounding the flow of specific forms of social capital are recreated. All social networks form relationships of mutuality, trust, and cooperation on the basis of which social capital is generated. What vary are the types and quality of resources available through exchanges of mutuality. Towanda Forrest is neither shunning mainstream values nor comporting herself as a pliant victim. At every step of her disfigured life, she has deployed knowledge and made decisions to control resources available in her environment.

Although it may seem a paradox in modern times, the passage from childhood to adulthood is ritualized, marked at every stage by symbols that denote fuller approximations to maturity. In the case of children born in affluence, those symbols designate a continued relationship with the market economy and high expectations about access to the opportunity structure. Middle-class parents encourage their children to obtain an education, not only because they value intellectual growth but because they "know" that credentials from "good" schools, high standardized test scores, and behaviors learned from the "right" contacts create a repertory of signals that can be parlayed into desirable jobs. Intimations about a future filled with promise flavor the conversation of middle-class parents and their children from the time they are very young.

Similar conversations do not ensue among many impoverished people because the resources and personal contacts that make promises seem real to children are simply not there. None of the markers that account for success in better neighborhoods exists in the Baltimore ghetto, where the number of social service delivery programs by far exceeds the number of banks. In that milieu, the symbolic repertory of impoverished children is not shaped through interaction with the market but by iteration with the apparatus that targets them as a problem to be resolved. Although fraught with contradictions, the birth of a child separates the boys from the men, the girls from the women. Despite the obfuscations of class, gender, and race, one thing is clear: giving birth to a child has a distinct symbolic meaning for the urban poor that overlaps with the same occurrence among more prosperous groups but is not identical.

Almost forty years ago, Robert K. Merton created an enduring typology of social action that assigned priority to the relationship between cultural goals and institutional means.[43] Among other categories, Merton distinguished between *conformists*, those who have internalized normative goals and possess the institutionalized means to implement them, and *innovators*, those who adhere to cultural norms but lack the institutional means to realize them.[44] A surprising offshoot of the analysis above is the recognition of impoverished ghetto dwellers as innovators bent on recreating meanings that are viable in limited environments characterized by residential segregation and exclusion from the spheres where resources are controlled.

Finally, two implications of this analysis for policy are worth notice. First is the insight that social networks matter. Meanings attached to behavior depend largely on whether a network is diversified, formed by subgroups with varying social statuses who act in various fields of activity. A diversified network makes it possible for individuals to tap resources through what Mark Granovetter calls *weak ties.* A problem with Towanda's social network is that, although it is loaded with strong family and friendship bonds, it lacks bridges to other social networks that control access to a larger set of opportunities and meanings. The prescription is to expand the social networks of impoverished children by bringing them into sustained contact with those who, by virtue of class and circumstance, know a different, richer reality than Towanda does.

A second, derived implication regards the efficacy of sexual education. My analysis makes clear that educational measures to curtail adolescent pregnancies are likely to have lackluster results when children view motherhood as the only avenue to adulthood. The expansion of the resource stockpile through which children can achieve maturity is a necessary precondition to reduce teenage pregnancies.

This chapter was written while I was in residence as a visiting scholar at the Russell Sage Foundation. It has benefited from discussions held with the Working Group in Immigration and Economic Sociology at the Russell Sage Foundation and from remarks offered by the Foundation's resident scholar, Robert K. Merton.

Notes

1. William J. Wilson, *The Truly Disadvantaged: The Inner City, The Underclass and Public Policy* (Chicago: University of Chicago Press, 1987).

2. Charles Murray, *Losing Ground: American Social Policy, 1950–1980* (New York: Basic Books, 1984); Lawrence Mead, *Beyond Entitlement: The Social Obligations of Citizenship* (New York: Free Press, 1986).

3. Douglas Massey, "American Apartheid: Segregation and the Making of the Underclass," *American Journal of Sociology* 96, no. 2 (September 1990):329–357. Massey's most recent research, however, also suggests that the most compelling factor in the concentration of ghetto poverty

is not the departure of middle-class African Americans but the unwillingness of whites to live in black areas.

4. The extent to which social networks are formed by individuals with differing social statuses, linked in a variety of ways, who play multiple roles in several fields of activity. See Jeremy Boissevain, *Friends of Friends: Networks, Manipulators and Coalitions* (New York: St. Martin's Press, 1974).

5. See Max Weber, *The Social and Economic Organization* (1922; reprint, New York: The Free Press, 1947); *The Sociology of Religion* (1922; reprint, Boston: Beacon Press, 1963); *The Protestant Ethic and the Spirit of Capitalism* (1904; reprint, New York: Charles Scribner's Sons, 1958); Georg Simmel, *The Philosophy of Money* (1907; reprint, Boston: Routledge & Kegan Paul, 1978); Karl Marx, *A Contribution to the Critique of Political Economy* (1859; reprint, New York: International Publishers, 1970).

6. Robert D. Putnam, "The Prosperous Community: Social Capital and Public Life," *The American Prospect* 13 (Spring 1993):37.

7. Relationships based on mutuality are not the only source of social capital. Also important are internalized norms and values, bounded solidarity, and enforceable trust as discussed by Alejandro Portes in the introductory chapter to this volume. My analysis of factors accounting for inclusion and exclusion in a social network are consistent with that discussion.

8. Mark Granovetter, "Economic Action and Social Structure: The Problem of Embeddedness," *American Journal of Sociology* 91 (1985):481–510.

9. Robin L. Jarrett, "Community Context, Intrafamilial Processes, and Social Mobility Outcomes: Ethnographic Contributions to the Study of African American Families and Children in Poverty" (Center for Urban Affairs and Policy Research, Northwestern University, 1992, mimeographed).

10. For an early treatment of this issue refer to Max Gluckman, *Custom and Conflict in Africa* (Oxford: Blackwell, 1956).

11. For further elaboration of this point see Philip Moss and Chris Tilly, " 'Soft' Skills and Race: An Investigation of Black Men's Employment Problems" (University of Massachusetts, Lowell, 1993, mimeographed).

12. The characteristics and functions of social networks of greatest potential interest to economic sociology were condensed in two volumes published coincidentally in the same year without apparent knowledge or at least mention of one another: Jeremy Boissevain, *Friends of Friends: Networks, Manipulators and Coalitions* (New York: St. Martin's Press, 1974) and Mark Granovetter, *Getting a Job: A Study of Contacts and Careers* (Cambridge: Harvard University Press, 1974). See also Harrison White, *Chains of Opportunity: System Models of Mobility in Organizations* (Cambridge: Harvard University Press, 1970).

13. Christopher Jencks, *Rethinking Social Policy: Race, Poverty, and the Underclass* (Cambridge: Harvard University Press, 1992), p. 18.

14. See, for example, Oscar Lewis, *Five Families: Mexican Case Studies in the Culture of Poverty: San Juan and New York* (New York: Basic Books, 1959).

15. In this respect, the works of Pierre Bourdieu and Michel Foucault should be of interest to economic sociology. See, for example, Michel Foucault, *The History of Sexuality*, Vol. 3, *The Care of the Self* (New York: Vintage, 1988). See also Pierre Bourdieu, "Social Space and Symbolic Power," *Sociological Theory* 7 (1989):14–25.

16. Robert K. Merton, "Three Fragments From a Sociologist's Notebooks: Establishing the Phenomenon, Specified Ignorance, and Strategic Research Materials," *Annual Review of Sociology* 13 (1987):1–28.

17. The most thorough rendition of the conservative view is Murray's *Losing Ground*. See also Douglas J. Besharov and Karen N. Gardiner, "Teen Sex: Truth and Consequences," *The American Enterprise* (January/February 1993):53–59. I use the term welfare state sparingly not to confuse it with public assistance programs. There is a difference between the latter, as they exist in the United States, and other, more comprehensive policies as found in most European countries. Welfare states assume that membership in the larger society affords individuals the right to certain economic privileges by virtue of their status as citizens. Public assistance programs differ in that they focus only on impoverished populations asked to yield some rights of citizenship to obtain economic relief. See Michael B. Katz, *The Undeserving Poor: From the War on Poverty to the War on Welfare* (New York: Pantheon, 1989).

18. In Christopher Jencks's words, "[Murray] made [a] claim that I take . . . seriously, namely that building a safety net for single mothers who do not work undermines traditional social norms about work and marriage." *Rethinking Social Policy: Race, Poverty, and the Underclass* (Cambridge: Harvard University Press, 1992), p. 13.

19. The alarm over teen pregnancies cannot be automatically attributed to racism. Other factors, including concern for the well-being of young mothers, are considered by legislators, government officials, and the public at large. Nevertheless, ideas about racial and cultural predispositions play a part also. In 1991, I interviewed ten top legislators and government officials in Baltimore. Seven answered in the affirmative when asked, "Do you believe that culture plays a role in the continuation of poverty among African Americans?" Five said yes when asked, "Do you believe that blacks are more likely to fall into poverty because of their race?" An equal number agreed that teen pregnancies were probably influenced by inherited cultural and biological propensities. The size and nonrandom character of the sample precludes generalizations. However, there is no reason to believe these opinions are uncommon.

20. Constance A. Nathanson, *Dangerous Passage: The Social Control of Sexuality in Women's Adolescence* (Philadelphia: Temple University Press, 1991). Kristin Luker, "Dubious Conceptions: The Controversy Over Teen Pregnancy," *The American Prospect* (Spring 1991):73–83. The most cursory glance at the historical record shows that the age and conditions under which people are deemed fit to procreate has varied. Matrimony and procreation have not always been paired. In foraging and hunting societies, childbearing tends to follow marriage at an early age, with marriage constituting primarily an alliance between kinship groups, not individuals. Early Puritans and Flemish Christians viewed pregnancy—and thus the demonstrated ability to reproduce—as a prerequisite for marriage. A delicious exponent of this tradition dating back to the fifteenth century is Jan Van Eyck's *Arnolfini's Marriage*, a masterpiece depicting a respectable Dutch merchant holding the hand of his visibly pregnant bride-to-be.

21. Christopher Jencks and Paul Peterson, *Urban Underclass* (Washington, D.C.: The Brookings Institution, 1991).

22. Marta Tienda and Haya Steir, "Intergenerational Continuity of Welfare Dependence: Ethnic and Neighborhood Comparisons" (paper presented at the Chicago Urban Poverty and Family Life Conference, Irving B. Harris Graduate School of Public Policy Studies, University of Chicago, 1991).

23. Murray, *Losing Ground.*

24. See Frank J. Furstenberg, Jr., *Unplanned Parenthood: The Social Consequences of Teen-Age Child-Bearing* (New York: Free Press, 1976); Frank F. Furstenberg, Jr., J. Brooks Gunn, and S. Philip Morgan, *Adolescent Mothers in Later Life* (Cambridge: Cambridge University Press, 1987) and Richard P. Taub, "Differing Conceptions of Honor and Orientations Toward Work and Marriage Among Low-Income African Americans and Mexican Americans" (paper presented at the Chicago Urban Poverty and Family Life Conference, Irving B. Harris Graduate School of Public Policy Studies, University of Chicago, 1991).

25. Daniel Patrick Moynihan, *The Negro Family: The Case for National Action* (Washington: U.S. Department of Labor, 1965).

26. Oscar Lewis, "The Culture of Poverty," in Daniel Patrick Moynihan, ed., *On Understanding Poverty: Perspectives From the Social Sciences* (New York: Basic Books, 1968). For a different and more recent treatment see Andrew Cherlin, *The Changing American Family and Public Policy* (Washington, D.C.: The Urban Institute Press, 1988), Chap. 6.

27. Ulf Hannerz, *Soulside: Inquiries into Ghetto Culture and Community* (New York: Columbia University Press, 1969).

28. Wilson, *The Truly Disadvantaged.*

29. Molly Rath, "Maryland Expanding Use of Norplant for Poor Women," Reuters Ltd., April 10, 1993.

30. See Tienda and Steir, "Intergenerational Continuity of Welfare Dependence."

31. An account of conditions prevailing in some inner-city public schools may be found in Jonathan Kozol, *Savage Inequalities: Children in America's Schools* (New York: Crown Publishers, 1991).

32. Recent works stress the importance of *respect* as a theme in the lives of the poor. See Philippe Buorgois, "In Search of Respect: The New Service Economy and the Crack Alternative in Spanish Harlem" (paper presented at the Conference on Poverty, Immigration, and Urban Marginality in Advanced Societies, Maison Suger, Paris, 1991). See also Taub, "Differing Conceptions of Honor and Orientations Toward Work and Marriage."

33. See Alvin Gouldner, "The Norm of Reciprocity: A Preliminary Statement," *American Sociological Review* 25 (1960):161–179; Mark Granovetter, "Economic Action and Social Structure: The Problem of Embeddedness," *American Journal of Sociology* 91, no. 3 (1985):481–510. James S. Coleman, "Social Capital in the Creation of Human Capital," *American Journal of Sociology* Supplement (1988):S95–121; Mark Granovetter, "The Old and the New Economic Sociology: A History and an Agenda," in Roger Friedland and A. F. Robertson, eds., *Beyond the Marketplace* (New York: Aldine de Gruyter, 1990).

34. Germane to this observation is the work of Pierre Bourdieu. See "Les trois états du capital culturel," *Actes de la Recherche en Sciences Sociales* 30 (November 1979):3–5.

35. Hannerz, *Soulside*; Loïc J. D. Wacquant and William J. Wilson, "The Cost of Racial and Class Exclusion," *Annals of the American Academy of Political and Social Science* 501 (1989):8–26; Taub, "Differing Conceptions."

36. Taub, "Differing Conceptions," p. 16.

37. Robert K. Merton, "Socially Expected Durations: A Case Study of Concept Formation in Sociology," in W. W. Powell and Richard Robbins, eds., *Conflict and Consensus: A Festschrift for Lewis A. Coser* (New York: The Free Press, 1984), p. 266.

38. Ibid., p. 266.

39. Alex Kotlowitz, *There Are No Children Here: The Story of Two Boys Growing Up in the Other America* (New York: Doubleday, 1991).

40. For a comprehensive treatment of this point see Jarrett, "Community Context." See also Glen H. Elder, Jr., "Families, Kin, and the Life Course: A Sociological Perspective," in Ross Parke, ed., *Advances in Child Development Research and the Family* (Chicago: University of Chicago Press, 1984). See also Linda M. Burton and Robin L. Jarrett, "Studying African American Family Structure and Process in Underclass Neighborhoods: Conceptual Considerations" (paper presented

at the Annual Meeting of the American Sociological Association, Cincinnati, Ohio, 1991).

41. Germane to this point is a comparison of Sweden, the Netherlands, Great Britain, Canada, France, and the United States conducted by the New York-based Guttmacher Institute. The United States has the highest adolescent pregnancy rates, but in the other five countries the overall level of support for unwed mothers is more generous. This raises questions about the extent to which teenagers are lured into having babies by the chance to collect a welfare stipend.

42. See Robert Aponte, "Urban Employment and the Mismatch Theory: Accounting for the Immigrant Factor" (University of Michigan, Ann Arbor, 1993, mimeographed).

43. Robert K. Merton, *Social Theory and Social Structure* (Glencoe, Ill.: Free Press, 1957).

44. The other categories were: *deviants* (those who, as in the case of criminals, adhere to prevalent values but shun institutional mechanisms), *rebels* (a smaller contingent of individuals who neither adhere to normative goals nor accept institutional means to realize them), *ritualists* (those who do not adhere to prevalent values but follow institutional dictates) and *escapists* (those who reject both conventional norms and institutional means).

7

Children of Immigrants: Segmented Assimilation and Its Determinants

ALEJANDRO PORTES

GROWING UP in an immigrant family has always been a difficult process of reconciling the language and cultural orientations of foreign-born parents with the demands for assimilation of the host society. In the American experience, the process has traditionally been portrayed as a seldom-resolved series of familial and social-psychological tensions which often culminate either in a rejection of the parental culture or a retreat from confrontation with outside society. Those children of immigrants who are able to move successfully between the two worlds represent a minority.[1] Studies of the second generation virtually ceased in the 1950s after the coming-of-age of the offspring of turn-of-the-century immigrants. In the 1990s, however, these studies have gained renewed vigor in the wake of accelerating immigration brought about by changes in United States immigration law. Unlike the earlier immigration wave, composed primarily of Europeans, contemporary immigrants came mostly from Latin American and Asian countries. Their numbers virtually guarantee that the second generation (native-born persons of foreign parentage) will surpass its earlier peak of about 28 million reached in 1940.[2]

More important than their numbers alone is the theoretical problem posed by the new second generation and its adaptation to American society. Children of immigrants grow up today in a social context different from that encountered by their predecessors, which

248

can alter significantly the effects of assimilation. Regardless of their particularities, studies of immigrant offspring in the past took for granted that acculturation into the values, norms, and practices of American society was a *sine qua non* for socioeconomic mobility.[3] Today this assertion is more problematic. As we shall see, there are circumstances at present in which assimilation does not lead to economic progress and social acceptance, but to precisely the opposite results. My purpose in this chapter is to examine the dilemmas confronting the second generation within the framework of conceptual developments in both economic sociology and the sociology of immigration. Their joint use will allow us to see the phenomena of intergenerational tension and sociocultural assimilation in a new light and to advance original propositions on their future course.

Segmented Assimilation and Its Variants

The dilemmas of contemporary second-generation adaptation are well illustrated by several recent studies. I present two examples that offer a suitable empirical background for the ensuing theoretical discussion.

The Haitian immigrant community of Miami is composed of some 100,000 legal and clandestine immigrants, many of whom sold everything in order to buy passage to America. First-generation Haitians are strongly oriented toward preserving a strong national identity, which they associate both with community solidarity and with social networks promoting individual success. In trying to instill national pride and an achievement orientation in their children, however, they come into conflict with the youngsters' everyday experiences in school. Little Haiti is adjacent to Liberty City, the main black inner-city area of Miami, and Haitian adolescents attend predominantly inner-city schools. Native-born minority youth stereotype Haitians as too docile and too subservient to whites and they make fun of French and Creole and of the Haitians' accent. As a result, second-generation Haitian children find themselves torn between conflicting ideas and values: to remain "Haitian" they would have to face social ostracism and continuing attacks in school; to become "American" (black American in this case), they would have to forgo their parents' dreams of making it in America on the basis of ethnic solidarity and preservation of traditional values.[4]

An adversarial stance toward the white mainstream is common among inner-city minority youth who, while attacking the newcomers' ways, instill in them an awareness of American-style discrimination. A common message is the devaluation of education as a vehicle for advancement of all black youth, a message that directly contradicts the immigrant parents' expectations. Academically outstanding Haitian American students have consciously attempted to retain their ethnic identity by cloaking it in black American cultural forms. Many others, however, have followed the path of least effort and become thoroughly assimilated. "Assimilation" in this instance is not to mainstream culture, but to the values and norms of the inner city. In the process, the resources of solidarity and mutual support within the immigrant community are dissipated.

A second recent study looks at the Punjabi Sikh community in the northern California town of "Valleyside," which consists of farmers and laborers brought from India to tend the fruit orchards on which the town's economy depend. By the early 1980s, second-generation Punjabi Sikh students already accounted for 11 percent of the student body at Valleyside High. An ethnographic study of Valleyside High School in 1980–1982 revealed a very difficult process of assimilation for Punjabi Sikh students. According to the author, Valleyside is "redneck country" and white residents are extremely hostile toward immigrants who look different and speak a different language:

> Punjabi teenagers are told they stink . . . told to go back to India . . . physically abused by majority students who spit at them, refuse to sit by them in class or in buses, throw food at them or worse.[5]

Despite these attacks and some evidence of discrimination from school staff, Punjabi students performed better academically than majority "Anglo" students. About 90 percent of the immigrant youth completed high school, compared to 70–75 percent among native whites. Punjabi boys surpassed the grade-point average (GPA) for their grades, were more likely to take advanced science and math classes, and expressed aspirations for careers in science and engineering. Punjabi girls, on the other hand, tended to enroll in business classes but paid less attention to immediate career plans, reflecting parental wishes that they should marry first. This gender difference is indicative of the continuing strong influence exercised by the immigrant community over its second generation. Punjabi parents pressured their children to avoid too much contact with white peers who may "dishonor" the immigrants' families and defined "becoming Americanized" as forgetting one's roots and adopting the most disparaged traits of the majority—such as leaving home at the age of eighteen, making decisions without parental consent, dating, and dancing. At the same time, parents urged children to abide by school rules, ignore racist remarks and avoid fights, and acquire useful skills including full proficiency in English.[6] The overall success of this strategy is remarkable because Punjabi immigrants were generally poor at the moment of arrival and confronted widespread discrimination from whites without the benefit of either governmental assistance or a well-established co-ethnic community.

The principal paradox that emerges from the study of today's second generation is apparent in the peculiar forms that adaptation is taking for its members. As the case of Haitians in Miami suggests, adopting the outlooks and cultural ways of the native-born is no longer always a step, as in the past, toward social and economic progress but may lead to exactly the opposite outcome. On the other hand, as the case of the Punjabi Sikhs illustrates, immigrant youth who remain firmly ensconced in their respective ethnic communities may, by virtue of this fact, have a better chance of educational and economic mobility through access to the resources that their communities make available.

This situation represents a significant analytic challenge because it stands the cultural blueprint for absorption of immigrant groups in American society on its head. As described in innumerable academic and journalistic writings, the expectation is that foreigners and their offspring will first acculturate and then seek entry and acceptance from the native-born population as a prerequisite for their social and economic advancement. Otherwise, they would remain confined to the ranks of the "ethnic" lower and lower-middle class.[7] This portrayal of the requirements for mobility in American society, so deeply embedded in the national consciousness, is contradicted by a growing number of recent real-life experiences.

At this point, it is necessary to pause in order to define more clearly the object of the study. A closer look at the existing evidence indicates that the consequences of assimilation have not changed signs entirely, but rather have become segmented. The important consideration is *to what sector* of the receiving society a particular immigrant group assimilates. Instead of a relatively uniform "mainstream" whose values and norms dictate a homogeneous path of integration, it is possible to distinguish today several alternative paths. One of them replicates the time-honored pattern of growing acculturation and parallel integration into the majority white middle class; a second leads straight in the opposite direction, to permanent poverty and assimilation into the underclass; a third links economic mobility with preservation of the immigrant community's solidarity.

This pattern of *segmented assimilation* immediately raises the question of what makes some immigrant groups susceptible to the downward route and what resources allow others to avoid this path. The possible causal factors are manifold and include, of course, the material resources and educational and occupational skills that different groups possess. These assets, commonly referred to as physical and human capital, represent the principal source of explanations advanced by economists for the differential success or failure of immigrants.[8] Although the significance of these individual resources is undeniable, I wish to focus attention on factors of a moral order associated with membership in a particular community. These factors belong more properly in the realm of social capital and involve the structures through which it is created. As we saw in the first chapter of this book, such structures include, in the case of immigrants, their modes of incorporation in the host society and the types of networks that subsequently emerge among their members.

Vulnerabilities and Resources

The available evidence indicates that children of immigrants are over-concentrated in urban areas and, within them, in the central cities. According to census data, 39.5 percent of children in households with at least one foreign-born parent lived in central city areas in 1980 as compared to 17.4 percent among children of native-born parents.[9] This overconcentration in the inner cities, which is a direct consequence of the lower economic resources of recent immigrants, has an unexpected consequence, namely to bring the offspring of these immigrants into close contact with downtrodden domestic minorities. During the last third of a century or so, American central cities have gradually become the repository of the children and grandchildren of earlier migrants who failed to move up the socioeconomic ladder. To a large extent, this failure was the direct consequence of outside discrimination coupled with changing requirements in the American labor market; but regardless of its causes, the end result was to foster the development of an adversarial outlook toward the mostly white mainstream.[10] The bearers of this outlook, who are the offspring of earlier immigrants and domestic migrants, can exercise a powerful influence on newly arrived youth by virtue of their numbers and their native-born status.

The main arena where this encounter between native minority youth and children of immigrants takes place is the public schools that both groups attend because of their physical proximity. The confrontation with inner-city values places the second generation in a serious dilemma, exemplified by the case of Haitian American children. It is worthwhile to delve deeper into the nature of this dilemma and the reasons why it so often ends with the abandonment of parental expectations and values. The dilemma has three aspects: 1) the outlook toward mainstream institutions of native minority youth and the social forces that support it; 2) the internal structure of the immigrant community; and 3) the social ties linking second-generation children to the aspects of the dilemma described in points 1 and 2.

Leveling Pressures

The cultural clash experienced by children of Haitian immigrants and by other groups to be described later involves the upward mobility expectations of the parents set in opposition to the downward leveling norms of the inner city. The social mechanism underlying these norms is the fear that a solidarity born out of common adversity would be undermined by the departure of successful members. Each success story saps the morale of a group, if that morale is built precisely on the limited possibilities for ascent under an oppressive social order.[11] In his field research in the Bronx, Bourgois illustrates the strong leveling pressures to which Puerto Rican youth with aspirations are subjected. They are forcefully denounced by their peers as "turnovers" who leave their own people behind in their quest "to be white."[12] Similarly, Wacquant and Wilson describe the South Side of Chicago as a "hyperghetto" in which solidarity cemented on common adversity discourages individuals from seeking or pursuing outside opportunities.[13]

Each instance of downward leveling norms has been preceded by extensive periods, often several generations, in which the upward mobility of a minority has been blocked. This has been followed by the emergence of collective solidarity based on opposition to those conditions and an accompanying explanation of the group's economic and social inferiority as caused by outside oppression. Although accurate from a historical standpoint, the emergence of such norms further reduces chances for individual advancement to the extent that youth are socialized into the futility of "making it" on the basis of one's own merits.[14] The arrival of sizable cohorts of children whose parentally inspired outlook is precisely the opposite is bound to elicit a strong reaction aimed at enforcing conformity with the dominant norms.

Note that, unlike most descriptions of social pathologies in American urban ghettos, the existence of downward leveling norms and the pressures experienced by second-generation youth to conform are not the outcome of "social disorganization" or anomie. On the contrary, the existence of such norms and the ability to enforce them depends on community structures and, in particular, on social networks. As Fernández Kelly notes in her analysis of families in the Baltimore ghetto, networks and social capital exist in the inner city, but the quality of resources that they make available and the conditions for gaining access to them are often at variance with those required for ascendance into mainstream society.[15] To the extent that such mobility is deemed desirable, leveling norms can be defined as another instance of the potential negative effects of social capital.

This discussion can be summarized in the following proposition:

I.   *The closer the propinquity of immigrant communities to downtrodden domestic minorities;*
     The stronger the social networks enforcing an adversarial stance among neighboring minorities;
     The greater the resources whose access is contingent on conformity to dominant norms.
     Then, the greater the incidence of downward assimilation among second-generation youth and the faster their abandonment of parental expectations.

An Example: Mexican Students in California   It seems appropriate to put some flesh onto these dry theoretical bones by illustrating this first hypothesis with an empirical example. The illustration comes from an ethnographic study of a high school in a small central California community whose economy has long been tied to agricultural production and immigrant farm labor. About 57 percent of the student population at "Field High" is of Mexican descent.[16] An analysis of school records for the class of 1985 showed that the majority of American-born Spanish-surname students who had entered the school in 1981 had dropped out by the senior year. Significantly, however, only 35 percent of the Spanish-surname students who had been originally classified as LEP (Limited English Proficient) dropped out. The figure was even lower than the corresponding one for native white students (40 percent). LEP status is commonly assigned to recently arrived Mexican immigrants.[17]

Ethnographic fieldwork at the school identified several distinct categories into which the Mexican-origin population was classified both by the staff and by the students themselves. *Recent Mexican immigrants* were at one extreme. They dressed differently and unstylishly. They claimed an identity as Mexican and considered Mexico their permanent home. The most academically successful of this group were those most proficient in Spanish, reflecting their prior levels of education in Mexico. Almost all were described by teachers and staff as courteous, serious about their schoolwork, respectful and eager to please as well as naive and unsophisticated. They were frequently classified as LEP.

Mexican-oriented students spoke Spanish at home and were generally classified as FEP (Fluent English Proficient). They had strong bicultural ties with both Mexico and the United States, reflecting the fact that most were born in Mexico but had lived in the United States for more than five years. They were proud of their Mexican heritage, but saw themselves as different from the first group, the *recién llegados* (recently arrived), as well as from the native-born *Chicanos* and *Cholos*, whom they derided as people who had lost their Mexican roots. Students from this group were active in soccer and the *Sociedad Bilingüe* and in celebrations of May 5th, the anniversary of the Mexican defeat of French occupying forces. Virtually all of the students of Mexican descent who graduated in the top 10 percent of their class in 1981 were identified as members of this group.

Chicanos were by far the largest Mexican-descent group at Field High. They were mostly American-born second- and third-generation students whose primary loyalty was to their in-group, seen as locked in conflict with white society. Chicanos referred derisively to successful Mexican students as "schoolboys" and "schoolgirls" or as "wannabes." According to Matute-Bianchi:

> To be a Chicano meant in practice to hang out by the science wing . . . *not* eating lunch in the quad where all the "gringos" and "schoolboys" hang out . . . cutting classes by faking a call slip so you can be with your friends at the 7-Eleven . . . sitting in the back of classes and not participating . . . *not* carrying your books to class . . . *not* taking the difficult classes . . . doing the minimum to get by.[18]

Chicanos merge imperceptibly into the last category, the *Cholos*, who are commonly seen as "low riders" and gang members. They are also native-born Mexican Americans, easily identifiable by their deliberate manner of dress, walk, speech, and other cultural symbols. Chicanos and Cholos are generally regarded by teachers as "irresponsible," "disrespectful," "mistrusting," "sullen," "apathetic," and "less motivated," and their poor school performance is attributed to these traits.[19] According to Matute-Bianchi, Chicanos and Cholos were faced with what they saw as a forced-choice dilemma between doing well in school or being a Chicano. To act "white" was regarded as disloyalty to one's group.

Notice that the first two groups described in the study—*mexicanos* and Mexican-oriented students—are both immigrant children, while the last two—*chicanos* and *cholos*—are both children and grand-children of immigrants. These last groups have had more time to experience American-style discrimination first-hand and, more importantly, to assimilate the reactive stance against it developed by significant segments of the Mexican American population in the past. The fact that those conveying this message are descendants of earlier Mexican immigrants, "people like us," adds to its authority and persuasiveness. This adversarial outlook protects the second generation's sense of self-worth against outside discrimination, but simultaneously retards its chances for upward mobility since school achievement is defined as antithetical to ethnic solidarity.[20]

Immigrant Social Capital

Since the nineteenth century, immigrant groups in the United States have been renowned for the solidarity displayed by their members and their success in promoting each other's enterprises. This pattern continues today and is supported by similar forces. With their education and skills from the home country devalued in the host society's labor market and facing pervasive discrimination by the native-born, immigrants have little recourse but to band together in search of moral support and economic survival.[21] This solidarity born from common adversity possesses two analytically distinguishable elements:

1. A common cultural memory brought from the home country and which comprises the customs, mores, and language through which immigrants define themselves and communicate with others;

2. An emergent sentiment of "we-ness" prompted by the experience of being lumped together, defined in derogatory terms, and subjected to the same discrimination by the host society.

The combination of these elements transforms immigrant groups into ethnic communities in a relatively short period of time. To the extent that the first element represents a continuation of cultural practices learned in the home country, it can be labeled *linear* ethnicity. To the extent that the second represents an emergent product of the experience of immigration, it may be labeled *reactive* ethnicity.[22] For the second generation, these two elements of solidarity have very different consequences. Reactive ethnicity has many points in common with the experience of earlier downtrodden minorities which underlies the emergence of an adversarial stance among their youth. Assimilation to the culture of the inner city is logically justified by a common situation of social inferiority and the need to respond jointly to an oppressive, white-dominated mainstream. Linear ethnicity, on the contrary, gives rise to an entirely different outlook based on the partial recreation of institutions brought from the home country. The emergence of immigrant churches, schools, restaurants, shops, and financial institutions patterned in the mold of the old country reinforces the first-generation stance in two ways: first, by creating a social environment that validates its norms and values; second, by creating opportunities within the immigrant community that are absent in the outside.[23]

The same is true for the second generation, whose attendance at ethnic churches, participation in ethnic festivities, and visits to ethnic shops consolidate its attachment to the immigrant community and hence pull it away from rapid acculturation. Similarly, the economic diversification of some immigrant communities creates niches of opportunity that members of the second generation can occupy often without need for an advanced education. Small-business apprenticeships, access to skilled building trades, and well-paid jobs in local government bureaucracies are among the ethnic niches documented in the recent literature. Fieldwork in the Chinese, Korean, Vietnamese, and Cuban communities indicates that up to one-half of recently arrived immigrants are employed by co-ethnic firms and that self-employment offers a prime avenue for mobility to both immigrants and their offspring.[24] Such community-mediated opportunities create a definite incentive for young people to remain within the ethnic fold and, more importantly, negate the premise of the inner-city minority stance that paths of mobility are blocked for those outside the white mainstream.

Social capital was defined in the introductory chapter as the ability to command scarce resources by virtue of membership in networks or broader social structures. In the case at hand, namely the adaptation of second-generation youth, the immigrant community provides two types of social capital: to parents and to the children themselves. For immigrant parents, social capital consists of the ability to call on co-ethnics to reinforce normative expectations vis-à-vis their offspring and to supervise their behavior. Coleman has referred to this process as the degree of "closure" of a community: to the extent that parents share a common outlook and are linked by close ties they will reinforce each other's normative control of their children. This type of social capital, of course, dissipates when communities become less cohesive.[25]

For the children, social capital consists of the ability to command resources controlled by the ethnic community along the lines described earlier. Quite clearly, the amount and quality of these resources depends on the physical, financial, and human assets possessed by fellow co-ethnics, but the *mobilization* of these resources and their availability to second-generation children depends on social capital. In other words, it makes little difference for immigrant youth that all members of their parents' generation are physicians or lawyers if they are spatially dispersed and feel little obligation toward each other. In such cases, there is little incentive for second-generation children to comply with parental normative expectations since this behavior does not yield any kind of privileged access to ethnic resources.

It follows from the preceding argument that density of networks within the immigrant community increases social capital with which to prevent downward assimilation. Density increases parental social capital for two reasons: first, it adds to the number of adults on whom parents can call for support; second, it decreases the centrality of children vis-à-vis their parents since adults tend to connect better within the ethnic community than dependent youth. As we saw in Chapter 1, centrality is associated with power which, in this instance, reverts to the parental generation. Yet children of immigrants within tightly knit communities are not only subject to adult expectations, but can also mobilize greater resources by virtue of their parents' and their own ethnic networks.

These arguments can be summarized in the following propositions:

IIa. The more immigrant solidarity is grounded in a common cultural
       memory and the replication of home country institutions (linear eth-
       nicity);
       The greater the density of social networks within these communities.
          Then, the greater the social capital available to: (1) parents for social
          control, and (2) their offspring for access to scarce community-
          controlled resources.
IIb. The greater 1 and 2.
       Then, the lower the probability of downward assimilation.

These propositions will be illustrated with additional empirical material after we examine the character of social ties within and outside the ethnic community.

Weak and Strong Ties

The preceding argument may be seen as contradicting some of the most influential notions advanced recently in economic sociology.

In his *Getting a Job* (and subsequent publications), Granovetter has elaborated the hypothesis that "weak ties" linking an individual to others are often more effective in furthering her/his goals than the "strong ties" of kin and other intimate relationships. Weak ties possess a number of advantages, including their larger scope, the non-redundant character of the information that they convey, and their more instrumental character. On the contrary, strong ties tend to be narrowly bound, provide overlapping information, and surround economic transactions with emotional content.[26]

In a related vein, Burt has recently advanced a theory of "structural holes," defined as the "gaps between nonredundant contacts."[27] When gaps do not exist within redundant networks (as is the case with strong ties), the actor (individual or firm) is said to be "constrained." When, on the other hand, an actor's network features more redundant holes but fewer nonredundant ones, the actor is said to possess greater "structural autonomy." The reason is that contacts that provide unique information (not available from other network members) yield gains that are additive rather than overlapping. Autonomous actors possess networks rich in such "weak ties" whose strength lies in their nonredundancy.[28]

My argument above, that linear ethnicity and density of networks increases social capital and hence long-term benefits for first- and second-generation immigrants, would appear to run against these theories. It does so only to a limited extent. Density of ethnic networks is not incompatible with weak ties insofar as a diversified ethnic community features a heterogeneous set of contacts which maximize the potential benefits of social capital for members. This is shown in Figure 7.1, which portrays ethnic networks for two hypothetical second-generation youths. The number of first-tier contacts (strong ties) of actor *A* and the related number of relationships of each contact in a "dense" community yields a much larger number of second- and third-tier contacts (weak ties) for *A* than for *B*. Since a number of secondary and tertiary contacts are nonoverlapping, the social capital available to *A* is much greater.

My second proposition does contradict Burt's theory of structural holes to the extent that it would predict greater long-term gain for "autonomous" second-generation youth. The reason is apparent from the contrasting situations portrayed in Figure 7.2. Intra-ethnic network gaps weaken the ability of parents to guide ("constrain") youth along their normative goal-oriented path and increase the ability ("autonomy") of offspring to explore alternative extra-ethnic contacts. To the extent that economic limitations place immigrant communities in close proximity to the inner city, the probability of such

Figure 7.1   Social Ties within Dense and Dispersed Immigrant Communities

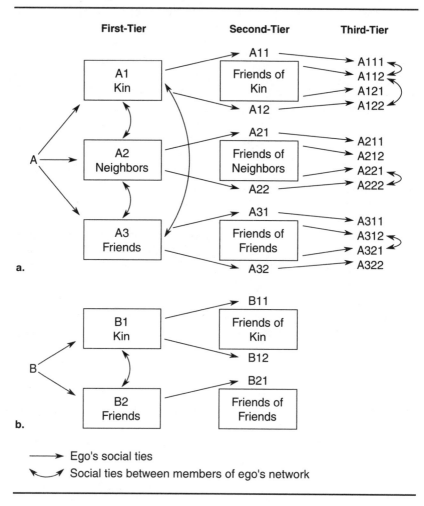

"structural holes" leading to downward assimilation is increased. In other words, the "nonredundant" information gained through this kind of autonomy is precisely of the sort that compromises the immigrants' economic mobility project by contradicting the premises on which it is grounded.

In Figure 7.2, the social networks of the more "constrained" individual *(A)* are dense enough to allow parents to monitor both intra- and extra-community relationships as well as to draw upon the sup-

Figure 7.2   Types of Relationships within Dense and Dispersed Immigrant Communities

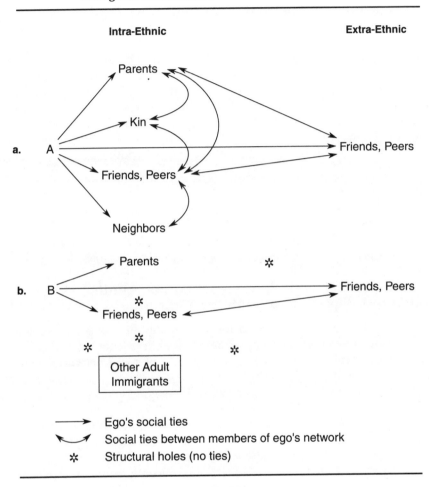

Intra-Ethnic   Extra-Ethnic

a.   A

Parents

Kin

Friends, Peers

Neighbors

Friends, Peers

b.   B

Parents   ✳

Friends, Peers

✳

Friends, Peers

✳

✳   ✳

Other Adult
Immigrants

———▶   Ego's social ties

Social ties between members of ego's network

✳   Structural holes (no ties)

port of ethnic community neighbors and friends. *B*'s parents, on the other hand, lack these resources because structural gaps isolate them both from other immigrants and from their child's outside relationships.

Another way of arriving at the same conclusion is to focus on the character, not the number of second-generation ties. Adolescent ties to their peers are commonly multiplex because the same individuals are simultaneously school mates, participants in the same extracurricular activities, and informal friends.[29] On the other hand, ties to isolated parents are uniplex since they are limited to the roles of adult and child within the family context. When the density of the immigrant community induces second-generation youth to take part in ethnically defined religious services, festivities, and other activities, the situation changes. Intergenerational ties are now defined not solely by the parental bond but by common membership in an overarching community. Other intra-ethnic ties are also multiplex through the same process, balancing the power and attraction of peer relationships on the outside. Figure 7.3 illustrates these contrasting situations.

This discussion leads to the following last hypothesis:

III. *The greater the multiplexity of social ties within the immigrant community;*
      The lesser the incidence of "structural holes" within these communities.
      Then, the greater the social capital available to immigrant parents and the lower the probability of downward assimilation.

An Empirical Test: Second-Generation Youth in South Florida and Southern California

There is at present no data set for any immigrant group that allows a rigorous test of the hypotheses advanced in this chapter. Concepts like social capital, density, and multiplexity of social networks have not been commonly incorporated into the arsenal of sociological survey research and the dependent variable—segmented assimilation—has only been used in one previous paper.[30] Hence, the title of this section is somewhat misleading since the empirical material to be presented does not so much represent a "test" as a first approach to these issues on the basis of available survey results.

The data for this analysis come from a recently completed survey of 5,267 second-generation adolescents in south Florida and southern California. The universe consisted of all eighth and ninth graders in the school systems of Miami (Dade County), Ft. Lauderdale (Broward County), and San Diego County who had at least one foreign-born parent and who themselves had been born in the United States or lived in the country for at least five years. A supplementary survey was conducted with children attending immigrant-oriented private schools in Miami. The eighth and ninth grades were selected to minimize the sample bias associated with large numbers of school dropouts in later grades. The final sample is about evenly balanced between the sexes and has an age range of thirteen to seventeen.[31]

Figure 7.3   Character of Relationships within Dense and Dispersed Immigrant Communities

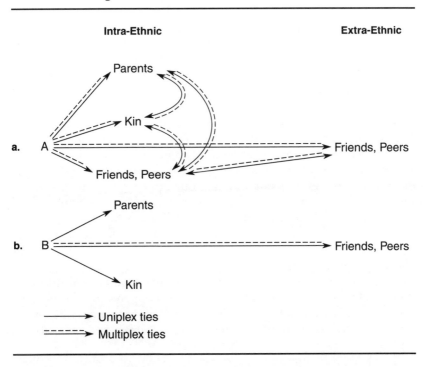

From this large data set, we selected four immigrant nationalities: Cuban American and Haitian American children in Miami/Ft. Lauderdale and Mexican American and Vietnamese American children in San Diego. To understand the ensuing results, a word must be said about the characteristics of their respective immigrant communities. Cuban and Vietnamese immigrations were the result of political convulsions in the respective countries and most of their original members were political refugees. Although federal resettlement programs attempted to disperse both groups throughout the nation, both eventually regrouped in certain localities: Cubans in the Miami metropolitan area and the Vietnamese in Orange and San Diego counties in southern California.[32]

Each refugee group formed highly dense communities in their places of concentration. The older and better-established Cuban community moved farther along the path of institutional development, including the creation of a network of parochial and private schools. Enrollment in these schools insulates Cuban American children from contact with downtrodden groups as well as from outside discrimination. The schools are bilingual and are staffed by other first-generation immigrants who share the parents' values. No such private school system has emerged among the Vietnamese in southern California, but this is compensated for by tight kin networks that monitor and encourage the children's performance in public schools. Both communities are very business oriented. A great deal has been written about the emergence of the Cuban enclave economy of Miami, but the growth of Vietnamese firms in southern California during the last decade has been nothing short of spectacular.[33]

Very different is the situation of Haitians in Miami and Mexicans in San Diego. Neither community possesses a well-developed ethnic economy that can generate autonomous opportunities for its members. Both communities have large numbers of transient and recent arrivals and individuals without legal status in the United States. Haitians have clustered in an impoverished neighborhood adjacent to Liberty City, the largest inner-city ghetto of Miami. Haitian churches, restaurants, and businesses have emerged in this area, inevitably dubbed Little Haiti. However, the institutional development of this ethnic community has been hampered by its recency, the tenuous legal status of much of its population, and widespread discrimination from outsiders who consider Haitians just another addition to the impoverished black inner city.[34]

The Haitian community lacks a private school system and their youth must attend public inner-city schools. There, initially well-mannered Haitian American youths are ridiculed for their accent, their docility, and their obedience to school staff. The parents' dream of upward mobility through education is put to a severe test by peers who deny that education can be of use to people of color. As recent immigrants, Haitian parents hold strongly to their values and aspirations and try to differentiate themselves from the impoverished native minorities nearby. However, theirs is a difficult situation because the institutional feebleness of their own community combines with the pressures of the inner city. In these circumstances, only the immediate family stands as a barrier to downward assimilation.[35]

Mexican immigrants are a much older presence in California, but the temporary and illegal status of many migrants and the menial jobs toward which they have been channeled for decades conspire against the emergence of a socially stable and economically strong community. The fluidity of the movement back and forth across the border and the continuous presence of new arrivals gives to Mexican neighborhoods an unsettled, transient character that weakens the development of stable institutions across generations.[36]

Many years of uninterrupted migration have created a sizable Mexican population in urban areas of southern California, but the relegation of its members to the lowest-paid jobs and unabated discrimination have turned some Mexican American areas into *the* core of the inner city. The adversarial reaction to this permanent situation of instability and subordination has its clearest expression in the emergence of Chicano and Cholo subcultures among native-born youth. As we saw previously, a key element of this stance is the denial of the usefulness of education and a consequent de-emphasis of both educational goals and achievement. This syndrome is summarized by a social anthropologist who has studied it in California schools as "learning not to learn."[37]

Table 7.1 presents a profile of the four selected second-generation groups in terms of their reported social relationships and attitudes. For comparison, I include similar figures for the rest of the sample, comprised of children of immigrants from approximately seventy different nationalities. Cuban American children attending private schools are the most self-enclosed in terms of their social relationships. The extreme intra-ethnic density of their peer interactions is highlighted by the fact that nine out of ten have as close friends other children of immigrants (primarily Cuban Americans). The figure drops to approximately five out of ten for the other groups. This high social insulation helps protect Cuban youth against outside discrimination. As shown in the second panel of Table 7.1, Cuban Americans are also the anomalous category with respect to discrimination since less than one-third report ever feeling discriminated against, while two-thirds of the other groups report such experiences.

When we turn to the question of whether education is perceived as a factor reducing or eliminating outside discrimination, 85 percent of Cuban Americans but only 47 percent of Haitian Americans believe that it can, with the other groups arrayed in between. The racial factor is obviously central to the Haitians' skepticism. These results indicate that even at an early age, children of nonwhite immigrants in close proximity to the inner city are both more aware of the existence of discrimination and more dubious about their chances to overcome it.

The last panel in the table shows an interesting difference in terms of the traditional outlook of youth from the more tightly knit immigrant communities. Asked whether the important thing for women is to meet the right man as opposed to getting an educa-

Table 7.1 Social Characteristics and Attitudes of Second-Generation Children in South Florida and Southern California[1]

	Florida		California			
	Cubans[2] (N = 171)	Haitians (N = 148)	Mexicans (N = 723)	Vietnamese (N = 355)	Others[3] (N = 3775)	p[4]
1. Co-Ethnic Friends Percent reporting that most close friends also have immigrant parents:[5]	94.2	45.9	49.2	54.4	64.4	.001
2. Perceptions of Discrimination Percent reporting having been discriminated against:	29.1	66.7	65.0	66.6	53.0	.001
3. Future Discrimination Percent believing that they will face discrimination even if they attain a high education:	15.1	52.7	35.4	35.5	29.9	.001
4. Female Upward Mobility Percent believing that the best way for a young woman to move up in life is to find the right man:	48.0	16.6	21.5	35.6	21.7	.001

[1] Eighth and ninth graders in Dade (Miami), Broward (Ft. Lauderdale), and San Diego schools who had at least one foreign-born parent and who themselves were born in the United States or had lived in the United States for at least five years in 1992.

[2] Cuban-origin students attending private schools in Miami.

[3] All other second-generation students in the sample. Parents come from 73 different countries.

[4] The probability of observed differences occurring by chance is less than 1 in 1,000 in all variables.

[5] In most cases, immigrant parents of close friends are of the same nationality as respondent's.

Table 7.2   Educational Characteristics of Second-Generation Children in South Florida and Southern California

	Florida			California		
	Cubans[1] (N=171)	Haitians (N=148)	Mexicans (N=723)	Vietnamese (N=355)	Others (N=3775)	p^2
1. Educational Aspirations Percent expecting to graduate from college:	97.1	86.1	62.0	77.4	80.2	.001
2. Occupational Aspirations Percent planning on a professional or executive occupation:	71.8	71.6	53.9	64.4	61.2	.001
3. Hours of Homework Percent reporting at least two hours of homework per day:	39.5	43.0	26.3	57.9	38.9	.001
4. Grade Point Average:[3]	3.35	2.96	2.44	3.36	3.07	.001
5. Standardized Math Achievement Score Mean percentile:[4]	78.80	46.27	31.82	60.45	55.94	.001
6. Standardized Reading Score Mean percentile:[4]	68.13	30.13	26.24	36.97	44.45	.001

[1] See definitions in Table 7.1.
[2] The probability of observed differences occurring by chance is less than 1 in 1,000 for all variables.
[3] Averages standardized to mean 3 and standard deviation 1 to adjust for different scales in different school systems.
[4] All scores are based on the Stanford achievement test standardized to national norms.

tion,[38], 48 percent of Cubans and 36 percent of Vietnamese opted for the first alternative, as opposed to much lower proportions among Mexicans and Haitians. Although other factors are undoubtedly at play, these large differences appear to reflect the greater "hold" that traditional parents' values have in more densely integrated ethnic communities.

Table 7.2 presents the distribution of educational characteristics for the same groups. Congruent with the long-standing plight of their community, Mexican American children have by far the lowest levels of educational and occupational aspirations. Aspirations are generally high among all second-generation youth but, for Mexican Americans, they fall 10 to 30 percentage points below those of other groups. On the contrary, Haitian American aspirations are quite high. The recency of the Miami Haitian community and the high hopes for the future held by immigrant parents are reflected in the optimism manifested by their offspring, despite their awareness of pervasive discrimination.

The same differences are observable in terms of hours of school homework. Mexican Americans report the lowest levels of homework, with only one-fourth spending at least two hours a day in these tasks. The proportion climbs to 43 percent among Haitian Americans, who even exceed the figure for Cuban Americans, again reflecting a resilient commitment to education. The hardest working group is Vietnamese Americans, the majority of whom dedicate two to six hours to after-school tasks. To the extent that such reports can be taken at face value, they are in line with the known emphasis of Vietnamese families on school achievement and the strong pressures in that direction brought to bear on their children.[39]

Homework and aspirations are not perfectly correlated with school performance. As the bottom rows of Table 7.2 indicate, the GPA, math and reading scores of Cuban and Vietnamese second-generation students exceed by significant margins those of their Haitian and Mexican counterparts, as well as the combined averages for all other nationalities. Despite higher aspirations, Haitian American scores are low and not significantly different from those of Mexican Americans. At the other extreme, Vietnamese Americans have impressively high math scores despite the fact that these children, unlike Cuban Americans, do not have the advantage of a private school education. Reading scores for Vietnamese children are much lower and near the average for all other nationalities, but they still surpass by a significant margin those of the bottom groups.

The observed differences in academic performance and in such key attitudinal variables as perceptions of discrimination are so far congruent with our expectations based on the preceding descriptions of each immigrant community. Cuban and Vietnamese immigrants have avoided so far the path of downward assimilation through the creation of their own cultural institutions and tightly knit family networks. Haitian parents struggle to implement the same goals against the severe handicaps of outside discrimination and close proximity to the inner city. For reasons already explained, Mexican immigrants face the most difficult circumstances.

Explaining the observed differences in terms of the characteristics of each first-generation immigrant community, however, runs up against the possibility that these differences can be fully accounted for by individual characteristics of immigrant parents and/or the children themselves. For example, paternal and maternal education, the child's length of residence in the United States, and her/his command of English may be the decisive factors affecting academic performance. Since these factors vary greatly among the four immigrant communities, failing to control for them may lead to the spurious conclusion that community variables significantly influence academic performance when, in fact, only individual and family variables do.

To examine this possibility, I regressed each indicator of academic performance on a vector of independent variables which comprise all individual/family characteristics that can plausibly bear on these outcomes plus dummy variables for each immigrant nationality. The vector of predictors includes the respondents' age, sex, grade (eighth or ninth), years of residence in the United States, knowledge of English, number of close friends who are co-ethnics, the father's occupational status, the mother's education, whether the family remains intact (father and mother present), and whether a language other than English is spoken at home.[40] Measurement scales of each of these variables are presented in the Appendix to this chapter. Dependent variables are the respondent's grade-point average in standardized scores and her/his math and reading percentile scores.

Table 7.3 presents results of this analysis. To take into account the possibility that determinants of performance differ by region, the analysis is replicated separately for Miami/Ft. Lauderdale and San Diego respondents. In each case, the effects of variables representing national origin are the net influence of belonging to a particular immigrant group in comparison to a reference category comprised of all other such groups and controlling for all individual/family predictors. The first panel of Table 7.3 shows that after controling for this vector of predictors, three of the four nationality variables retain a strong independent effect on GPA. Net of all other variables, being

Table 7.3 Least Square Regressions of Grade Point Average, Math and Reading Scores on Selected Predictors; Children of Immigrants, 1992

Variable[1]	Full Sample		
	1.GPA[2]	2.Math[3]	3.Reading[3]
School Grade	12.047**	5.690**	4.565**
	(7.43)	(5.63)	(5.10)
Sex (Girls)	35.961**	1.303	2.217*
	(13.59)	(1.60)	(3.07)
Age	−18.079**	−5.747**	−3.828**
	(9.23)	(9.40)	(7.04)
Length of U.S. Residence	−13.316**	−0.101	2.358**
	(8.45)	(0.23)	(5.34)
Knowledge of English	3.334**	2.655**	4.786**
	(4.23)	(9.72)	(19.72)
Friends' Ethnicity (Co-Ethnics)	6.545*	3.896**	1.553*
	(2.92)	(5.57)	(2.52)
Father's Occupation	0.594**	0.231**	0.201**
	(5.40)	(6.89)	(6.74)
Mother's Education	4.180**	1.572**	1.905**
	(3.87)	(4.75)	(6.46)
Language at Home (English Only)	4.800	1.111	3.210
	(0.88)	(0.68)	(2.18)
Two-Parent Household	24.248**	4.073**	2.002*
	(8.84)	(4.79)	(2.65)
Cuban	25.675*	12.558**	13.664**
	(2.69)	(4.43)	(5.38)
Haitian	4.385	−3.971	−10.017**
	(0.56)	(1.62)	(4.56)
Mexican	−38.496**	−14.99**	−7.672**
	(9.40)	(11.69)	(6.76)
Vietnamese	39.406**	10.964**	3.177*
	(7.43)	(6.54)	(2.61)
R	.411	.458	.526
R^2	.169	.210	.277
N	4990	4422	4518

* $p < .01.$ ** $p < .001.$

[1]See Appendix for details of measurement. Words in parentheses indicate highest score in dichotomous variables.

[2]b-regression coefficients taken to the fifth significant digit and multiplied by 100. Coefficients are interpretable as percentages of a standard deviation unit in the dependent variable. T-ratios in parentheses.

Miami/Ft. Lauderdale			San Diego		
1.GPA[2]	2.Math[3]	3.Reading[3]	1.GPA[2]	2.Math[3]	3.Reading[3]
5.012	6.248**	5.867**	17.303**	5.687**	2.385
(1.07)	(4.54)	(4.97)	(3.82)	(3.78)	(1.73)
26.888**	1.318	1.240	45.880**	1.168	3.303*
(7.12)	(1.19)	(1.31)	(12.73)	(0.97)	(3.02)
−19.534**	−5.787**	−3.311**	−14.074**	−6.264**	−4.140**
(6.98)	(6.90)	(4.61)	(5.27)	(6.95)	(5.00)
−10.294**	−0.436	1.305	−11.200**	0.264	3.615**
(4.35)	(0.63)	(2.18)	(5.31)	(0.36)	(5.46)
10.111**	2.305**	4.889**	1.366	2.578**	4.587**
(7.12)	(5.24)	(13.01)	(1.42)	(7.16)	(13.84)
4.236	3.635**	1.233	10.400**	3.656**	1.906
(1.27)	(3.67)	(1.45)	(3.52)	(3.68)	(2.09)
0.608**	0.235**	0.181**	0.466*	0.208**	0.244**
(4.01)	(5.29)	(4.74)	(2.96)	(4.04)	(5.18)
5.810**	1.526**	1.341**	2.763	1.443*	2.398**
(3.73)	(3.33)	(3.40)	(1.89)	(2.99)	(5.43)
14.276	0.803	3.137	−14.388	0.178	3.280
(2.14)	(0.41)	(1.88)	(1.49)	(0.06)	(1.15)
24.883**	5.433**	2.280	16.402**	3.191	0.883
(6.56)	(4.87)	(2.38)	(4.06)	(2.34)	(0.71)
21.459	11.444**	15.565**	—	—	—
(2.13)	(3.93)	(6.24)			
14.162	−5.138*	−9.739**	—	—	—
(1.74)	(2.69)	(4.62)			
—	—	—	−59.437**	−14.540**	−9.396**
			(12.46)	(9.10)	(6.39)
—	—	—	23.059**	12.764**	2.672
			(4.21)	(6.96)	(1.59)
.380	.372	.458	.491	.500	.566
.144	.138	.210	.241	.250	.321
2574	2365	2360	2415	2055	2157

[3]b-regression coefficients are interpretable as percentile point change in the dependent variable per unit change in each predictor. T-ratios in parentheses.

a member of the Cuban community of Miami or the Vietnamese community of San Diego is associated with significantly better academic performance. The opposite is true for Mexican American students in southern California. Haitian ethnicity has no independent effect indicating that, in this case, the lower-than-average GPA is entirely accounted for by individual and family characteristics. Exactly the same results are obtained when the sample is broken down by region. In Miami/Ft. Lauderdale, Cuban but not Haitian ethnicity has a strong and positive net effect on GPA; in San Diego, the Mexican and Vietnamese effects are both significant but they run in opposite directions.

The second and third panels of Table 7.3 present the corresponding results for standardized reading and math performance tests. In each case, the effects of individual and family predictors are reasonable. For example, grade in school, knowledge of English, and parental education and occupation significantly improve math scores, and the same set of variables plus length of residence has a similar effect on reading scores. However, these combined effects do not eliminate the influence of national origin which runs, without exception, in the expected directions. Vietnamese and Cuban children perform significantly better than the average in both math and reading tests, while Mexican and Haitian youth perform worse after controlling for all individual and family variables. Both Mexican effects are statistically significant; in the Haitian case both effects are negative but one is not significant.

I interpret these findings as providing indirect evidence of the role of community social resources in facilitating second-generation upward mobility and fending off the threat of downward assimilation. While not central to this analysis, other results in Table 7.3 also support this conclusion. For example, limiting close friendships to the ethnic community tends to have a consistently positive effect on academic performance. In contrast, length of residence in the United States has a significantly negative effect on grade point average. Both results run contrary to conventional wisdom about the effects of acculturation, but are congruent with a theory that emphasizes the role of community social capital in implementing the immigrant parents' mobility project.[41]

Additional evidence in support of this general interpretation comes from a separate multivariable analysis of determinants of the observed interethnic differences in experiences of discrimination. Results of this logistic regression are presented in Table 7.4. The vector of potentially relevant individual and family variables includes, in this case, the respondent's sex, age, area of residence,

Table 7.4   Logistic Regression of Experiences of Discrimination on Selected Predictors; Second-Generation Youth, 1992

Predictor[1]	B[2]	SE[3]	Significance	Exp[4]
Area of Residence:[5]				
Miami	−.450	.056	.001	.638
Ft. Lauderdale	.184	.081	.021	1.202
Sex (Female)	.124	.058	.031	1.132
Age	−.024	.034	n.s.[6]	—
Length of U.S. Residence	−.041	.036	n.s.	—
Two-Parent Household	−.103	.061	n.s.	—
Father's Education	−.023	.025	n.s.	—
Mother's Education	.044	.024	n.s.	—
Father's Occupation	.002	.002	n.s.	—
Knowledge of English	.052	.017	.003	1.052
Knowledge of Parents' Language[7]	−.008	.009	n.s.	—
Friends' Ethnicity (Co-Ethnics)	.269	.050	.001	1.310
Ethnicity:[8]				
Cuban	−.402	.086	.001	.669
Haitian	.752	.184	.001	2.122
Mexican	.216	.108	.046	1.248
Vietnamese	.221	.128	n.s.	—
Constant	.929	.617	—	—
Model Chi Square	304.37		.001	

[1]See Appendix for details of measurement; words in parentheses indicate highest score in dichotomous variables.

[2]Logistic regression effects.

[3]Standard error.

[4]Indicates the relative increase/decrease in the odds of experiencing discrimination per unit change in each predictor variable.

[5]San Diego is the omitted area. Listed effects are deviations from the overall effect.

[6]Not significant.

[7]For children whose parents' language is English, scores in this variable are equivalent to their knowledge of English.

[8]All other immigrant nationalities is the reference category; effects are relative to it.

knowledge of English, knowledge of the parental language, friends' ethnicity, and parental education and occupation. After controlling for this lengthy array of variables, significant differences in reported experiences of discrimination persist. Children who belong to institutionally complete ethnic groups, such as Cuban Americans in south Florida, are effectively shielded from outside discrimination. Children from the tightly knit Vietnamese community do not suffer more discrimination than the average for all immigrant groups, despite their identifiable phenotypical traits. On the other hand, Mexican American and Haitian American children experience significantly greater discrimination even after equalizing for individual and family variables. This effect is attributable to the inability of feebler immigrant communities to protect their children from negative outside messages.

Conclusion

The evidence presented in this chapter is only preliminary. Together these ethnographic and survey results add up to a plausible case for our theoretical argument but do not demonstrate it. The hypotheses indicate, however, the kind of variables required to put them to a more rigorous test. Unlike most research conducted in the past, these data requirements focus on the character of immigrant communities rather than of their individual members. This is also the general direction in which recent developments in economic sociology and the sociology of immigration point. For too long, research on immigrant and ethnic groups has been dominated by a strong individualistic bent where the social context in which economic success or failure takes place is either absent or is introduced in an ad hoc fashion. The argument developed in this chapter suggests the opposite: systematic attention to such context, in particular the character of ethnic communities, is necessary in order to make sense of individual results. For this purpose, a combination of intensive qualitative observation and survey methods is required.

Fifty years ago, the dilemma of Italian youngsters studied by Child consisted of assimilating to the American mainstream, choosing to sacrifice in the process their parents' cultural heritage or taking refuge in the ethnic community against the challenges of the outside world. In the contemporary context of segmented assimilation, the options have become less clear. Children of nonwhite immigrants may not even have the opportunity to gain access to the white mainstream, no matter how acculturated they become. Joining those native circles to which they do have access may prove a ticket to permanent subordination and disadvantage. Under these circumstances, embedding the adaptation of second-generation youth within the networks of the ethnic community may not be a symptom of escapism, as in the past, but a rational strategy for capitalizing on otherwise unavailable material and moral resources. Yet the successful implementation of this strategy also depends on the history and characteristics of that community and the social context that surrounds it. As the case of Haitian Americans in south Florida indicates, good intentions and high aspirations are not enough when structural forces place individuals in conditions of insurmountable disadvantage.

I wish to thank the other contributors to this book, in particular Bryan Roberts and Patricia Fernández Kelly, for their comments. An earlier version of this chapter, coauthored with Min Zhou, was published in *The Annals of the American Academy of Political and Social Sciences* 530 (November 1993):74–96. None of these colleagues bears responsibility for the contents of this version. The data on which the chapter is partially based were collected by the project, "Children of Immigrants: The Adaptation of the Second Generation," supported by grants from the Spencer Foundation, Mellon Foundation, Russell Sage Foundation, and National Science Foundation (grant no. SES-9022555).

Notes

1. Irving L. Child, *Italian or American? The Second Generation in Conflict* (New Haven: Yale University Press, 1943).

2. Jeffrey S. Passel and Barry Edmonston, "Immigration and Race: Recent Trends in Immigration to the United States," Paper #PRIP-UI-22, The Urban Institute, Washington D.C., May, 1992.

3. W. Lloyd Warner and Leo Srole, *The Social Systems of American Ethnic Groups* (New Haven: Yale University Press, 1945); Thomas Sowell, *Ethnic America: A History* (New York: Basic Books, 1981).

4. This account is based on fieldwork in Miami conducted in preparation for a survey of immigrant youths in public schools. The survey and preliminary results are described in the final section of this paper. See also Alex Stepick, "Haitian Refugees in the U.S.," Report no. 52, Minority Rights Group, London, 1982; Alex Stepick and Alejandro Portes, "Flight into Despair: A Profile of Recent Haitian Refugees in South Florida," *International Migration Review* 20 (Summer 1986):329–350.

5. Margaret A. Gibson, *Accommodation without Assimilation: Sikh Immigrants in an American High School* (Ithaca, N.Y.: Cornell University Press, 1989), p. 268.

6. Gibson, *Accommodation without Assimilation*. The study is summarized in Rubén G. Rumbaut, "Immigrant Students in California Public Schools: A Summary of Current Knowledge," Report #11, Center for Research on Effective Schooling for Disadvantaged Children, The Johns Hopkins University, 1990, pp. 22–23.

7. Warner and Srole, *The Social Systems*.

8. See for example Barry R. Chiswick, "The Effect of Americanization on the Earnings of Foreign-Born Men," *Journal of Political Economy* 86 (October 1978):897–921; George J. Borjas, "Self-Selection and the Earnings of

Immigrants," *American Economic Review* 77 (1987):531–553; Cordelia W. Reimers, "A Comparative Analysis of the Wages of Hispanics, Blacks, and Non-Hispanic Whites," in G. J. Borjas and M. Tienda, eds., *Hispanics in the U.S. Economy* (New York: Academic Press, 1985), pp. 27–75.

9. Leif Jensen, "Children of the New Immigration: A Comparative Analysis of Today's Second Generation" (paper commissioned by the Children of Immigrants Research Project, Department of Sociology, The Johns Hopkins University; reprinted as Working Paper #1990–32, Institute for Policy Research and Evaluation, The Pennsylvania State University, University Park, August 1990).

10. See Philippe Bourgois, "In Search of Respect: The New Service Economy and the Crack Alternative in Spanish Harlem" (paper presented at the conference on Poverty, Immigration, and Urban Marginality in Advanced Societies, Maison Suger, Paris, May 10–11, 1991). Also Loïc J. D. Wacquant and William J. Wilson, "The Cost of Racial and Class Exclusion in the Inner City," *Annals of the American Academy of Political and Social Science* 501 (1989):8–26.

11. Alejandro Portes and Julia Sensenbrenner, "Embeddedness and Immigration: Notes on the Social Determinants of Economic Action," *American Journal of Sociology* 98 (May 1993):1320–1350.

12. Bourgois, "In Search of Respect."

13. Wacquant and Wilson, "The Cost of Racial and Class Exclusion."

14. Carole Marks, *Farewell-We're Good and Gone, the Great Black Migration* (Bloomington, Ind.: Indiana University Press, 1989); Mario Barrera, *Race and Class in the Southwest: A Theory of Racial Inequality* (Notre Dame, Ind.: Notre Dame University Press, 1980); Frank A. Bonilla and Ricardo Campos, "A Wealth of Poor: Puerto Ricans in the New Economic Order," *Daedalus* 110 (Spring 1981):133–176; Candace Nelson and Marta Tienda, "The Structuring of Hispanic Ethnicity: Historical and Contemporary Perspectives," *Ethnic and Racial Studies* 8 (January 1985):49–74.

15. Fernández Kelly, this volume.

16. The name is fictitious.

17. M. G. Matute-Bianchi, "Ethnic Identities and Patterns of School Success and Failure among Mexican-Descent and Japanese American Students in a California High School," *American Journal of Education* 95 (November 1986):233–255. Results of the study are summarized in Rumbaut, "Immigrant Students."

18. Matute-Bianchi, "Ethnic Identities and Patterns," p. 253.

19. Rumbaut, "Immigrant Students," p. 25.

20. Portes and Sensenbrenner, "Embeddedness and Immigration."

21. Robert E. Park, "Human Migration and the Marginal Man," *American Journal of Sociology* 33 (May 1928):881–893; William I. Thomas and Flor-

ian Znaniecki, *The Polish Peasant in Europe and America*, ed. and abr. Eli Zaretsky (1918–1920; reprint, Chicago: University of Illinois Press, 1984); Oscar Handlin, *The Uprooted: The Epic Story of the Great Migrations That Made the American People*, 2nd enlarged edition (1951; reprint, Boston: Little, Brown, 1973). For more recent examples, see Victor Nee and Brett de Bary Nee, *Longtime Californ': A Documentary Study of an American Chinatown* (New York: Pantheon Books, 1973); Min Zhou, *New York's Chinatown: The Socioeconomic Potential of an Urban Enclave* (Philadelphia: Temple University Press, 1992); and Ivan Light and Edna Bonacich, *Immigrant Entrepreneurs: Koreans in Los Angeles 1965–1982* (Berkeley: University of California Press, 1988).

22. The difference between these types is explained at greater length in Alejandro Portes and Rubén G. Rumbaut, *Immigrant America: A Portrait* (Berkeley: University of California Press, 1990), Chap. 4.

23. Zhou, *New York's Chinatown*; Ivan Light, *Ethnic Enterprise in America: Business and Welfare among Chinese, Japanese, and Blacks* (Berkeley: University of California Press, 1972); Thomas Bailey and Roger Waldinger, "Primary, Secondary, and Enclave Labor Markets: A Training System Approach," *American Sociological Review* 56 (August 1991):432–444; Alejandro Portes, "The Social Origins of the Cuban Enclave Economy of Miami," *Sociological Perspectives* 30 (October 1987):340–372.

24. Roger Waldinger, "The Making of an Immigrant Niche" (manuscript, Department of Sociology, University of California, Los Angeles, 1992); Kenneth Wilson and W. Allen Martin, "Ethnic Enclaves: A Comparison of the Cuban and Black Economies in Miami," *American Journal of Sociology* 88 (1982):135–160; Alejandro Portes and Min Zhou, "Gaining the Upper Hand: Economic Mobility among Immigrant and Domestic Minorities," *Ethnic and Racial Studies* 15 (October 1992):491–522.

25. James S. Coleman, "Social Capital in the Creation of Human Capital," Supplement, *American Journal of Sociology* 94 (1988):S95–121.

26. Mark S. Granovetter, *Getting a Job: A Study of Contacts and Careers* (Cambridge: Harvard University Press, 1974).

27. Ronald S. Burt, *Structural Holes: The Social Structure of Competition* (Cambridge: Harvard University Press, 1992).

28. Ibid.

29. See the discussion of uniplex and multiplex ties in Chapter 1.

30. Alejandro Portes and Min Zhou, "The New Second Generation: Segmented Assimilation and its Variants," *The Annals of the American Academy of Political and Social Sciences* 530 (November 1993):74–96.

31. Alejandro Portes, Rubén G. Rumbaut, and Lisandro Perez, *Children of Immigrants: The Adaptation Process of the Second Generation* (research project funded by the Spencer, Mellon, Russell Sage, and National Science

Foundations, Department of Sociology, The Johns Hopkins University, in progress).

32. Robert L. Bach, Linda W. Gordon, David W. Haines, and David R. Howell, "The Economic Adjustment of Southeast Asian Refugees in the United States," in *World Refugee Survey, 1983* (Geneva: United Nations High Commission for Refugees, 1984), pp. 51–55; Rubén G. Rumbaut, "The Structure of Refuge: Southeast Asian Refugees in the United States, 1975–85," *International Review of Comparative Social Research* 1(Winter 1990):95–127; Sergio Diaz-Briquets and Lisandro Perez, "Cuba: The Demography of Revolution," *Population Bulletin* 36 (April 1981):2–41; Alejandro Portes and Robert L. Bach, *Latin Journey: Cuban and Mexican Immigrants in the United States* (Berkeley: University of California Press, 1985).

33. U.S. Bureau of the Census, *Survey of Minority-Owned Business Enterprises, 1977* (Washington, D.C.: U.S. Department of Commerce, 1981); Portes and Zhou, "Gaining the Upper Hand."

34. Alex Stepick, "The Refugees Nobody Wants: Haitians in Miami," in G. J. Grenier and A. Stepick, eds., *Miami Now!* (Gainesville: University of Florida Press, 1992), pp. 57–82.

35. Alejandro Portes and Alex Stepick, *City on the Edge: The Transformation of Miami* (Berkeley: University of California Press, 1993).

36. Douglas Massey, Rafael Alarcón, Jorge Durand, and Humberto González, *Return to Atzlán: The Social Process of International Migration from Western Mexico* (Berkeley: University of California Press, 1987); Douglas S. Massey and Luis Goldring, "Continuities in Transnational Migration: An Analysis of 13 Mexican Communities" (paper presented at the Workshop on U.S. Immigration Research: An Assessment of Data Needs for Future Research, sponsored by the National Research Council, Washington, D.C., September 17–18, 1992); Portes and Bach, *Latin Journey*.

37. Marcelo M. Suarez-Orozco, "Towards a Psychosocial Understanding of Hispanic Adaptation to American Schooling," in H. T. Trueba, ed., *Success or Failure? Learning and the Languages of Minority Students* (New York: Newbury House Publishers, 1987), pp. 156–168.

38. The item was phrased as follows:

> Mary said: "For a woman, the important thing is to meet the right man so that she can marry and have a nice family."
> Jane said: "For a woman, the important thing is to get an education so that she can be financially independent."
> Who do you think is right?

39. Rubén G. Rumbaut and Kenji Ima, "Determinants of Educational Attainment Among Indochinese Refugees and Other Immigrant Students" (paper presented at the annual meeting of the American Socio-

logical Association, Atlanta, August 1988); Rubén G. Rumbaut and Kenji Ima, *The Adaptation of Southeast Asian Refugee Youth: A Comparative Study* (Washington, D.C.: U.S. Office of Refugee Resettlement, 1988).

40. The data contain separate measures of father's and mother's education and father's and mother's occupational status. However, the simultaneous inclusion of both parental indicators creates problems of collinearity due to the high intercorrelation of educational indicators and missing data problems due to the large number of nonworking mothers. For these reasons, the analysis includes indicators of only one parental variable for each dimension. Results pertaining to the effects of national origin are not affected, however, by the simultaneous inclusion of both parental variables.

41. The significance of family social capital is made evident by the strong positive effects of intact families on all indicators of achievement. Unlike those discussed in the text, this effect is not incompatible with predictions advanced by earlier theories.

Appendix: Variable Measurement

Variable[1]	Measurement Scale
Length of U.S. Residence	Native-born (coded highest) to "less than 9 years."
Knowledge of English	Summated index of respondents' report of ability to read, write, speak, and understand English. —Each item is coded as follows: Very Well = 4; Well = 3; Not Well = 2; Not at All = 1.
Father's Occupation	Treiman International Occupational Prestige Scores.
Mother's Education	Years completed, categorized in a 5-point scale from: "Less than high school" to "College graduate or more" (coded highest).
Knowledge of Parents' Language	Summated index of respondents' report of ability to read, write, speak, and understand the parental language, if other than English. —Each item is coded as follows: Very Well = 4; Well = 3; Not Well = 2; Not at All = 1.

[1] Omits variables with self-explanatory measurements; these include all dichotomous variables defined by their labels.

Index

Boldface numbers refer to figures and tables.

281

Cornelius, W., 80n
Cornell, L. L., 70, 85nn
correlations: of ranks of self-employment rates and incomes, 184, **185**
cost-benefit calculations: and individual migration decisions, 19–20
coupling/decoupling, 145–156; balance between, 156; and economic conditions, 153–154; and ethnic advantages, 154, 155; and ethnic separation, 147–148, 153; factors affecting, 150; and noneconomic claims, 145–146, 147–148; and overseas Chinese, 142–146, 156; and retention of ethnicity, 148; *see also* boundaries
credit: and advantages of minorities, 155–156; and Chinese entrepreneurship, 143; obtaining, in Modjokuto, 132; *see also* rotating credit associations
Cuba, immigrants from: as cultural exiles, 63, 65–66, 78; and ethnic enclave in Miami, 28; and family demographic characteristics, 72–73; and income advantage of entrepreneurs, 27; and informal economy in Miami, 30; and modes of incorporation, **26;** and returns to human capital, 24; and second-generation identity, 65–66; and use of Spanish, 65–66; *see also* Cuban Americans
Cuba, immigration from: and size of Miami population, 92; and U.S. expansionism, 20
Cuban Americans: attitudes of, toward female social mobility, 265–268; community in Florida, described, 263–264; defined, for study of segmented assimilation, 262–263; discrimination against, 265, **266;** and downward assimilation, 269; educational aspirations and characteristics of, **267**, 268; effects of ethnicity on academic performance, 269–272, **270–271;** effects of ethnicity on discrimination, 272–274, **273;** ethnicity of friends, 265, **266;** occupational aspirations of, **267;** social characteristics and attitudes of, in south Florida and southern California, **266**
cultural analysis: objections to, 169; *see also* interaction theory of entrepreneurship
cultural capital: defined, 213; and economic sociology, 220–223; in Tabanan, 135; toponomical nature of, 215
cultural capital in ghetto, xv, 213–242; factors affecting forms and effects of, 215; and social capital, 213, 220, 222,

241; as symbolic reperto[r]
240–241
cultural diversity: and entr[y]
202
cultural exiles: and collectiv[e]
durations, 63, 64–66; exa[m]
66
cultural explanations of behavior: *vs* situational explanations, 225–227; *vs.* situational explanations, 223
cultural memory: and downward assimilation, 258; and ethnic solidarity, 256
cultural repertory: and American mores in ghetto, 215; of blacks, 141, 142
culture: adversarial (*see* adversarial culture); and change, 202–203; Chinese, as basis for networks in Modjokuto, 143; class, described, 170; concept of, misused, 221; and entrepreneurship, 202–203; of poverty, 221; temporal, in an African American ghetto, 54; vocational, of bourgeoisie, 170; welfare, 225–226; *see also* ethnic culture
cumulative causation, 17–19; and local labor markets, 88, 115
Curran, J., 206n
Curry, L., 99, 121n

Dalton, M., 8, 10, 36nn
data aggregation: implications of, for interaction theory, 200
Daughters of the American Revolution (DAR), ix–x, xin
DaVanzo, J., 124n, 125n
Davis, W. G., 145, 151, 159n, 160n, 161n, 164n
deindustrialization: and international migration, 21–22
demand: definitions of, 166–168; for entrepreneurs, 172–175; general, and self-employment ranks, 183–184; for labor, locational aspects of, 107; market opportunity as, 167; in regression procedure, 191; variables used in analysis of self-employment rates, 186–188, 189–191; as viewed by different disciplines, 204nn; *see also* interaction theory; supply/demand interactions
demand, aggregate: defined, 176, 190; and demand effects, 176–177; effects of, on self-employment rates, **192–194**, 197; operationally defined, **186–188**, 190; in regression procedure, 191
demand effects on self-employment rates, 175–177, **192–194**, 196–198, 199–201; general, 175–176, 199; and